# AMERICAN–
# SOVIET
# RELATIONS

Recent Titles in
Contributions in Political Science
*Series Editor: Bernard K. Johnpoll*

The Fiscal Congress: Legislative Control of the Budget
*Lance T. Leloup*

Improving Prosecution? The Inducement and Implementation of
Innovations for Prosecution Management
*David Leo Weimer*

Creating the Entangling Alliance: The Origins of the North Atlantic
Treaty Organization
*Timothy P. Ireland*

The State as Defendant: Governmental Accountability and the
Redress of Individual Grievances
*Leon Hurwitz*

Ethnic Identities in a Transnational World
*John F. Stack, Jr., editor*

Reasoned Argument in Social Science: Linking Research to Policy
*Eugene J. Meehan*

The Right Opposition: The Lovestoneites and the International
Communist Opposition of the 1930s
*Robert J. Alexander*

Quantification in the History of Political Thought: Toward a
Qualitative Approach
*Robert Schware*

The Kent State Incident: Impact of Judicial Process on Public Attitudes
*Thomas R. Hensley*

Representation and Presidential Primaries: The Democratic Party
in the Post-Reform Era
*James I. Lengle*

Heroin and Politicians: The Failure of Public Policy to Control
Addiction in America
*David J. Bellis*

The Impossible Dream: The Rise and Demise of the American Left
*Bernard K. Johnpoll*

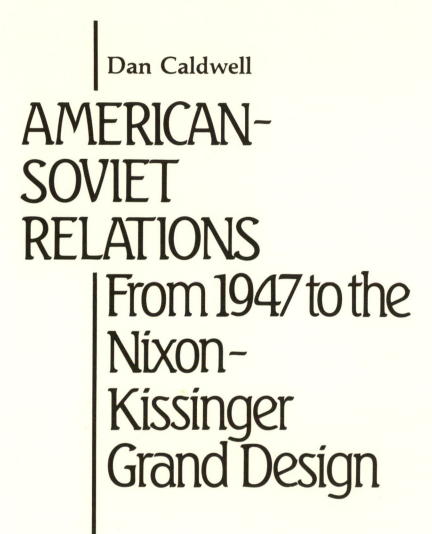

Dan Caldwell

# AMERICAN-
# SOVIET
# RELATIONS

## From 1947 to the Nixon-Kissinger Grand Design

CONTRIBUTIONS IN POLITICAL SCIENCE, NUMBER 61

GREENWOOD PRESS

Westport, Connecticut • London, England

**Library of Congress Cataloging in Publication Data**

Caldwell, Dan.
    American-Soviet relations.

    (Contributions in political science ; no. 61 ISSN
0147-1066)
    Bibliography: p.
    Includes index.
    1.  United States—Foreign relations—Russia.
2.  Russia—Foreign relations—United States.
3.  United States—Foreign relations—1945-
4.  Russia—Foreign relations—1945-    I.  Title.
II.  Series.
E183.8.R9C28      327.73047         80-27333
ISBN 0-313-22538-9 (lib. bdg.)

Library of Congress Catalog Card Number: 80-27333
ISBN: 0-313-22538-9
ISSN: 0147-1066

First published in 1981

Greenwood Press
A division of Congressional Information Service, Inc.
88 Post Road West
Westport, Connecticut 06881

Printed in the United States of America

10 9 8 7 6 5 4 3 2 1

TO LORA
*With appreciation and love*

# CONTENTS

# TABLES

# PREFACE

The two principal objectives of this study are to describe American-Soviet interactions in the crisis management, economic, and strategic-military issue areas from 1947 through 1976, and to analyze the attempt by Richard Nixon and Henry Kissinger to develop and implement a grand design and grand strategy for achieving a new international system.

This book has three major parts. Part I describes the procedures, rules, and organizations—or regimes—that the United States and the Soviet Union have developed since 1947 to manage conflicts of interest in various functional areas. Part I also examines the Nixon-Kissinger grand design and grand strategy for a new American foreign policy. In essence, the first four chapters provide a panoramic view of post-World War II Soviet-American relations.

Employing the methodology of structured, focused comparison, Part II compares a case from the acute cold war with a case from the détente period for the three issue areas under examination. Three matched pairs of cases are analyzed to examine the similarities and differences in Soviet and American foreign policy behavior in the crisis management, arms control, and economic issue areas during the acute cold war and détente periods.

Part III, the conclusion of this study, assesses how Soviet and American foreign policy behavior differed among the three periods and three issue areas under investigation and the degree to which

Nixon and Kissinger were able to cope with and to encourage further development of interdependence between the United States and the Soviet Union.

## A Note on Sources

Writing on such recent and controversial subjects as Soviet-American relations and the Nixon-Ford-Kissinger approach to foreign policy raises some problems concerning data collection and interpretation. Very few Soviet governmental documents on these subjects are available, and many of the U.S. documents remain classified. However, given the salience of these subjects, it is important to analyze them with the available, though fragmented, data.

As U.S. governmental reports and memoranda are declassified, and if and when Soviet sources become available for analysis, some of the interpretations and hypotheses of this study undoubtedly will have to be modified. However, until these additional documents are available publicly, I believe that I have consulted the most important materials available at the present time in providing a systematic description of Soviet-American relations and a critical analysis of the Nixon-Kissinger approach to the Soviet Union. During the course of my research, I have made use of the speeches, writings, and memoirs of Richard Nixon, Gerald Ford, and Henry Kissinger; congressional hearings related to U.S.-Soviet relations, détente, and arms control; secondary accounts written by historians, political scientists, and journalists; selected primary sources published in the United States and the Soviet Union; and a series of confidential interviews that I conducted with former members of the Nixon and Ford administrations.

## Acknowledgments

This study was strengthened substantially by forty-five interviews with former governmental officials and foreign policy analysts who served in the Nixon and Ford administrations. In some instances, those whom I interviewed allowed me to attribute information that they provided; however, in most cases I had to agree to conduct the interviews on a confidential basis. I would like to thank those people who granted me interviews, providing me with many useful insights.

Alexander L. George of Stanford University meticulously read and commented on a previous draft of this study, and I am more grateful to him for his help and encouragement than I can adequately express. Robert O. Keohane, Alexander Dallin, Walter Clemens, and John Lovell also read the entire manuscript, and I appreciate their many comments and criticisms.

In addition, a number of other scholars read and commented on one or more chapters. I would like to thank Barton Bernstein, Richard Cottam, Paul Marantz, Henry Nau, Robert North, John Oneal, William Potter, Dennis Ross, B. Thomas Trout, and Lawrence D. Weiler.

A preliminary version of chapter 7 was presented in 1977 at a seminar sponsored by the International Security Studies Program of the Woodrow Wilson International Center for Scholars, Washington, D.C., where Robin Edmonds, Joseph Kruzel, General Brent Scowcroft, and Helmut Sonnenfeldt provided useful comments. I would like to thank Samuel F. Wells, Jr., the director of the International Security Studies Program, and James Billington, the director of the Wilson Center, for the time that they allowed me to spend at the center from July to August 1977. I also received helpful comments on this paper from Colonel Richard G. Head, James King, and Robert Weinland.

Several organizations have supported the research and writing of this study. Most of all, I thank the members of the Stanford Arms Control and Disarmament Program and the director of the program, John Wilson Lewis, for their support. The University Consortium on World Order Studies and the Faculty Sabbatical Leave and Release Time Committee of Pepperdine University provided support for the preparation of this manuscript, and I appreciate their help. Dr. John Nicks and Dr. Norman Hughes of Seaver College, Pepperdine University provided me with encouragement during the final revision of the manuscript, and I am grateful to them. For research assistance, I am indebted to Brian Baker and Dave McCormick.

Gaye Passell, Betty Lee, and the Word Processing Staff of

Pepperdine University supervised the typing of several drafts of the study, and Bo Caldwell proofread the final manuscript. My parents provided boundless encouragement, as they always have, and I thank them for their constancy.

I owe my greatest personal thanks to my wife, Lora, who read and criticized drafts of the study, greatly improving its clarity and readability. More importantly, Lora provided me with support and encouragment when it seemed that the project would never be done. I dedicate this book to her with heartfelt thanks and love. Our children, Beth and Ellen, were constant reminders that there are far more joyful things in life than writing a book.

# AMERICAN–
# SOVIET
# RELATIONS

# INTRODUCTION

"The case of international tension is like a cabbage," Nikita Khrushchev once remarked. "If you tear off the leaves one by one you come to the heart. And the heart of this matter is relations between the Soviet Union and the United States."[1] This book focuses on the heart of the matter—Soviet-American relations from 1947 through 1976. International relations scholars have devoted more attention to the analysis of this bilateral relationship than any other, and for good reason: the survival and well-being of the post-World War II world depended upon the stability of relations between the two superpowers.

Numerous histories of postwar U.S.-Soviet relations have been written. Rather than employing purely historical analysis, this study seeks to uncover similarities and differences in Soviet and American foreign policy behavior in three distinct time periods and three issue areas. Historians and political scientists have divided the postwar era into various periods. In a 1972 article, for instance, Zbigniew Brzezinski divided the cold war into six phases.[2] In this study, I have divided the 1947-1976 period into three periods: the acute cold war (1947-1962), the limited détente (1963-1968), and the détente periods (1969-1976). Although this periodization represents a sweeping generalization, it provides a means of assessing the ups and downs in Soviet-American relations during the postwar epoch.

Rather than attempting to analyze the full panoply of superpower interactions, I have chosen to limit my analysis to three issue areas: crisis management, economics, and strategic-military relations. I chose these issue areas because of their salience; to a large extent, relations between the United States and the USSR in the three areas under examination determined the tenor of overall relations.

Throughout history, statesmen have developed rules and norms for the regulation of interaction between two or more actors in various functional or geographic areas. These rules or norms may be implicit or explicit. The norms of the classical balance of power system, for example, were largely tacit, whereas the rules governing international economic relations established at Bretton Woods in 1944 were quite explicit.

Regimes are the norms, procedures, and/or organizations created to manage the activities of international actors within issues areas in which there are mutually perceived needs for cooperation to regulate existing conflicts of interest or to promote some mutual interest.[3] Political scientist Hayward Alker has defined regimes as "governing rule systems or productive, causally effective rules structures."[4] In recent years, scholars have described and analyzed international regimes in the science-technology, oceans, monetary, and strategic-military issue areas.[5] Robert Keohane and Joseph Nye have also described and analyzed Canadian-American and Australian-American bilateral regimes.

An obviously necessary (but not sufficient) prerequisite for the establishment of a regime is interaction between at least two international actors. Interstate and transnational interactions over time may result in the development of regimes. In this study regimes have been identified by analyzing formal Soviet-American agreements and treaties, official statements, and the actual behavior of the two superpowers.

The regime concept is a potentially valuable tool of policy analysis for several reasons. First, the concept allows analysts to focus on shared norms within particular issue areas. Too often in the past international relations scholars have emphasized system-wide norms and ignored issue-area norms. Second, analyses of regimes in different issue areas may contribute to a better understanding of how international norms are established and maintained. Third, the regime concept may assist policymakers in the identification of possible areas and means of cooperation that otherwise might be ignored.

Despite its potential usefulness in policy analysis, the regime concept is underspecified at present. Some analysts have treated regimes dichotomously; either the regimes exist or they do not. Recent analysts employing this concept (Keohane and Nye, Alker) have drawn a threefold distinction: nonregimes, quasi-regimes, and regimes. Although this distinction is a step in the right direction, analysts should attempt greater differentiation. Characteristics that should be specified include the following: (1) regime type— what functional activity does the regime regulate; (2) scope—is the regime bilateral or multilateral, regional or global, public or private; (3) is the regime implicit or explicit; (4) is the regime partial or comprehensive? Once analyses of regimes with different characteristics are completed, it may be possible eventually to develop a typology of regimes that has both theoretical interest and policy relevance. The construction of such a typology should contribute both to the explanation of regime development and change and to efforts, such as Nixon's and Kissinger's, to facilitate the creation, expansion, and explication of regimes.

In addition to describing the development of Soviet-American economic, crisis management, and strategic-military regimes, part I of this study also describes and analyzes Nixon's and Kissinger's attempts to devise and implement a new American foreign policy. Richard Nixon and Henry Kissinger entered office in 1969 having pledged to end the Vietnam War and to seek a new "structure of peace." Rather than attempting to deal with problems of American foreign policy on an issue-by-issue *ad hoc* basis, Nixon and Kissinger formulated a grand design of a new international system and a grand strategy for achieving this system. The grand design was Nixon's and Kissinger's desired end state of their new international system; the grand strategy was the means for achieving the new international system. In their grand design, Nixon and Kissinger envisioned a triangular configuration of power among the United States, the Soviet Union, and the People's Republic of China. In his memoirs, Kissinger described the grand design and grand strategy:

We moved toward China . . . to shape a global equilibrium. It was not to collude against the Soviet Union but to give us a balancing position for constructive ends—to give each communist power a stake in better relations with us. Such an equilibrium could assure stability among the major powers, and even eventual cooperation, in the Seventies and Eighties.[6]

During their first four years in office, Nixon and Kissinger outlined their grand design and grand strategy in annual "state of the world" reports; however, they never fully explicated the desired end state of their new international system. Instead they emphasized the ongoing processes of normalizing relations with the People's Republic of China (a process referred to as rapprochement) and establishing better relations with the Soviet Union (a process referred to as détente).

In the early 1970s, détente was one of the most widely used and least understood concepts in the lexicon of international relations. Like other prevalent concepts in the field of international relations—"national interest," "balance of power," and "national security," to name a few—usage of détente was confusing and in some cases even contradictory. Ambiguity has not always clouded the meaning of détente, however. As Harold Nicolson has pointed out in his primer on diplomacy, during the eighteenth and nineteenth centuries, statesmen commonly understood the term to mean the lessening of tensions between two or more states.[7] In this sense, the contemporary détente in Soviet-American relations actually began in the aftermath of the Cuban missile crisis when the two superpowers moved to lessen tensions in several issue areas, most notably crisis management and arms control. Going well beyond its classical diplomatic meaning, Nixon and Kissinger used détente to refer to a process of developing greater Soviet-American interdependence through the establishment of regimes in various issue areas.

American presidents since Franklin Roosevelt have been faced with the twofold task of developing long-range policies to deal with the Soviet Union and at the same time gaining public and congressional support for such schemes. Roosevelt felt that the establishment of the United Nations with its provision for great power consultation in the Security Council would provide a framework for dealing and working with the Soviets in the postwar world.[8] But U.S.-Soviet competition made the UN mechanism ineffectual and, following crises in Iran, Greece, and Turkey, President Harry Truman proposed the doctrine of containment. Truman and his advisers faced the difficult task of gaining public and congressional acceptance of and support for the new policy.[9] There were, in fact, important domestic constraints in the United States on the choice and design of a long-range American foreign policy for dealing with the Soviet Union. A very important means of providing for domestic support of a long-range foreign policy is through the acquisition of policy legitimacy.[10] If a president is able to build his policy on the underlying beliefs and values of American society, then it is far easier to gain consensus support for his policy. Just as Truman and his advisers faced a new international environment in the mid-1940s, Nixon and Kissinger confronted a new international milieu in the 1970s. Nixon's and Kissinger's attempt to legitimate their grand design and grand strategy is reviewed and evaluated in this study.

Whereas part I provides a broad overview of Soviet-American relations from 1947 through 1976, part II provides a more focused examination of U.S. and Soviet foreign policy behavior in three matched pairs of cases. In recent years, a number of scholars have emphasized the need for a systematic comparison of case studies.[11] Alexander George and his colleagues have utilized a method of "structured, focused comparison," according to which the analyst prepares a set of standardized, general questions that reflect the theoretical concerns of the study.[12] These questions are then applied to the analysis of each case. Based on the results of these applications, the analyst modifies original questions to account for previously neglected factors. Comparison of the case studies enables the analyst to develop context-dependent generalizations about the phenomenon under study. Because of the utility of this approach for the analysis of decision-making variables and because of its usefulness in developing policy-related theory, I have chosen to use the structured, focused comparison methodology in chapters 5, 6, and 7.

My principal objective in part II is to assess the degree to which American and Soviet foreign policy behavior varied under different systemic conditions and in various issue areas. In order to examine this question, I have selected cases from the acute cold war (1947-1962) and détente (1969-1976) system-periods and the crisis management, arms control, and economic issue areas. I did not examine cases from the limited détente period (1963-1968) in order to highlight the differences between U.S. and Soviet foreign policy behavior.

Many historical cases could serve as the basis for a structured, focused comparison of détente. Important cases of détente during the nineteenth century include Anglo-French relations (1815-1817), Russo-German relations (1875-1877), and Anglo-French relations following the Fashoda incident of 1898. The Nixon-Kissinger conception of détente as a system-developing process, however, went well beyond the classical diplomatic meaning of the term as simply the lessening of tensions between two or more states. Because the primary focus of this study is the Nixon-Kissinger grand design and grand strategy, I have chosen cases from the post-World War II international systems. Prior to selecting cases for intensive investigation, I listed the most significant cases of Soviet-American interaction during the two periods and in the three issue areas under examination.[13] After considering these cases in light of my research design and objectives, I selected for analysis the cases listed in table 1.

**Table 1**
**CASES SELECTED FOR ANALYSIS**

|  | Period | |
|---|---|---|
| **Issue Area** | *1947-1962* | *1969-1976* |
| Economic | Trade negotiations, 1958-1961 | Trade Agreement, 1972 |
| Arms Control | London subcommittee negotiations, 1955-1957 | SALT, 1969-1972 |
| Crisis Management | Cuban missile crisis, 1962 | October War, 1973 |

There were several general reasons for my choice of cases. First, I wanted to select those that were important enough to involve the principal decision makers of both the United States and the Soviet Union. Second, I wanted to select those for which public data were accessible. Third, I wanted matched pairs of cases, one from the acute cold war period and the other from the détente period, that would be comparable along a number of similar dimensions. My exploratory analysis of the cases enabled me to identify a number that superficially appeared similar.

My choice of cases was also influenced by factors particular to each one. The Soviet turn to the West between 1958 and 1961 represented a serious attempt to develop a substantial trade with the West. Although extensive trade developed between the Soviet Union and the states of Western Europe and Japan, Soviet-American trade remained minimal, and U.S. cold war economic obstacles largely remained in place until the early 1970s. The 1972 Trade Agreement called for the resolution and removal of most of these barriers. A systematic comparison of these two important cases therefore should contribute to an understanding of the motivations and behavior of American and Soviet policymakers in the economic issue area.

Soviet and American leaders fundamentally disagreed over the issue of the inspection and verification of nuclear disarmament. In addition, the Soviet Union did not explode its first nuclear weapon until 1949. Because of the verification issue and because of the Soviet refusal to forgo the development of nuclear weapons, there were no serious efforts to control nuclear arms until the mid-1950s. The UN Subcommittee on Disarmament conducted a series of negotiations in London between 1955 and 1957 that most observers viewed as serious and substantive. Although these negotiations failed to produce any tangible results, the bilateral U.S.-Soviet Strategic Arms Limitation Talks did result in several important agreements.

As a number of analysts have pointed out, the Cuban missile crisis was the dénouement of the acute cold war. This event, rivaled in its seriousness only by the Berlin crises of 1948 and 1961, undoubtedly played a part, if not the major role, in catalyzing the détente that followed in its aftermath. Although the stakes were obviously not as high in the Soviet-American crisis during the

October War, this crisis, nevertheless, was one of the most serious U.S.-Soviet confrontations of the post-1962 period. A comparison of these two cases contributes to an understanding of the antecedents, as well as effects, of détente upon Soviet and American foreign policy behavior.

The conclusion of the study assesses the utility of the theoretical concept of regime in describing and evaluating Soviet-American relationships, as well as the Nixon-Ford-Kissinger policies. I also analyze the major reasons for the failure of these policies toward the Soviet Union.

## Notes

1. *New York Times*, May 11, 1959, p. 3.

2. Zbigniew Brzezinski, "How the Cold War Was Played," *Foreign Affairs* 51-1 (October 1972): 181-209.

3. Robert O. Keohane and Joseph S. Nye, *Power and Interdependence: World Politics in Transition* (Boston: Little, Brown, 1977), p. 5.

4. Hayward R. Alker, Jr., "A Methodology for Design Research on Interdependence Alternatives," *International Organization* 31-1 (Winter 1977): p. 36.

5. Keohane and Nye, *Power and Interdependence*; John Gerard Ruggie and Ernst B. Haas, eds., "International Responses to Technology," special issue of *International Organization* 29-3 (Summer 1975); David C. Gompert, Michael Mandelbaum, Richard L. Garwin, and John H. Barton, *Nuclear Weapons and World Politics: Alternatives for the Future* (New York: McGraw-Hill, 1977); and Seyom Brown, Nina Cornell, Larry Fabian, and Edith Weiss Brown, *Regimes for the Ocean, Outer Space, and Weather Modification* (Washington, D.C.: Brookings Institution, 1977).

6. Henry A. Kissinger, *White House Years* (Boston: Little, Brown, 1979), p. 192.

7. Harold Nicolson, *Diplomacy*, 3d ed. (London: Oxford University Press, 1963).

8. Robert Dallek, *Franklin D. Roosevelt and American Foreign Policy, 1932-1945* (New York: Oxford University Press, 1979).

9. John Lewis Gaddis, *The United States and the Origins of the Cold War, 1941-1947* (New York: Columbia University Press, 1972).

10. B. Thomas Trout, "Rhetoric Revisited: Political Legitimation and

the Cold War," *International Studies Quarterly* 19-3 (September 1975): 251-84.

11. Sidney Verba, "Some Dilemmas in Comparative Research," *World Politics* 20 (October 1967); Harry Eckstein, "Case Study and Theory in Macropolitics," in Fred I. Greenstein and Nelson Polsby, eds., *The Handbook of Political Science* (Reading, Mass.: Addison-Wesley, 1975); Bruce Russett, "International Behavior Research: Case Studies and Cumulation," in Michael Haas and Henry Kariel, eds., *Approaches to the Study of Political Science* (Scranton, Pa.: Chandler Publishing Company, 1970).

12. Alexander L. George, "Case Studies and Theory Development: The Method of Structured, Focused Comparison," in Paul Gordon Lauren, ed., *Diplomacy: New Approaches in History, Theory, and Policy*, (New York: Free Press, 1979), pp. 43-68.

13. For the lists of cases that I examined, see Dan Caldwell, "American-Soviet Detente and the Nixon-Kissinger Grand Design and Grand Strategy," (Ph.D., diss., Stanford University, 1978), pp. 293-95.

# PART I

# AMERICAN AND SOVIET POLICIES AND REGIMES, 1947–1976

# CHAPTER 1

# COLD WAR POLICIES
# AND REGIMES

The mistrust between the leaders of the West and the Soviet Union that existed prior to World War II was exacerbated by the war and was a factor that dominated East-West relations for most of the three decades following 1945. During the war, relations between the Soviet Union and its allies were not cordial but a matter of expediency for both sides. With some justification, Joseph Stalin felt that Franklin Roosevelt and Winston Churchill unnecessarily delayed the opening of a second front and the shipment of materiel to Soviet forces. Although Roosevelt believed that he could influence Stalin through personal charm, Churchill distrusted the Soviet leader and suspected him of desiring to control Eastern Europe.

During the two years immediately following World War II, the configuration of international politics changed substantially. Having suffered greatly from the war, both the vanquished and the victorious states, with the exception of the United States, were in social, economic, and political disarray, and a civil war raged in China. However, the United States, which had suffered significant casualties in the war, remained untouched by the conflict and thus emerged from it as the most powerful state in the world, accounting for 50 percent of the world's gross national product in 1945.

Despite the predominant position of the United States within the international system at the end of World War II, most Americans favored a return to its prewar position in the world. Congress was besieged with demands "to bring the boys home." The rapidity and the magnitude of the American demobilization following World War II was unprecedented in world history; in June 1945, there were twelve million men and women on active duty in the U.S. military services. Within two years, the size of the U.S. military had shrunk to one and one-half million, and President Truman observed, "So far as I was concerned, the program we were following was no longer demobilization—it was disintegration of our armed forces."[1]

The beginning of the cold war was never formally declared, but a series of events during February and March 1946 left little doubt that postwar relations between the United States and the Soviet Union would be marked by competition and conflict rather than cooperation. On February 9, 1946, Stalin delivered a public speech, arguing that capitalism and communism were incompatible and that the Soviet Union would not return to a peacetime footing. *Time* magazine called Stalin's speech "the most warlike pronouncement uttered by any top-rank statesman since V-J Day." One week later twenty-two people were arrested in Canada on charges of trying to steal information on the atomic bomb for the Soviet Union. On March 5, 1946, in an address delivered at Fulton, Missouri, former British Prime Minister Winston Churchill warned, "From Stettin in the Baltic to Trieste in the Adriatic, an iron curtain has descended across the continent . . ." Commenting on the Soviet approach to international relations, Churchill went on, "I am convinced that there is nothing they [the Soviets] admire so much as strength, and there is nothing for which they have less respect than weakness, particularly military weakness."[2]

In March 1946, the first major Soviet-American postwar crisis occurred. In 1942, Great Britain and the Soviet Union had deployed troops into Iran in order to deny access to Iranian oil and transportation routes from the Axis powers. Both Allies agreed to withdraw their forces six months after the termination of hostilities. During the last months of 1945, however, disturbing reports reached Washington that the Soviets planned to stay in Iran. On the same day that Churchill delivered his "iron curtain" speech, the United States sent a stiff note to the Soviet Union demanding the immediate withdrawal of its forces from Iran. The text of this message was released to the press, at that time an unusual procedure.

In the weeks following, tension increased dramatically; *News-week* even compared the atmosphere to the fall of 1938 when the Munich crisis had dominated public events.[3] The Soviet Union failed to respond to the U.S. note and began to move its troops toward Tehran rather than in the direction of the Russian border. When given evidence of Soviet troop movements, Secretary of State James Byrnes reportedly beat his fist into his other hand and commented, "Now we'll give it to them with both barrels."[4] The United States sent another telegram to the Soviet Union demanding an explanation of its maneuvers and also submitted the issue to the UN Security Council for consideration, an action that the Soviets regarded as "unfriendly." Despite the fact that Soviet-Iranian negotiations were in progress, the United States continued to support a consideration of the issue by the Security Council. At the beginning of April, the Soviet and Iranian governments reached an agreement for the withdrawal of Soviet troops, and the crisis was ended.

The episode over Iran highlighted the necessity for a reassessment of American policy toward the Soviet Union and the necessity for a systematic conceptualization of Soviet foreign policy. Such a framework was provided by the *charge d'affaires* at the U.S. Embassy in Moscow, George Kennan, who sent the secretary of state an 8,000-word telegram concerning the sources of Soviet foreign policy conduct.[5]

People selectively and subjectively respond to stimuli from their environment. Political leaders not only seek to understand their environment, they also seek to mold the environment in ways that benefit their particular state. In order to make sense out of reality and to gain public support for their policies, leaders must develop a coherent structure into which the facts of international political life may be fit. Legitimation is the process by which "leaders lay down the rules, promulgate policies, and disseminate symbols which tell followers how and what they should do and feel."[6]

Policy legitimacy is a basic requirement of any political system and is sought actively by most political leaders. Fundamentally a government's domestic and foreign policies must reflect to some degree "a quality of oughtness" as determined by the normative values of a particular society. People do not view the world as it is; they view it through glasses tinted by the most salient political values and symbols of their particular society. The need for a broad consensus on public policy goals and the means for achieving those objectives is particularly important within democratic societies such as the United States.

B. Thomas Trout, in describing the legitimation of Soviet and American cold war policies during the 1945-1947 period,[7] noted that legitimation occurred in two phases: an attentive phase in which new, legitimate symbols were introduced and an assertive phase in which these symbols were used to legitimate new foreign policies. During the attentive phase of the cold war, U.S. policy makers attempted to formulate a coherent structure in which to fit incoming facts about the Soviet Union. Although most American policymakers viewed the Soviet Union as an important international actor in the postwar world, there was substantial disagreement concerning the character of the Soviet Union and how to deal with it.

Kennan's report provided a structure into which U.S. policymakers' misgivings toward the Soviet Union could be fit. He described the polarization of the Soviet and American systems and recommended a sophisticated U.S. strategy for dealing with the Soviet Union. In essence, Kennan sought to contain Soviet expansionist efforts and, achieving this, to induce changes within the Soviet Union over the long run. Kennan's description of the condition of Soviet-American relations and his prescriptions for U.S. policy were complex yet coherent.

In February 1947, the British announced that they would withdraw their aid from Greece and Turkey. President Truman, Secretary of State George Marshall, and Under Secretary of State Dean Acheson met with congressional leaders to explain the necessity of filling the vacuum created by British withdrawal. According to Acheson, Secretary Marshall did not present a convincing case, and the responsibility for justifying the new U.S. foreign policy fell on Acheson, who recalled in his memoirs:

No time was left for measured appraisal. In the past eighteen months, I said, Soviet pressure on the Straits, on Iran, and on northern Greece had brought the Balkans to the point where a highly possible Soviet breakthrough might open three continents to Soviet penetration. Like apples in a barrel infected by one rotten one, the corruption of Greece would infect Iran and all to the east. It would also carry infection to Africa through Asia Minor and Egypt, and to Europe through Italy and France . . . [8]

Several of the central beliefs held by American policymakers throughout the acute cold war are reflected in this statement. There is a great emphasis on the credibility and indivisibility of U.S. commitments; if the United States did not respond to Soviet moves in Greece, then the Soviet Union would be free to act anywhere. Acheson's "rotten apples" analogy was expressed by later policy-makers as the domino theory.

On March 12, 1947, President Truman went before the Congress and requested military aid for Greece and Turkey in order "to support free people who are resisting attempted subjugation by armed minorities or by outside pressures."[9] In retrospect, it appears that Truman's speech, Acheson's and Marshall's writings and speeches, and Kennan's telegram provided the cornerstones on which American cold war foreign policies were built. Whereas Kennan had presented recommendations based on complex and long-range analysis, Truman and Acheson had simplified and distorted the world situation in order to legitimate containment. Kennan later complained in his memoirs, "We obviously dislike to discriminate. We like to find some general governing norm to which, in each instance, appeal can be taken, so that individual decisions may not be made on their particular merits but automatically, depending on whether the circumstances do or do not fit the norm."[10] By mid-1947, the basic components of U.S. containment policy had been articulated by members of the Truman administration and overwhelmingly accepted by the Congress and the American public. The cold war had begun.

Most historians and political scientists point to 1947, the year in which President Truman pledged aid to Greece and Turkey, as the beginning, and 1962, the year in which the United States and the Soviet Union confronted one another over Soviet missiles in Cuba, as the end of the acute cold war period. This conventional labeling of the fifteen-year period from 1947 through 1962, however, must be qualified, for there were significant changes that should be recognized, particularly within the Soviet Union. Despite the rhetoric of the Soviet constitution, Joseph Stalin ruled the USSR dictatorially from the time of his takeover from Lenin until his death in 1953.

The succession of Nikita Khrushchev to the primary leadership position of the Soviet government and the policies that he espoused during his tenure in office mark a second phase of the acute cold war period. Although Khrushchev's intentions vis-à-vis the West were (and remain) ambiguous, it is clear that he sought at least limited agreements with Western states, whereas Stalin had sought political, social, and economic autarky for the Soviet Union.

Although the change in leadership from Stalin to Khrushchev had important ramifications for Soviet domestic and foreign policy, leadership changes within the United States during the acute cold war, while having some effects on domestic policy, did not significantly affect the conduct of U.S. foreign policy. President Truman announced the doctrine of containment in 1947 and was supported by a bipartisan coalition, including, importantly, such pre-World War II isolationists as Arthur Vandenberg. Despite differences over U.S. tactics in the Korean War, Truman's successor, Dwight Eisenhower, supported the major cold war aim of American foreign policy—to contain communism—a goal also supported by Presidents John Kennedy and Lyndon Johnson.

Despite various conflicts of interest during the acute cold war, the United States and the Soviet Union developed a number of rules and procedures for crisis management and nuclear deterrence. They were unable, however, to establish comprehensive regimes in the arms control and economic issue areas.

## Soviet and American Strategic Nuclear Policies

### THE ABORTIVE ATTEMPT AT NUCLEAR DISARMAMENT, 1945-1946

The bombings of Hiroshima and Nagasaki ended the most destructive war in human history and demonstrated the new capability of the United States to engage in cataclysmic warfare. Once Japan surrendered, American leaders had to decide how nuclear power should be used. Because there were many potential beneficial uses, it was unwise as well as impractical to attempt to bury the nuclear secret. At the same time, nuclear weapons represented an advance of several magnitudes in weapons design, and it was highly desirable to control the spread of these weapons to other countries. Thus, in November 1945, President Truman, British Prime Minister

Clement Attlee, and Canadian Prime Minister William King met in Washington, D.C., and agreed on the need for international action to provide for the peaceful use of nuclear energy and the prohibition of nuclear weapons.

From 1945 to 1949 the United States was the only state that had nuclear weapons. Many people doubted the effectiveness of strategic bombing, and history provided no precedent for the power of atomic weapons. Perhaps because of the revolutionary nature of these arms, Americans had difficulty in developing political or military strategies for the use of these weapons to gain limited objectives.

In deciding what to do with nuclear weapons, American policymakers faced at least five different options. To some who did not appreciate the implications of the new weapons, the answer was simple: do nothing. There were two proponents of this alternative. The idealists believed that peaceful uses of atomic energy would provide an abundant source of energy for all states and that the atomic age represented an age of plenty. Realists, on the other hand, argued that it made no difference what progress other states might make in nuclear research; the United States could always stay ahead. Therefore there was no reason to try to control nuclear weapons.[11] A second alternative would be for the United States to share its knowledge of nuclear power for peaceful purposes with any state desiring such information. The implementation of this proposal, it was assumed, would engender a climate of goodwill and trust.

The third alternative, relatively rare, envisioned the threat to use nuclear weapons for political and military purposes. Some believed that nuclear weapons could be used to threaten other states in order to achieve certain diplomatic objectives such as the democratization of Eastern European states. But this alternative overlooked the uniqueness of nuclear weapons; U.S. leaders had little experience in traditional diplomacy and no experience in attempting to translate strategic-nuclear power into effective political-military influence.

The fourth option called for the use of nuclear weapons against the Soviet Union. Although such an attack on Soviet nuclear facilities would guarantee the U.S. monopoly on nuclear weapons, "the idea of a preventive war," Arnold Wolfers pointed out in

1946, "is so abhorrent to American feeling that no government in this country . . . could hope to gain popular support for such an adventure."[12] In addition, following the end of the war, the Soviets maintained a very large standing army that could be used to attack Western Europe. For these reasons, preemptive war against the Soviet Union was neither a desirable nor a feasible option for the United States.

The final alternative for dealing with nuclear weapons was to devise a system for controlling or eliminating them. In December 1945, a committee chaired by Under Secretary of State Dean Acheson was appointed to study the control of nuclear energy, and the following month a group of consultants headed by David Lilienthal was appointed to work with Acheson's committee. After three months of work, the Acheson-Lilienthal report was completed and released to the public. It called for the creation of an international authority to own and exercise control over all nuclear research and development. The proposed International Atomic Development Authority (IADA) would also be granted the power to manage, inspect, and license all nuclear facilities. This proposal called for the implementation of an agreement banning nuclear weapons and the termination of U.S. nuclear weapons production and development to be deferred until the IADA was established.

The principal provisions of the Acheson-Lilienthal report were adopted by Bernard Baruch, whom President Truman had appointed to present the U.S. nuclear proposal to the UN. Baruch modified the Acheson-Lilienthal proposal by specifiying that if violations were charged against a member of the UN Security Council, the alleged violator would not be allowed to exercise its veto power. The Soviet Union opposed the Baruch Plan on the issue of the veto and presented a counterproposal, the Gromyko Plan, calling for a ban on the use or fabrication of nuclear weapons and for the destruction of existing stockpiles of weapons. This plan did not contain provisions for effective verification of its implementation. The Baruch and Gromyko plans were the first efforts by the United States and the Soviet Union to achieve nuclear disarmament. When these negotiations failed, the attention of policymakers focused on the means to manage the revolutionary weapons of mass destruction in a new nuclear age.

MANAGING NUCLEAR WEAPONS: THE DEVELOPMENT OF
STRATEGIC NUCLEAR DETERRENCE

Soon after the bombing of Hiroshima and Nagasaki, a small group of civilian strategists in the United States began thinking about the implications of atomic weapons. In 1946, a collection of remarkably prescient essays was published, edited by Bernard Brodie, concerning the impact of atomic weapons on world politics. One of the contributors to this volume pointed out, "To speak of it as just another weapon was highly misleading. It was a revolutionary development which altered the basic character of war itself."[13] In one of his essays, Brodie presented eight postulates on the effect of the bomb on the character of war:

1. The power of the present bomb is such that any city in the world can be effectively destroyed by one to ten bombs.
2. No adequate defense against the bomb exists, and the possibilities of its existence in the future are exceedingly remote.
3. The atomic bomb not only places extraordinary military premium upon the development of new types of carriers but also greatly expands the destructive range of existing carriers.
4. Superiority in air forces, though a more effective safeguard in itself than superiority in naval or land forces, nevertheless fails to guarantee security.
5. Superiority in numbers of bombs is not in itself a guarantee of strategic superiority in atomic bomb warfare.
6. The new potentialities which the atomic bomb gives to sabotage must not be overrated.
7. In relation to the destructive powers of the bomb, world resources in raw materials for its production must be considered abundant.
8. Regardless of American decisions concerning retention of its present secrets, other powers besides Britain and Canada will possess the ability to produce the bombs in quantity within a period of five to ten years hence.[14]

Taken together, these propositions constituted an early formulation of the theory of deterrence: if nuclear weapons could not be eliminated or controlled, then their use should be deterred by persuading "one's opponent that the cost and/or risks of a given course of action he might take outweigh its benefits."[15] The concept of deterrence, as old as humanity, had taken on new meaning in the nuclear age.

During the period of the U.S. nuclear monopoly (1945-1949), Soviet leaders publicly characterized nuclear weapons as militarily insignificant and charged that the new weapons could not materially influence the outcome of any war. They also rhetorically claimed that nuclear war would only adversely affect the capitalist states. Given the relative rapidity with which the Soviet Union developed nuclear weapons and the tremendous cost of this development, it appears that Soviet leaders placed substantially more importance upon the acquisition of nuclear weapons than their public pronouncements indicated. In August 1949, the Soviet Union exploded its first nuclear weapon, ending the U.S. nuclear monopoly. Great Britain exploded its first nuclear weapon in 1952.

Once the USSR developed nuclear arms, Soviet decision makers, like American policymakers four years before, were confronted with the question of what to do with them. Stalin based his analysis of the implications of nuclear weapons for the conduct of war upon his thinking about conventional war. He believed that the new weapons did not call for a drastic change in Soviet military strategy. Thus he viewed nuclear weapons as an adjunct to Soviet conventional forces and emphasized the maintenance of the large Soviet conventional forces.

The revolution in modern weaponry was carried one step further on November 1, 1952, when the United States exploded its first hydrogen (thermonuclear) bomb. The resulting explosion had the equivalent power of one million tons of TNT, was one thousand times more powerful than the Hiroshima bomb, and was about one hundred thousand times more powerful than the largest conventional bombs used in World War II. The Soviet Union exploded its first hydrogen bomb in August 1953. This event, coupled with the death of Stalin in March 1953, opened the way for a rethinking of Soviet nuclear strategy. In contrast to earlier Soviet leaders, Georgi Malenkov first claimed that nuclear war would result in the destruction of both capitalist and socialist societies. Khrushchev denounced Malenkov's ideas but later accepted the view that a general war between the socialists and capitalists would result in the "annihilation of almost all life" in both camps. He went on to assert that the socialist camp would prevail, however, in such a conflict. The recognition by Soviet leaders that nuclear war would be disastrous for all states was important to the development of a strategic nuclear regime. If deterrence were to work, the significant actors had to believe that they were vulnerable to punishment by the other members of the system. If an actor believed, even mistakenly, that it was invulnerable to attack, deterrence would fail.

In the United States, the change of leadership from Truman to Eisenhower in 1953 caused a change in U.S. nuclear policy. Eisenhower promised to end the Korean War and to take a "new look" at U.S. military forces and strategy in order to reduce defense expenditures. In order to obtain maximum deterrence for minimum cost ("bigger bang for the buck"), Eisenhower decided to embark on a policy of massive retaliation whereby, according to John Foster Dulles, the United States would respond to aggression by retaliating "instantly, by means and places of our own choosing."[16] In essence, this policy was an attempt to translate strategic nuclear power into tactical military power. The doctrine of massive retaliation was primarily a declaratory rather than an operational policy and was, probably by design, very ambiguous.

Because of the ambiguity and the questionable assumptions of massive retaliation, a number of people attacked the doctrine in the late 1950s. Critics included former State Department officials Chester Bowles and Dean Acheson, former U.S. Army Chief of Staff Maxwell Taylor, and academicians such as William Kaufmann, Henry Kissinger, and Bernard Brodie. The critics charged that massive retaliation would not be effective in deterring local aggression since potential belligerents would fail to believe that the United States would risk nuclear war to deter local aggression. Massive retaliation became an issue in the 1960 election, and, following his election, President John F. Kennedy announced a new strategic doctrine emphasizing the development of forces designed to provide a flexible response to the action of opponents.

Although Soviet military strategy since World War II differed from that of the United States in significant respects (namely, Soviet emphasis on a war-fighting nuclear capability, as well as deterrence), it also reflected U.S. strategic concepts. Following several years of ambiguous policies during the mid- to late 1950s, the Soviet Union seemed to implement its own massive retaliation policy. In fact, in retrospect it appears that the basic assumption of massive retaliation—that strategic nuclear threats could be used as an instrument of diplomacy—contributed to the making of the most serious crisis of the acute cold war, the Cuban missile crisis.

### CONTROLLING NUCLEAR WEAPONS

Although the United States and the Soviet Union failed to achieve nuclear disarmament in the late 1940s, several significant tacit rules were established. Both superpowers believed that control of nuclear weapons should not be turned over to their respective allies. Similarly, the leaders of both nations believed that they should discourage and prevent, where possible, the proliferation of nuclear weapons.

The UN General Assembly established the UN Atomic Energy Commission in 1946 and the Commission for Conventional Armaments in 1947 to provide some control over nuclear power and conventional weapons; however, by 1950 both organizations were moribund, and in January 1952 the General Assembly created the UN Disarmament Commission to replace the two organizations. No real progress was made in this forum, and, following Stalin's death and the election of Dwight Eisenhower, a new disarmament forum, the Subcommittee on Disarmament, was created in 1954 by the UN. Discussions were held between 1955 and 1957, and several important proposals were presented by the members of the subcommittee. For a number of reasons, the Soviet Union withdrew from the negotiations in September 1957, marking what was probably the final chance to limit nuclear weapons to three nations.

President Eisenhower attributed the Soviet withdrawal from the negotiations to the Soviet development of intercontinental ballistic missiles (ICBM), which may also have stimulated new interest in arms control.[17] The fact that ICBMs could reach the United States from the Soviet Union (or vice-versa) in thirty minutes caused some strategic analysts to shift their focus from the means of employing nuclear weapons to the means of controlling weapons of mass destruction. This new interest in incremental ways to reduce arms levels and to assure deterrence stability was reflected in a number of academic studies published during the early 1960s.[18] In the foreword to the volume edited by Donald Brennan, Jerome Wiesner pointed out:

One idea stands out very clearly in these chapters: the general consensus that civilization is faced with an unprecedented crisis. There is a growing realization that if the arms race is allowed to continue its accelerating pace, our country will have less security, not more, with each passing year. As a result, there is an ever-increasing likelihood of war so disastrous that civilization, if not man himself, will be eradicated.[19]

While the substantive issues of arms control were being widely discussed, several organizations were created to further the objectives of arms control. In 1957, businessman Cyrus Eaton established a conference of Soviet and American scientists to discuss the problems of nuclear weapons and arms control. The Pugwash conferences (so-named since initially they met at Eaton's estate, Pugwash) have played an important role as a transnational Soviet-American organization and have provided an informal communications channel for U.S. and Soviet scientists. Pugwash also served to educate Soviet scientists about American-developed strategic concepts and doctrines. In the view of Wolfgang Panofsky, director of the Stanford linear accelerator and a Pugwash participant, "The reason we have a solid ABM Treaty today is that both sides were educated at the [Pugwash] conferences."[20]

Despite the inability of the United States and the USSR to conclude a nuclear disarmament agreement during the acute cold war, they did take several limited steps toward the development of an arms control regime. Throughout the 1950-1957 period, both states discussed various arms control proposals at UN-sponsored conferences, and informal talks took place at the Pugwash Conferences. By the late 1950s, the superpowers tacitly agreed to follow nonproliferation policies. In 1959 the deployment of weapons of mass destruction to Antarctica was prohibited. In the United States, the Arms Control and Disarmament Agency (ADCA) was created in 1961 to coordinate U.S. policymaking in the arms-control issue area. Very limited progress was made during the acute cold war period toward the establishment of an arms control regime.

THE COLD WAR NUCLEAR DETERRENCE REGIME

In addition to the limited progress on the control of nuclear weapons, the United States and the Soviet Union were able to agree tacitly on several rules that served to stabilize their nuclear relationship. Taken together, the rules constituted a strategic deterrence regime. The first two were essential to the maintenance of this regime:

1.  Each superpower should be able to attack the other superpower with nuclear weapons sufficient to inflict unacceptable damage.
2.  The military forces of one superpower should not be deployed against the military forces or the territory of the other superpower since such action could result in uncontrollable escalation.

The essence of nuclear deterrence is expressed in the first rule: each superpower should have sufficient power to deliver a devastating attack on the other. Nuclear deterrence is most stable when both superpowers have forces that are secure and able to retaliate even in the event of an attack. Throughout the acute cold war, the homelands of the United States and the Soviet Union remained off-limits for conflict. The military forces of the two states never directly engaged one another since leaders of both countries feared that such a hostile confrontation could easily escalate into an uncontrollable conflict. Fear of escalation also led to the maintenance of the threshold between conventional and nuclear weapons, although both superpowers made rhetorical threats to use nuclear weapons in certain situations.

Because the superpowers observed these two rules, the cold war nuclear regime remained balanced and stable. A number of important secondary rules also contributed to the maintenance of the regime:

3.  Control of nuclear weapons should not be turned over to the allies of superpowers.
4.  The superpowers should discourage the proliferation of nuclear weapons and provide non-nuclear states with technical assistance in the development of nuclear power for peaceful purposes.

As early as 1946, some strategic analysts clearly recognized the dangers of nuclear proliferation.[21] The desire to limit the spread of nuclear weapons led to the creation of the UN Atomic Energy Commission in 1946. Despite the dangers of nuclear proliferation, both the Soviet Union and the United States contributed to the problem in the first half of the 1950s. The Soviets, for example, provided technical assistance to the Chinese in their nuclear program, and the United States stimulated many other states' interest in nuclear power as a result of its Atoms for Peace program. By the late 1950s, however, American and Soviet leaders recognized the dangers associated with these programs and tacitly agreed to limit their role in providing information about nuclear power. When the Soviets stopped providing the Chinese with technical advice, a major crisis ensued that contributed to the Sino-Soviet split. The United States and the Soviet Union agreed to share their knowledge of nuclear energy for peaceful purposes with other states that would promise to follow the anti-proliferation safeguards established by the IAEA, which, looking back on his administration's arms control and disarmament efforts, President Eisenhower concluded was the one "considerable accomplishment."[22]

The superpowers considered themselves responsible for the continued stability of the nuclear strategic regime and for this reason, as well as for others, would not provide their allies with nuclear forces that they controlled independently of the superpower. Of course, the Soviet Union was unwilling to provide its Eastern European satellites with nuclear weapons. For its part, the United States supplied its North Atlantic Treaty Organization (NATO) forces with nuclear weapons but retained command and control over these forces. In contrast to the predictions of many analysts in the late 1940s that a large number of states would develop nuclear weapons, the record of nonproliferation since 1945 is reasonably good due largely to American-Soviet tacit cooperation in this area.

5.   It is permissible to threaten the use of nuclear weapons in order to gain political-military advantages.

On a number of occasions during the acute cold war, Soviet and American leaders threatened to use nuclear weapons. For instance,

President Eisenhower threatened the North Koreans with the "nuclear option" in February 1953.[23] This threat was apparently ineffectual, and during the next six months the United States dropped several other hints that it would use nuclear weapons unless an armistice was reached. In July 1953, an armistice was signed. The Soviet Union threatened to use nuclear weapons on several occasions, most notably during the 1956 Suez crisis.

All but the last of these tacit rules of nuclear deterrence contributed to the stability of the Soviet-American strategic-military regime. The use of nuclear threats in order to make political-military gains, however, proved to be potentially destabilizing, and following the Cuban missile crisis, the United States and the Soviet Union agreed to stop attempting to use their strategic forces against one another to make political diplomatic gains.

## Soviet and American Economic Policies

### THE WAXING OF THE ECONOMIC COLD WAR, 1945-1953

Stalin's traditional Russian distrust of the West was heightened by his experiences with Churchill and Roosevelt during World War II and contributed to Stalin's desire after the war to make the Soviet Union independent of the West. Such autonomy, Stalin believed, could be achieved by integrating the Eastern European and Soviet economies. He based his new economic policies on the theory of the "parallel market."[24] According to this theory, a tremendous new market of nearly one billion people had been created by World War II and the civil war in China. Stalin wanted to deny capitalist countries access to this market and in doing so permanently undermine the economic position of the West. He believed that two results would follow: social discontent within capitalist countries and fierce commercial rivalry among capitalist states for the remaining markets.

On June 5, 1947, Secretary of State George Marshall delivered his famous commencement address at Harvard University and stated that the United States was willing to assist with the rebuilding of the devastated European states; however, Marshall pointed out, "The initiative, I think, must come from Europe. . . . The program should be a joint one, agreed to by a number, if not all, European nations."[25] In response to Marshall's proposal, the British and French governments invited all of the countries of Eastern and Western Europe to a conference to formulate a program for European recovery. The Soviet Union was also invited and even attended the conference briefly. It withdrew from the conference, however, and informed all of the Eastern European states that they were forbidden from participating in any American-sponsored economic recovery scheme.

In support of Stalin's economic grand design for Eastern Europe and the Soviet Union, the Council of Mutual Economic Assistance (CMEA) was founded in January 1949. Its members were the Soviet Union, Albania, Bulgaria, Czechoslovakia, East Germany, Hungary, Poland, Rumania, Yugoslavia, and the People's Republic of China. Over 50 percent of Soviet trade was conducted with CMEA countries from 1949 through the 1970s.[26] The Soviet Union exercised tight control over Eastern European trade and demanded that Soviet interests be given precedence over Eastern European interests. For example, Soviet authorities arrested two senior Eastern European trade officials and charged them with being nationalistic and anti-Soviet for attempting to obtain better economic terms for their respective countries' dealings with the Soviet Union. Several of these officials were subsequently executed for their "crimes."[27]

After the offer of Marshall Plan aid was rejected by the Soviet Union and Eastern Europe, the United States turned to a policy of economic warfare vis-à-vis the East. The fundamental assumption of U.S. policymakers after 1947 was that an economically strong Soviet Union and Eastern Europe constituted a threat, and the West and Western governments should therefore do nothing to strengthen these states economically. The United States and its Western European allies sought to restrict East-West trade through three mechanisms: export, financial, and import restrictions.[28]

*Export restrictions.* In 1947, the United States enacted export controls applicable to trade with the Soviet Union. The Soviet blockade of Berlin in April 1948 stimulated the passage of the Export Control Act of 1949, which called for a comprehensive system of controls. In January 1950, the Western European countries and the United States established the Consultative Group-Coordinating Committee (COCOM), an organization founded to coordinate the embargo of the Soviet Union. In pursuit of this objective, COCOM compiled and maintained lists of embargoed goods; at the height of the cold war over a thousand items were proscribed. The outbreak of the Korean War in June 1950 provided the impetus for tightening the strategic embargo of the East. In 1951 the U.S. Congress passed the Mutual Defense Assistance Control Act (Battle Act), which called for the cessation of U.S. economic, military, or financial assistance to any country that provided embargoed goods to the Soviet Union. No cutback or elimination of aid ever occurred; the threat of such action was apparently sufficient to deter trade by Western countries with the Soviet Union in strategic goods.

*Financial restrictions.* During World War I, the United States loaned approximately $22 billion to the states of Europe and the Soviet Union, but with the onset of the depression in the early 1930s, many states defaulted on their loans. As a means to pressure debtor countries, in 1934 Congress passed the Johnson Debt Default Act, which stipulated that no U.S. citizen or corporation could buy or sell securities of or lend money to a government in default on debts to the United States. However, most Western, as well as Eastern European governments, were in default; Bulgaria and Albania were the only communist countries that had not defaulted. Therefore, to make loans to Western Europe possible under the Marshall Plan, the Johnson Act was amended to exclude any member country of the World Bank and the International Monetary Fund from the provisions of the Johnson Act. Yugoslavia was the only communist member of these institutions. Thus, most Eastern European states, as well as the Soviet Union, which had also incurred a substantial debt under Lend-Lease, were subject to the provisions of the act, while Western European states were exempt. According to East-West trade expert Samuel Pisar, the United States was the only Western state that placed such restrictions on the extension of private credit to the Eastern bloc.[29]

*Import restrictions.* The Trade Agreements Extension Act of 1951 withdrew most-favored-nation (MFN) treatment from all Eastern bloc countries, except Yugoslavia. This action resulted in the application of the high tariffs of the Smoot-Hawley Act of 1930 to goods imported from the East. In many cases, the high tariff levels removed the potential profit from trading and therefore severely restricted East-West trade.

By 1951, the rules and institutions founded by the United States and its Western European allies and Japan were firmly established and operating. A measure of their effectiveness is reflected in the decline of Soviet-American trade.

### THE WANING OF THE ECONOMIC COLD WAR, 1954-1962

The death of Stalin in March 1953 and the de facto Korean War armistice of July 1953 marked significant turning points for Soviet and American cold war policies. Stalin's theory of "parallel markets" had not proved correct; the West had not suffered grievously because of the inaccessibility of Eastern markets. In fact, some in Eastern Europe and the Soviet Union believed that the communist states had suffered more than the West had. Some businessmen in the noncommunist world believed that the Stalinist autarkic policies had hurt Western economies. As a result of these beliefs, efforts were made to increase East-West trade, and between 1953 and 1954 Soviet trade turnover with noncommunist states increased significantly from $1 billion to $1.375 billion. By 1955 Soviet trade with the noncommunist world constituted over one-quarter of all Soviet trade. Table 2 depicts the growth of Soviet trade with the West from 1959 through 1960.

The renewed Soviet interest in trade with the West apparently was stimulated by a desire to obtain advanced industrial equipment and credits. In his memoirs, Khrushchev recalled a meeting with Nelson Rockefeller:

> We were interested in talking to Rockefeller about the possibility of getting credit from the United States, something on the order of six billion dollars. But the Americans were already pressing us to repay them the money we owed them for the Lend Lease. We told them we were willing to pay them a certain amount, but not all, of what we owed. . . . if they would give us six billion dollars' credit. We had some discussions about this, but nothing ever came of it.[30]

Thus despite an apparent Soviet interest in expanding Soviet-American commercial relations, the Lend-Lease issue remained an

Table 2

### SOVIET TRADE TURNOVER, 1951-1960
### (MILLIONS OF DOLLARS)

| Year | Total Turnover | With Other Soviet Bloc States | | With Free World | |
|------|------|------|------|------|------|
| | *Value* | *Value* | *Percent* | *Value* | *Percent* |
| 1951 | 4,500 | 3,640 | 81 | 860 | 19 |
| 1952 | 5,200 | 4,160 | 80 | 1,040 | 20 |
| 1953 | 5,750 | 4,750 | 83 | 1,000 | 17 |
| 1954 | 6,250 | 4,875 | 78 | 1,375 | 22 |
| 1955 | 6,300 | 4,900 | 78 | 1,400 | 22 |
| 1956 | 7,225 | 5,350 | 74 | 1,875 | 26 |
| 1957 | 8,320 | 6,000 | 70 | 2,320 | 30 |
| 1958 | 8,647 | 6,378 | 74 | 2,269 | 26 |
| 1959 | 10,514 | 7,913 | 75 | 2,601 | 25 |
| 1960 | 11,193 | 8,015 | 72 | 3,178 | 28 |

*Source:* U.S. Department of Commerce, cited by U.S. Congress, Joint Economic Committee, *A New Look at Trade Policy Toward the Communist Bloc: The Elements of a Common Strategy for the West* (Washington, D.C.: Government Printing Office, 1961), p. 75.

obstacle, symbolic of the enduring perception of U.S. policy-makers that the cold war should be fought with economic as well as military instruments.

Stalin's isolationist economic policy halted the import of technology from the West, which, according to some experts, had been very important to Russian economic and industrial development since the revolution.[31] In some categories of equipment, contact with Western technological developments had been lost for a decade and a half, and in some industrial sectors, the Soviet Union lacked the factories to produce needed products. In these areas, the Soviets turned to the West. For instance, from 1953 to 1954, the Soviet government ordered over two hundred vessels (primarily fishing trawlers) from Western shipyards.

By the convening of the Twentieth Party Congress in February 1956, Stalin's isolationist economic policy had been discredited, and trade with the West resumed on a limited but significant basis. At the Congress, Khrushchev denounced the abuses perpetrated by Stalin in his famous "secret speech."[32] Unnoticed by many Western observers who focused their attention on Khrushchev's speech, Anastas Mikoyan disavowed many of Stalin's economic theories, contending that Stalin had not fully understood modern capitalism and the "fact of the growth of capitalist production." He went on to attack the theory of parallel markets: "In our analysis of the state of the economy of contemporary capitalism we can hardly find helpful, or hardly correct, the well-known assertion of Stalin . . . to the effect that following the split of the world market 'the volume of production in these countries will shrink.' "[33]

In response to Soviet efforts to increase trade in the mid-1950s, the U.S. government reduced the COCOM embargo lists in 1954 and again in 1956. This was only a small step toward lessening the obstacles in the way of increased Soviet-American trade since important financial restrictions (such as the Johnson Act) and import restrictions (denial of MFN) remained in effect.

From 1958 through 1961, Khrushchev proposed the expansion of Soviet-American trade on a number of occasions. For instance, in June 1958 he wrote to Eisenhower and called for large industrial purchases (including entire factories) by the Soviet Union from the United States, but Eisenhower's response was "curt and unenthusiastic."[34] While Khrushchev suggested a significant widening of trade and, by inference, therefore, a substantial modification of Soviet and American cold war economic policies, Eisenhower proposed that trade proceed according to the existing rules and procedures.[35] Although the United States refused to change significantly financial, export, and import restrictions on East-West trade, Western European states increasingly engaged in trade with the East from the mid-1950s.

Throughout the acute cold war, American and Soviet foreign economic policies were out of phase; when the United States offered Marshall plan aid to Eastern Europe and the Soviet Union, Stalin was not interested, and when Khrushchev, reversing Stalin's isolationist economic policies, expressed a desire to expand Soviet-American trade, the United States maintained its cold war policy of economic warfare vis-à-vis the East.

## Soviet-American Crisis Management

Fortunately the United States and the Soviet Union fought the cold war primarily with words and economic and military aid rather than with bullets; however, on three occasions (Berlin, 1948; Berlin, 1961; and Cuba, 1962), the superpowers directly confronted one another in major crises that threatened to escalate into war. On a number of other occasions, conflicts that initially involved the superpowers or their respective allies threatened to escalate into superpower confrontations.

American and Soviet leaders were aware and afraid of the dangers of escalation and for this reason developed a set of implicit norms for dealing with potential or actual superpower crises. These norms, taken together, constituted a Soviet-American regime for crisis management. To be sure, this regime evolved during the entire course of the cold war and was almost completely implicit. The rules for crisis management and nuclear deterrence were similar in several important respects. For instance, the avoidance of escalation to nuclear war and the desire to avoid direct confrontations between the military forces of the superpowers were fundamental to both regimes. Although the rules for crisis management clearly do not characterize Soviet and American foreign policy behavior in each individual crisis, they do describe the general behavior of the two superpowers during the acute cold war.

The development of nuclear weapons had raised new and disturbing questions about the use of force in world politics. Would any conflict involving U.S. and Soviet forces ultimately lead to the use of nuclear weapons? Under what circumstances would they be used? Could nuclear weapons be controlled? The answers to these questions were far from obvious during the early part of the acute cold war.

### EARLY POSTWAR SOVIET-AMERICAN CRISES

By the end of World War II, it was clear that the war had resulted not only in the physical destruction of much of Europe; it had also destroyed the European-oriented international state system that had evolved from the Peace of Westphalia of 1648. Although the United States was more powerful, wealthier, and unscathed by the war relative to the European and Asian states and was therefore the most logical leader of a new postwar security system, American leaders did not view this as their country's natural (or even desirable) role during the first year and a half following the end of the war. But the crises over Greece, Turkey, and Iran catalyzed the development of the doctrine of containment.

Relations between the United States and the Soviet Union continued to worsen throughout 1947 and the first half of 1948. In March 1948, the Soviets walked out of the Allied Control Council, the organization charged with the responsibility of governing Germany and located in Berlin. Several weeks later the Soviets imposed rail and road restrictions on Allied traffic from West Germany to Berlin. The Western occupying forces responded by airlifting supplies to their forces in Berlin. In June, the Soviets gradually decreased Western traffic to Berlin until finally, on June 24, they imposed a full blockade of the city.

At one end of the spectrum, several of Truman's advisers recommended that the United States respond to the Soviet blockade with a strategy of coercive diplomacy, while several others recommended that the United States withdraw from Berlin altogether. Rejecting these two extremes, Truman responded to the blockade with a quickly organized airlift designed to buy time for negotiations. Initially U.S. planners believed that it would be impossible to airlift the supplies needed to sustain the population of West Berlin; however, the airlift proved to be an effective means of breaking the ground blockade without directly confronting Soviet or East German forces. Although the Soviet Union threatened to interfere with these flights, it never did so, and a set of ground rules evolved during the first days of the crisis.[36] The Allied resupply effort was sufficient to supply the residents of Berlin with their vital needs, and rather than escalating the conflict, the Soviets and Allied powers negotiated a settlement to the conflict in 1949.

Since it was the first crisis in which Soviet and American military forces confronted one another directly, the Berlin crisis was very important in establishing the initial rules for Soviet-American crisis interaction. Above all, both superpowers demonstrated caution and restraint. Bernard Brodie has pointed out that "in retrospect it is difficult to find evidence of any threat of force by the

Soviet leaders to deny us ground access to Berlin.''[37] As the Soviets implemented the blockade over a span of three months, the Western powers did little to make their protest effective. For their part, the Allies neither escalated the conflict nor threatened coercive action even after the imposition of the total blockade on June 24. According to Alexander George and Richard Smoke, from the Soviet perspective, the blockade, a "classical example of a low-risk, potentially high-gain strategy," was controllable and reversible.[38] From the American standpoint, the blockade created a crisis that could easily escalate into a direct military conflict between Soviet and American forces. But by exercising great caution, Soviet and American leaders passed the first major test of crisis management.

In a sense, cold war crises provided opportunities for leaders to learn how to manage diplomatic and military means at their disposal so that armed conflict could be minimized or avoided altogether. In the 1948 Berlin crisis, decision makers developed a number of rules of crisis management. Similarly, the Korean War was an extremely important experience for U.S. decision makers since they were forced by events to consider the unresolved questions of the new nuclear era: How can conflicts be controlled and under what conditions should nuclear weapons be used? In his memoirs, Khrushchev indicates that Stalin encouraged North Korea's Kim Il-sung concerning his plans for attacking South Korea without giving the implications of such an attack serious thought.[39] Although historians continue to debate the degree to which the Soviet Union supported and/or pressured the North Koreans to attack, it seems inconceivable that such action would have been taken by Kim Il-sung without the knowledge and approval of the Soviet Union.

On June 25, 1950, when North Korea launched a massive attack on South Korea, U.S. officials were taken by surprise and had no military contingency plans for such an event. President Truman met with a small group of advisers and decided to intervene with U.S. military forces. Although the problems associated with the conduct of limited war differ in some respects from those of crisis management, each type of conflict management requires the exercise of similar restraints. Both situations require close control over military operations by political leadership due to the inherent tension between military and political objectives. Understandably the military commander wants to use the coercive force at his disposal as effectively as possible in order to minimize losses to his forces. The political leaders of a state, in contrast, often want force to be used in a limited, controlled manner so that the conflict will not escalate into a costly general war. Based on the U.S. experience in the Korean War in general and on the Truman-MacArthur controversy in particular, several scholars have developed useful prescriptions for American decision makers in managing crises;[40] however, these prescriptions are applicable primarily to the United States and do not address the question of what reciprocal rules for crisis management are followed (or should be followed) by the parties involved in a crisis situation.

Although the Soviet Union was not directly involved in the Korean War with its own military forces, the war contributed to the development of a Soviet-American crisis management regime. Most importantly, the Korean War remained limited. Limitations on the conduct of war may assume several different forms. First, the war may be limited to a certain geographic area. In the Korean War, American officials stated that U.S. forces would not invade China; however, when General Douglas MacArthur launched his offensive, the Chinese feared an invasion of their homeland and launched a counteroffensive. This type of action accentuates the critical importance of communications in limiting war: messages must be clearly understandable and credible. Second, limits may be placed on the types of weapons used in a war; neither chemical-biological nor nuclear weapons were used in the Korean War. Third, limits may be placed on acceptable targets. Fourth, the participants must be limited. Finally, the pace of the conflict may be controlled.[41] The Korean War provides a number of examples in which these various types of limitations were observed, both effectively and ineffectively.

At the onset of the Korean War, the cold war became the central fact of world politics, and the United States assumed the leadership of the Western states, a position that it had shunned following the end of World War II. With the Berlin blockade and the Korean War, Soviet and American leaders learned how to control, manage, and limit political-military crises. This education was costly in human lives and dollars but relatively inexpensive when compared to the possible alternative of general war.

Throughout the cold war the education process continued. In 1961, tensions increased concerning Berlin and at the Vienna summit meeting in June, Khrushchev gave Kennedy an *aide-memoire* demanding that East and West Germany negotiate a means of reunification within six months and that West Berlin become an international city. The Soviets also increased harassment of highway (*Autobahn*) and air traffic to West Berlin. Some of John Kennedy's advisers, most notably Dean Acheson, recommended that the United States reject the Soviet proposals outright and prepare for a confrontation, including, if necessary, a military confrontation with the Soviets. Kennedy rejected Acheson's call for a declaration of a national emergency but requested and received from Congress increased appropriations for U.S. forces in Europe, authority to call up reserves and increase draft calls, authority to implement economic sanctions against East European states, and a tax increase to pay for these measures. On August 13, the East German government anounced that East Germans would not be allowed to travel to West Berlin. Although the United States officially protested this action, it took no action to remove the barbed wire barriers, and within several days the East Germans began to build a permanent wall, presumably with the approval, if not the encouragement, of the Soviet Union. Kennedy responded by reinforcing the Allied garrison in West Berlin, appointing General Lucius Clay as the American commander, ordering a movement of U.S. troops along the *Autobahn* to exercise access rights, and dispatching Vice-President Lyndon Johnson to West Berlin. Although there were several dramatic confrontations, most notably at "Checkpoint Charlie," no shots were fired in the 1961 Berlin crisis. In fact, there is evidence to suggest that the East German troops were not equipped with live ammunition, suggesting that Eastern forces were fearful of the outbreak and escalation of violence in the conflict.[42]

Soviet and American foreign policy behavior during the Cuban missile crisis, perhaps the most serious U.S.-Soviet crisis of the entire acute cold war period, provided further evidence that Soviet and American decision makers were afraid of possible escalation resulting from a direct superpower military confrontation.

Rather than reviewing the history of cold war confrontations, I will describe the implicit norms that developed in the course of Soviet-American cold war crisis interaction. Although scholars who have analyzed the phenomenon of Soviet-American crisis management have commented on the development of rules and norms, no one has systematically described these rules.[43] Undoubtedly the rules were violated by the Soviet Union or the United States (or both) in particular crises, but I believe that an explicit listing and discussion of these rules will contribute to a better understanding of the Soviet-American cold war crisis management regime.

RULES CONCERNING THE USE OF FORCE

1. Force should not be used against the military units or territory of the other superpower.
2. The escalation of conflicts should be considered very carefully and avoided if possible.

One of the most striking aspects of the acute cold war period is that despite the dominant atmosphere of hostility in Soviet-American relations, on only three occasions did military units of the two superpowers directly confront one another. Soviet and American military units were cautious and restrained in the Berlin airlift of 1948, and in the 1961 Berlin crisis, both sides again demonstrated restraint.

During numerous other incidents and crises, Soviet and American leaders used their military forces against the forces of the other superpower sparingly and cautiously. For instance, in 1960 the Soviets shot down an American U-2 flying over their country. Rather than escalating the conflict, President Eisenhower acknowledged that the flight was officially sponsored by the U.S. government and did not question the legal right of the Soviet action.

3. If armed force is used during a crisis, the military units of superpowers' allies should be used if possible.
4. Each superpower recognized on a de facto rather than de jure basis the sphere of influence of the other superpower and would not intervene militarily into a recognized sphere of influence area.

In situations where the objectives at stake are not important enough to warrant the direct involvement of the superpowers' military forces, the United States and the Soviet Union have used proxy military forces of allied states or friendly groups, a strategy that enables the superpower to avoid the direct use of its own military forces and at the same time to scale down the level of risk. The Soviet Union employed proxies on a number of occasions during the acute cold war: East Germany in the 1948 and 1961 Berlin crises, North Korea and China in the Korean War, and the Arab states in the 1956 Middle East War. The United States has provided support for proxy forces in the following cases: Iran (1946), Greece (1947), Congo (1960), the Bay of Pigs (1961), and Vietnam (1961-1965).

Despite their aggressive rhetoric, both the Soviet Union and the United States recognized each other's spheres of influence. In the 1948 and 1961 Berlin crises, Soviet actions appeared to be limited probes designed to test American resolve. When it became apparent that U.S. decision makers placed a high value on remaining in the city, the Soviets accepted the pre-crisis status quo regarding U.S. forces in Berlin. Despite the Eisenhower-Dulles talk about the rollback of communism in Eastern Europe, the United States took no action to stop Soviet forces from intervening in Hungary in 1956. Significantly it was the Soviet violation of the American sphere of influence in Latin America that led to the Cuban missile crisis, one of the three most serious crises of the acute cold war.

5. Except in extreme situations (for example, in the case of a Soviet attack on Western Europe), nuclear weapons should not be used, even in a situation of tactical advantage, since their use would significantly increase the probability of escalation to general nuclear war.

With most weapons—firearms, artillery, bombers, ships—there is an expectation that they will be used if it is expedient to do so. With nuclear weapons, the superpowers recognize that there are very few times when the use of such weapons would be expedient. American and Soviet leaders (at least since Khrushchev) fear that such use might cause a conflict to escalate into general nuclear war.

COMMUNICATION RULES

6. Communication by deed is more effective than verbal or narrative communication.

7. Threats of the use of force, including threats to use nuclear weapons, are permissible as a means to accentuate signals.

Effective communication is a prerequisite for effective crisis management by the superpowers individually and between them bilaterally. In an age of near-instantaneous global communications, the problems of communications can be mistakenly minimized or forgotten. As recently as 1960 during the Congo crisis, for example, the American embassy in Leopoldville could only communicate with Washington, D.C., via a civilian ham operator in Frankfurt who happened to pick up their transmissions and who then telephoned messages to Supreme Headquarters Allied Powers Europe (SHAPE) headquarters where the messages were relayed to Washington.[44]

The problem of communications between the Soviet Union and the United States is even more important and complicated than the example illustrates. Communications may be direct or indirect. Direct forms of communication include telephone, telegraph, diplomatic notes, public speeches, or visits, and indirect forms include actions such as troop movements, air force and naval deployments, and changes in diplomatic practices. Since no direct communications links between the United States and the Soviet Union existed during the acute cold war (other than the embassies in Washington and Moscow), Soviet and American political leaders usually communicated messages by their actions rather than words. Leaders of both superpowers apparently believed that actions were more credible and less ambiguous in their meaning. Consequently scholars and policymakers devoted a great deal of time and energy to the analysis of superpower signaling.

### BARGAINING RULES

8. Bargaining is largely tacit.
9. The United States and the Soviet Union seek to limit their risks in crises; however, the risk-taking calculus for each superpower is strongly influenced by differing historical traditions and ideologies.

During the acute cold war, Soviet-American bargaining during crises tended to be tacit, with the presentation of proposals by deed rather than by words. To be understood clearly, successful proposals have to be simple, recognizable, and conspicuous.[45] American and Soviet foreign policy behavior during crises did not always conform to these requirements; however, in successful cases of Soviet-American crisis management, these attributes were usually present.

Some evidence suggests that during the acute cold war Soviet leaders primarily sought control over risks, even if they were high, while American decision makers raised the risks only if they were clearly willing to escalate a conflict.[46] Thus although the attitudes of Soviet and American decision makers concerning risk acceptance differed, both nevertheless sought to limit risks.

### ALLIANCE MANAGEMENT RULE

10.  The United States and the Soviet Union should exercise firm control to prevent the escalation of conflict.

The cold war was primarily a matter between the Soviet Union and the United States and secondarily between the states of Eastern and Western Europe. Because of the disproportionate power held by the two superpowers relative to the European countries, decision making during crises was centered in Washington and Moscow. Although the United States and the USSR would usually advise or consult with their respective allies, the allies never were given an equal voice in deciding the response to a particular crisis.

## Conclusion

Following the end of World War II, Soviet-American relations worsened, and conflict threatened to break out between the world's two most powerful states. Despite the intense rivalry that existed between the United States and the Soviet Union, certain interests were so important that both countries' leaders decided that limited cooperation in several areas was highly desirable. The fear of a Soviet-American general war involving the use of nuclear weapons led U.S. and Soviet leaders to develop rules and procedures for the management of nuclear weapons; in other words, a nuclear deterrence regime was created (table 3 summarizes the rules of the acute cold war regimes). The fear of another world war also motivated

**Table 3**

**ACUTE COLD WAR POLICIES AND REGIMES**

| Strategic Military Issue Area | Economic Issue Area | Crisis Management Issue Area |
|---|---|---|
| Nuclear deterrence regime established | Nonregime | Implicit regime established |
| Each superpower should be able to attack the other with nuclear weapons sufficient to inflict unacceptable damage | Soviet policies: Stalin: Autarky Khrushchev: Turn to the West | Rules concerning the use of force Force should not be used against the military units or territory of the other superpower |
| The military forces of one superpower should not be deployed against the military forces or territory of the other superpower | U.S. policies: Marshall Plan aid offered and refused; U.S. then sought to isolate the USSR and Eastern Europe from the Western international system | Avoid escalation of conflict Use proxy military forces De facto spheres of influence recognized |
| It is permissible to threaten the use of nuclear weapons in order to gain political-military advantages | | Except in extreme situations, nuclear weapons should not be used |
| Disarmament: Nonregime | | Communication rules Communicate by deed rather than words |
| U.S.: Presented the Baruch Plan, which called for international control of nuclear power, provided on-site inspections were permitted | | Threats of the use of force, including nuclear threats, are permissible |
| USSR: Presented the Gromyko Plan, which called for the destruction of all nuclear weapons and then inspection | | |

*—Continued*

**Table 3** —*Continued*

| Strategic Military Issue Area | Economic Issue Area | Crisis Management Issue Area |
|---|---|---|
| Arms Control: Weak, limited regime<br><br>Control of nuclear weapons should not be turned over to allies of the superpowers<br><br>The U.S. and USSR should discourage the proliferation of nuclear weapons and provide non-nuclear states with technical assistance in the development of nuclear power for peaceful purposes<br><br>Deployment of weapons to Antarctica prohibited (1959)<br><br>Pugwash conferences | | Bargaining rules<br><br>Bargaining is largely tacit<br>Risks should be limited<br>Alliance management rule<br><br>Firm control over allies should be exercised to avoid escalation |

Soviet and American leaders to develop certain rules for crisis avoidance and crisis management. These rules evolved throughout the 1947-1962 period, and by the end of the period the rules were well established, even though they were informal and tacit.

In areas that did not threaten the most vital mutual interest of the two superpowers, survival, the U.S. and Soviet leaders were not sufficiently motivated to create agreed rules, procedures, and institutions for managing potential or actual conflicts of interest. Thus Soviet-American economic relations remained moribund throughout the acute cold war; attempts at nuclear disarmament failed completely; and very limited progress was made in the arms control issue area. The findings in this chapter suggest that in periods of high tension, the greater the perceived salience of an issue, the greater the probability that a regime will be established.

## Notes

1. Harry S. Truman, *Memoirs: Years of Decisions* (Garden City, N.Y.: Doubleday, 1955), p. 509.
2. *Vital Speeches* 12 (March 15, 1946): 329-32.
3. *Newsweek* 27 (March 25, 1946): 24.
4. Quoted by John Lewis Gaddis, *The United States and the Origins of the Cold War* (New York: Columbia University Press, 1972), p. 311.
5. A revised version of Kennan's dispatch was published under the pseudonym "X"; see "The Sources of Soviet Conduct," *Foreign Affairs* 25 (July 1947): 566-82.
6. J. Schaar, "Legitimacy in the Modern State," in P. Green and S. Levinson, eds., *Power and Community* (New York: Pantheon, 1970), p. 285.
7. B. Thomas Trout, "Rhetoric Revisited: Political Legitimation and the Cold War," *International Studies Quarterly* 19 (September 1975): 252.
8. Dean Acheson, *Present at the Creation: My Years in the State Department* (New York: W. W. Norton, 1969), p. 293.
9. *Public Papers of the Presidents: Harry S. Truman: 1947* (Washington, D.C.: Government Printing Office, 1963), p. 179.
10. George F. Kennan, *Memoirs, 1925-1950* (Boston: Little, Brown, 1967), p. 322.
11. The idealist and realist support of a do-nothing nuclear policy is described by William T. R., Fox, "International Control of Atomic Weap-

ons," in Bernard Brodie, *The Absolute Weapon: Atomic Power and World Order* (New York: Harcourt, Brace and Company, 1946), pp. 179-81.

12. Arnold Wolfers, "The Atomic Bomb in Soviet-American Relations," in Brodie, *Absolute Weapon*, p. 117.

13. Frederick S. Dunn, "The Common Problem," in Brodie, *Absolute Weapon,* p. 4.

14. Bernard Brodie, "War in the Atomic Age," in Brodie, *Absolute Weapon*, pp. 24-63.

15. Alexander L. George and Richard Smoke, *Deterrence in American Foreign Policy: Theory and Practice* (New York: Columbia University Press, 1974), p. 11.

16. John Foster Dulles, "Speech to the Council on Foreign Relations," *Department of State Bulletin* 30 (January 25, 1954): 107-10.

17. Dwight D. Eisenhower, *Waging Peace, 1956-1961* (Garden City, N.Y.: Doubleday, 1965), pp. 472-73.

18. Hedley Bull, *The Control of the Arms Race* (New York: Praeger, 1961); Donald G. Brennan, ed., *Arms Control, Disarmament, and National Security* (New York: George Braziller, 1961); and Thomas C. Schelling and Morton Halperin, *Strategy and Arms Control* (New York: Twentieth-Century Fund, 1961).

19. Jerome B. Wiesner, foreword to Brennan, *Arms Control*, p. 14.

20. Public lecture by Wolfgang Panofsky, Stanford University, January 21, 1976.

21. Brodie, "War in the Atomic Age," p. 63.

22. Eisenhower, *Waging Peace, 1956-1961*, p. 468.

23. Dwight D. Eisenhower, *The White House Years: Mandate for Change: 1953-1956* (Garden City, N.Y.: Doubleday, 1963), p. 181.

24. Samuel Pisar, *A New Look at Trade Policy toward the Communist Bloc*, report prepared for the Joint Economic Committee (Washington, D.C.: Government Printing Office, 1961), p. 72.

25. Quoted by Louis J. Halle, *The Cold War as History* (New York: Harper and Row, 1967), p. 129.

26. See table 2-2 in Marshall I. Goldman, *Détente and Dollars: Doing Business with the Soviets* (New York: Basic Books, 1975), p. 24.

27. Ibid., p. 23.

28. For a summary of the Western rules and institutions created to support these controls, see "Appendix I: Restrictions on East-West Trade," in ibid, pp. 289-91.

29. Pisar, *New Look at Trade Policy*, p. 71.

30. Nikita Khrushchev, *Khrushchev Remembers*, ed. and trans. Strobe Talbott (Boston: Little, Brown, 1970), 1: 399.

31. Anthony C. Sutton, *Western Technology and Soviet Economic Development*, vol. 1: *1917-1930*, vol. 2: *1930-1945*, vol. 3: *1945-1965* (Stanford, Calif.: Hoover Institution Press, 1968, 1971).

32. Reprinted in Khrushchev, *Khrushchev Remembers*, 1: 559-618.

33. Quoted by Pisar, *New Look at Trade Policy*, p. 11.

34. Ibid., p. 13.

35. For the texts of both Khrushchev's and Eisenhower's letters, see *Department of State Bulletin* (August 4, 1958): 200-2.

36. Alexander L. George, David K. Hall, and William R. Simons, *The Limits of Coercive Diplomacy: Laos, Cuba, Vietnam* (Boston: Little, Brown, 1971), pp. 20-21.

37. Bernard Brodie, *Escalation and the Nuclear Option* (Princeton: Princeton University Press, 1966), p. 45.

38. George and Smoke, *Deterrence in American Foreign Policy*, p. 118.

39. Khrushchev, *Khrushchev Remembers*, 1: 367-73.

40. George, Hall, and Simons, *Limits of Coercive Diplomacy*, pp. 8-15; Glenn D. Paige, *The Korean Decision* (New York: Free Press, 1968), pp. 361-64; Ole R. Holsti, *Crisis, Escalation, War* (Montreal: McGill-Queens University Press, 1972); Thomas W. Milburn, "The Management of Crisis," in Charles F. Hermann, ed., *International Crises: Insights from Behavioral Research* (New York: Free Press, 1972), pp. 259-80; Glenn H. Snyder, "Crisis Bargaining," in Hermann, *International Crises*.

41. Several of these types of limitations are described by Edward L. Warner III, "Escalation and Limitation in Warfare," in Richard G. Head and Ervin J. Rokke, eds, *American Defense Policy*, 3d ed. (Baltimore: Johns Hopkins University Press, 1973).

42. Hannes Adomeit, "Soviet Risk-Taking and Crisis Behaviour: A Theoretical and Empirical Analysis" (Ph.D. diss., Columbia University, 1977).

43. Both Coral Bell and Phil Williams repeatedly refer to "the conventions of crisis," but neither author explicitly describes the rules of crisis management. See Coral Bell, *The Conventions of Crisis: A Study in Diplomatic Management* (London: Oxford University Press, 1971), and Phil Williams, *Crisis Management: Confrontation and Diplomacy in the Nuclear Age* (New York: John Wiley, 1976).

44. This example is quoted by Alastair Buchan, *Crisis Management: The New Diplomacy* (Boulogne-sur-Seine: Atlantic Institute, 1966), p. 45.

45. Thomas C. Schelling, *Arms and Influence* (New Haven: Yale University Press, 1966), p. 137.

46. Jan F. Triska and David D. Finley, *Soviet Foreign Policy* (New York: Macmillan, 1968).

# CHAPTER 2

# THE LIMITED DÉTENTE REGIMES

Both John Kennedy and Nikita Khrushchev were cognizant of the dangers of a Soviet-American military confrontation, but the Cuban missile crisis dramatically highlighted the possibility of nuclear war between the two superpowers. In a letter written to Khrushchev on October 27, 1962, during the latter part of the crisis, President Kennedy referred to the possibility of a Soviet-American détente:

I would like to say again that the United States is very much interested in reducing tensions and halting the arms race; and if your letter signified that you are prepared to discuss a détente affecting NATO and the Warsaw Pact, we are quite prepared to consider with our allies any useful proposals.[1]

After the crisis, Kennedy and Khrushchev initiated efforts to lessen tension between their two countries and to lessen the probability of nuclear war. The Hot Line Agreement and the Limited Test Ban Treaty, both signed in 1963, were the first fruits of these efforts. In keeping with the classical diplomatic meaning of détente as the lessening of tensions between two or more states, the period following the Cuban missile crisis has been characterized as one of reduced Soviet-American tensions and the end of the acute cold war. Because a number of factors precluded a comprehensive lessening of tensions between the United States and the Soviet

Union, the 1963-1968 period can appropriately be called the limited détente era.

## The Limited Détente International System

The Cuban missile crisis was not the only factor that contributed to the waning of the acute cold war; it was, rather, the catalyst for change. There were a number of other developments in the international system that significantly affected Soviet-American relations in this period. Among the most important developments were: the fragmentation of the cold war American and Soviet alliance systems; the full economic and political recovery of many countries that had suffered heavily in World War II; the achievement of strategic nuclear parity by the Soviet Union with the United States; the assertion of nationalism in both developed and developing states; the ability of many new states to maintain their independence vis-à-vis the Soviet Union and China without having to depend on the United States for protection; the increasing importance of economic forms of power within the international system; and leadership changes in the United States, the Soviet Union, and China.

During the early 1960s, Sino-Soviet relations were openly hostile, and in the aftermath of the Cuban missile crisis the Chinese openly castigated the Soviet Union for capitulating to the United States. Mao Zedong viewed the Limited Test Ban Treaty of 1963 as further proof of a U.S.-Soviet condominium. This agreement, in fact, symbolically marked an important realignment of the major actors in the international system. Following the signing of the hot-line and test ban agreements, American, Soviet, and Chinese decision makers recognized that the United States and the Soviet Union were no longer total enemies; rather they were "limited adversaries."[2] Partially in response to the Soviet-American lessening of tensions in 1963, the Chinese emphasized the importance of developing their own nuclear weapons and of becoming independent of the Soviet Union. In October 1964, the People's Republic of China detonated its first nuclear device, followed by four more detonations over the next two years. In June 1967, the Chinese exploded their first hydrogen bomb. The Sino-Soviet split and the subsequent development of a Chinese nuclear weapons capability marked a dramatic development in the international system, which, following these developments, was no longer unambiguously bipolar.

Although not as serious as the Sino-Soviet split, the Soviet-Eastern European alliance system showed certain signs of tension by the late 1950s and early 1960s. One of the clearest and most important indicators of this tension was the Soviet intervention into Hungary in 1956. Soon after the crisis, the United States provided economic assistance to Poland, which with Yugoslavia were the only Communist states to be granted most-favored-nation status by the United States. In October 1963, President Josip Tito of Yugoslavia visited Washington, evidence of a closer U.S.-Yugoslavian relationship. In the mid-1960s a number of academic and governmental figures in Czechoslovakia argued that Eastern Europe had fallen far behind Western Europe scientifically and technologically and that extensive internal reform as well as substantially increased contact with the West would be required to reap the benefits of the scientific-technological revolution of the modern age. Rumania's President Nicolae Ceausescu also sought increased contact with the West and greater autonomy from the Soviet Union. In addition, he, unlike the Czech leaders, maintained close relations with China and pursued conservative domestic policies.

Fragmentation and decentralization were not unique to the Soviet alliance system. In the West the states of Western Europe and Japan had fully recovered both economically and politically from the devastation caused by World War II and were no longer as dependent upon the United States as they had been immediately following the war. This recovery marked a second major development in the limited détente international system. During the late 1950s, the Western European states began to assert their independence from the United States, and by the early 1960s, Charles de Gaulle symbolized this new assertion of nationalist sentiment when he blocked the entry of Great Britain into the Common Market. Earlier de Gaulle had announced the creation of a French nuclear force, which he claimed would "completely change the conditions of our [French] defense, those of our intervention in faraway lands and those of the contribution that we would be able to make to safeguard our allies."[3] In 1966, France with-

drew its military forces from NATO accentuating the tensions
of NATO members' "troubled partnership."

With the election of Willi Brandt as chancellor in 1966, West
Germany began to make overtures to Eastern Europe for improving
relations. Brandt was quick to point out, however, that *Ostpolitik*
did not lessen the Federal Republic's commitment to NATO.

A third major development in the limited détente international
system was the achievement of strategic nuclear parity by the Soviet
Union. At the time of the Cuban missile crisis, Soviet strategic
forces were significantly inferior to U.S. forces. According to
estimates, in 1962 the Soviet Union had no more than seventy-five
ICBMs while the United States had almost three hundred.[4] After
the Cuban missile crisis (some analysts say as a result of the crisis),
the Soviet Union embarked on a substantial buildup of strategic
forces and by the late 1960s had achieved parity with the United
States.

The assertion of nationalism by developing states was a fourth
major development in the 1963-1968 period. In these countries
nationalist feelings, which were evident in the 1950s, increased in
the 1960s and resulted in demands for national independence;
many former colonies were granted independence during the 1960s.
In many cases, the newly independent states did not have an adequate administrative infrastructure to meet the demands of their
societies, and for this reason, as well as many others, the gap
between the developed and developing states continued to grow.

In several important cases, states with significant factions desiring independence were either not granted full independence or,
once granted independence, the internal factions could not reach a
satisfactory settlement concerning the structure of the new government. Designed to register France's defeat and to provide France
with a face-saving means of disengagement, the Geneva Agreements left Vietnam divided and the basic question of who was to
govern Vietnam unanswered. U.S. forces in an advisory role replaced the withdrawing French forces, and by the end of 1963 there
were sixteen thousand American troops in South Vietnam.

In the mid-1950s India initiated a policy of nonalignment.
Following India's example, many newly independent and small
states by the early 1960s were able to maintain their independence

vis-à-vis the Soviet Union and China without having to depend on the United States. The emergence of the nonaligned bloc was thus a fifth important development and closely related to the emergence of nationalist sentiment.

Despite the continued significance of military power during the 1962-1968 period, the importance of economic matters increased and marked the sixth major development in the limited détente international system. At the end of World War II the U.S. gross national product (GNP) constituted 50 percent of the world's GNP. Throughout the acute cold war, the United States had the capability to exercise hegemonic power over the international economic system. With the full economic recovery of the states of Western Europe and Japan, the U.S. percentage of the world's GNP gradually declined; nevertheless, the United States retained consensual hegemonic control over the Western economic system until the mid- to late 1960s when its allies refused to continue to finance the "key currency" status of the dollar. By the end of the 1960s, the ability of the United States to control the noncommunist international economic system was clearly waning.

During the limited détente period, important leadership changes took place in the United States, the Soviet Union, and China, and these changes, in turn, had important effects on the relations among these states. William Zimmerman has pointed out that "from 1959 on, Khrushchev generally adopted the position that 'reasonable men' or 'realists' were in the majority in the American ruling group."[5] Khrushchev considered Kennedy to be one of the realists who favored the lessening of tensions with the Soviet Union rather than one of the Dulles-type "madmen" who, Khrushchev thought, were bellicose and entirely unreasonable. Some important Soviet leaders, such as Marshal Rodion Malinovsky, did not accept Khruschev's dichotomous characterization of U.S. leaders. Among those Soviet leaders who accepted Khrushchev's view, there was a great deal of uncertainty, following Kennedy's assassination, whether Lyndon Johnson was one of the "realists" or "madmen."

If Soviet leaders were uncertain about Johnson, there was no such doubt about Barry Goldwater during the 1964 election campaign. To the Soviets, Goldwater was an archetypal cold warrior, one of the "madmen" of "American ruling circles." There was undoubtedly a sense of relief in the Kremlin when Johnson was elected; however, this did not last long, for in February 1965 the United States initiated the bombing of North Vietnam. Several months later, Premier Alexei Kosygin angrily charged, "The government of the United States is in essence pursuing the foreign policy line proposed by Goldwater at the time of the elections but rejected by the American people. It is carrying out an aggressive policy directed against the countries of Socialism."[6]

The ouster of Khrushchev was due to a complex mix of domestic and international factors, and, although it is impossible to determine which of these factors was the most important, it is possible to identify some of the foreign policy issues that played a role. First, Khrushchev's successors did not totally accept his dichotomous view of American leaders. Second, following the ouster, there was a change in the style of the Soviet leadership in foreign policy matters from Khrushchev's impulsive and adventuristic style to the hesitant, cautious, methodical style of Leonid Brezhnev, Kosygin, and Nikolai Podgorny. Third, during the latter part of Khrushchev's reign, there were reports that Khrushchev was planning to improve relations with the Federal Republic of Germany. Following the change in leadership, all such reports stopped. Fourth, the new Soviet leaders sought, without success, to improve relations with China. One of the major reasons that the Sino-Soviet gap proved unbridgeable was the Soviet Union's apparent willingness to act as a mediator between the North Vietnamese and the United States in the Vietnam War.[7] Chinese leaders viewed this objective as a betrayal of international communism and, more importantly, a withdrawal of Soviet support of Chinese foreign policy objectives in Southeast Asia.

According to Donald Zagoria, the ouster of Khrushchev in 1964 and the U.S. escalation of the Vietnam war in 1965 caused the leaders of the Chinese army and some party members to press the case for reestablishing ties with the Soviet Union.[8] Army Chief of Staff Marshall Luo Ruiqing and Party leaders Deng Xiaoping and Liu Shaoqi wanted a reconciliation in order to deter further U.S. escalation in Vietnam and an attack on China. Opposing this group was a faction that favored concentrating on China's internal economic development. Although domestic concerns were central issues in the Cultural Revolution, the split between those who advocated and those who opposed reconciliation with the Soviet Union undoubtedly contributed to the political turmoil. The Cultural Revolution caused a major reshuffling of the Chinese leadership, and eventually a faction led by Mao, Lin Biao, the Zhou Enlai emerged as dominant. Significantly, this faction rejected the army's advocacy of a hard-line Vietnam policy and reconciliation with the Soviet Union. In fact, this faction viewed the Soviet Union as a greater enemy than the U.S.

The seven major developments in the limited détente international system—the fragmentation of alliance systems, the recovery of the states devastated by World War II, the achievement of parity by the Soviet Union, the assertion of nationalism, increased autonomy for nonaligned states, the increasing importance of international economic issues, and the leadership changes in the United States, the Soviet Union, and China—were not isolated phenomena but were, in some respects, closely related. For instance, the assertion of nationalism contributed to the Sino-Soviet split as well as to the Vietnam War, and the Vietnam War undoubtedly contributed to the growing U.S. balance-of-payments problems of the 1960s. These developments not only affected the international system; they had an important effect on Soviet-American relations and on the rules, procedures, and organizations that American and Soviet leaders sought to build to manage interactions in various issue areas.

## The Development of a Soviet-American Arms Control Regime

In the early 1960s, some strategic analysts argued that, even if disarmament could not be achieved, the control and limitation of certain types and numbers of weapons would be desirable. Additionally, rules could be developed for the conduct of war in case deterrence failed and, furthermore, arms control could provide economic savings.[9] The feasibility of one arms control measure—the banning of nuclear tests—had been studied by a group of international experts in 1958, and a moratorium on nuclear tests was observed from November 1958 until August 1961 when the Soviets resumed such tests. Negotiations for an agreement designed to limit nuclear tests were conducted, but without avail, throughout 1962 at the newly created Eighteen-Nation Disarmament Committee (ENDC).

In a report to the Supreme Soviet in December 1962 concerning the Cuban missile crisis, Khrushchev noted that in the age of nuclear weapons, it was necessary to show "more sobermindedness and a greater desire to remove the roadblocks that cause friction among states" and that "sensible norms" of international relations should be strengthened.[10] To these ends, Khrushchev called "upon the Western powers to remove the last barriers to an agreement on ending nuclear tests for all time to come."[11] Negotiations in the ENDC faltered over the issue of verification, which remained contentious throughout the spring of 1963. On June 10, President Kennedy in a commencement address delivered at American University spoke of the need to "re-examine our attitude toward the Soviet Union" and emphasized the need for a nuclear test ban treaty.[12] Kennedy's speech was well received in Moscow, and rapid progress was made; on August 5, 1963, the Limited Test Ban Treaty was signed in Moscow. Although some analysts characterize this treaty as merely a "clean air bill . . . ."[13] it was the most significant arms control agreement concluded since the Washington Naval Treaty of 1922, and it was thought that it would, in addition to reducing fallout, limit proliferation, slow the pace of the arms race, and lead to an improvement in Soviet-American relations.

Once the danger of fallout was reduced, other arms control problems could be addressed. The prohibition of weapons of mass destruction in space was first proposed at the UN Disarmament Subcommittee talks in 1957; however, the Soviets linked a ban on nuclear weapons in outer space and "general and complete disarmament." Following the successful conclusion of the Limited Test Ban Treaty, the Soviets changed their position and announced that they were willing to discuss steps to prevent the spread of nuclear arms to outer space. In October 1963, the UN General Assembly unanimously passed a resolution calling upon all states to refrain from introducing weapons of mass destruction into outer space. This resolution formed the basis of a treaty drafted by the

United States and the Soviet Union and signed in January 1967. Like the 1959 Antarctica Treaty, the Outer Space Treaty is a non-armament agreement in which the signatories seek to prohibit the deployment of weapons from certain areas.

Proliferation became a major concern of both great and small powers in the late 1950s and early 1960s. Between 1958 and 1961, a number of small states in the UN General Assembly, led by Ireland, presented resolutions calling for nonproliferation. The Cuban missile crisis caused increased interest among a number of Latin American states in the prohibition of nuclear weapons from Latin America. In fact, one month after the crisis, Bolivia, Brazil, Chile, and Ecuador submitted a draft resolution to the UN proposing a Latin American denuclearized zone. This led to a series of negotiations during the next three years, which resulted in the Treaty for the Prohibition of Nuclear Weapons in Latin America. The treaty, signed by fifteen Latin American states in February 1967, obliged the signatories to use nuclear material and facilities solely for peaceful purposes and to prohibit the installation or storage of nuclear weapons on their respective territories.

The superpowers were also concerned about the prospect of proliferation. In early 1963, President Kennedy noted that ten states might develop nuclear weapons by 1970 and perhaps fifteen or twenty by 1975. He regarded the possibility that a future president would have to face a world of fifteen to twenty nuclear powers as "the greatest possible danger."[14]

The French and Chinese nuclear explosions dramatized the dangers of nuclear proliferation and represented a direct threat to the Soviet Union, but the Soviets refused to discuss nonproliferation as long as the United States was considering the Multilateral Force (MLF), a proposal calling for a force of naval vessels equipped with nuclear weapons and staffed by crew members drawn from NATO countries. For the Western proponents of the MLF, the proposal was a means to advance European integration and to avoid proliferation simultaneously. To its opponents in the West, the MLF muddied the issues of NATO defense and sidestepped serious arms control. The Soviet Union strenuously opposed the MLF, believing that the United States was simply attempting to provide nuclear weapons to West Germany. In 1965 the United

States for various reasons abandoned the MLF, which opened the way for negotiations on the proliferation problem. At the 1966 and 1967 sessions of the ENDC and in informal meetings between Secretary of State Dean Rusk and Foreign Minister Andrei Gromyko in 1967, the United States and the Soviet Union were able to submit separate but identical texts of a draft treaty. At the instigation of the non-nuclear weapons states, this draft was changed in several respects and then signed on July 1, 1968.

The Non-Proliferation Treaty (NPT) prohibited non-nuclear weapons states from acquiring nuclear weapons by manufacture or transfer and obliged states possessing nuclear weapons to assist non-nuclear states in developing peaceful nuclear energy. The signatories also pledged to pursue negotiations relating to the cessation of the arms race. Because the treaty prevented the acquisition of nuclear weapons by West Germany, the Soviet Union viewed it as very important.

As a means of improving relations with the Soviet Union, President Johnson in 1964 and again in 1966 proposed a policy of "building bridges with the East." In 1966, he stated, "Our common task is this: to search for every possible area of agreement that might enlarge the prospect for cooperation between the United States and the Soviet Union. . . . [The Vietnam] conflict does not have to stop us from finding new ways of dealing with one another."[15] In support of this new accommodative approach, Secretary of Defense Robert McNamara, supported by Secretary of State Rusk and President Johnson, privately proposed negotiations on strategic arms to the Soviet leadership in late 1966.[16] In June 1967, President Johnson and Premier Kosygin met at Glassboro, New Jersey, and discussed various issues relating to the strategic balance. On the day that the NPT was signed, July 1, 1968, the United States announced that agreement had been reached with the Soviet Union to enter discussions on strategic arms limitations. During August, American and Soviet officials planned the opening of the Strategic Arms Limitations Talks (SALT). A joint announcement concerning the opening and schedule of the talks was prepared for release on August 21. On August 20, however, Soviet and East European forces invaded Czechoslovakia, and the United States postponed the opening of the talks indefinitely.

Significant arms control measures were achieved during the limited détente period. Taken together, these agreements constituted an international arms control regime. The procedures and rules of this regime resulted in reduced amounts of radioactive fallout, the de-nuclearization of outer space, and the slowing of nuclear proliferation. Additional negotiations were begun in 1967 on the prohibition of the stationing of weapons of mass destruction on the seabed, and the United States and the Soviet Union agreed in principle to open negotiations on the limitation of strategic arms.

## Toward the Development of a
## Soviet-American Economic Regime

Throughout the acute cold war, Soviet-American trade was a highly politicized issue, and the comparative advantages for the expansion of U.S.-Soviet trade were pushed into the background by cold war tensions. In 1953 at the height of the acute cold war, East-West trade as a percentage of total world trade was 1.3 percent; by 1965 this figure had grown to 2.6 percent.[17] Table 4 shows the levels of Soviet trade with the noncommunist world and with the United States for the years 1960 through 1971. Although Soviet-American trade increased during the limited détente period, it was greatly surpassed by Soviet trade with the rest of the noncommunist world. With the exception of 1964, Soviet trade with the United States throughout the 1963-1968 period remained at a level of about $100 million. During this same period, however, Soviet trade with the West increased from a level of $2.6 billion to $4.2 billion. Thus, although Soviet trade with the West increased substantially, the U.S. share of the trade declined. This finding is significant since attempts were made by both Soviet and American leaders throughout the limited détente period to increase U.S.-Soviet trade.

Khrushchev wanted to increase trade with the West during the late 1950s and early 1960s in order to gain access to modern technologies for Soviet industry. Averell Harriman recalled, ''In 1963 when we were negotiating the Limited Test Ban Agreement, Mr. Khrushchev raised the question [of most-favored-nation status for

Table 4

### SOVIET TRADE WITH THE WEST, 1960-1971 (MILLIONS OF DOLLARS)

| Year | Exports | | Imports | | Turnover[b] | | United States |
|------|---------|---|---------|---|-------------|---|---------------|
| | West[a] | United States | West | United States | West | United States | (% of total) |
| 1960 | 983 | 25 | 1080 | 60 | 2063 | 85 | 4.1 |
| 1961 | 1069 | 24 | 1093 | 51 | 2162 | 74 | 3.4 |
| 1962 | 1115 | 17 | 1283 | 27 | 2398 | 44 | 1.8 |
| 1963 | 1218 | 25 | 1400 | 28 | 2618 | 53 | 2.0 |
| 1964 | 1282 | 21 | 1734 | 163 | 3016 | 184 | 6.1 |
| 1965 | 1438 | 34 | 1601 | 65 | 3039 | 99 | 3.3 |
| 1966 | 1711 | 47 | 1742 | 63 | 3453 | 110 | 3.2 |
| 1967 | 1886 | 39 | 1782 | 63 | 3668 | 102 | 2.8 |
| 1968 | 2051 | 43 | 2144 | 57 | 4195 | 99 | 2.4 |
| 1969 | 2230 | 61 | 2495 | 117 | 4725 | 177 | 3.7 |
| 1970 | 2345 | 64 | 2780 | 115 | 5125 | 179 | 3.3 |
| 1971 | 2710 | 60 | 2860 | 144 | 5570 | 204 | 3.7 |

Source: Data adapted from Department of Commerce data quoted by E. Douglas Kenna in U.S. Congress, Joint Economic Committee, *Soviet Economic Outlook*, Hearings, 93d Congress, 1st sess., 1973, p. 23.

[a]All Western noncommunist countries.
[b]Refers to total dollar value of exports plus imports.

the Soviet Union] and said in his blunt way, 'Those who want peace encourage trade.' "[18] Despite the apparent Soviet interest in expanding Soviet-American trade, the United States maintained its cold war export restrictions; in fact, in 1962 the Export Control Act was extended to prohibit the export of goods that could have "economic significance," in addition to those goods that were restricted for national security reasons. The United States pressured its NATO allies and Japan to support the export restrictions published by the Consultative Group Coordinating Committee (COCOM). Increasingly during the early 1960s, however, the Western European states and Japan ignored the COCOM restrictions and met the Soviet demand for advanced industrial equipment. While COCOM's power declined, U.S. export restrictions remained in effect; yet, despite these restrictions, the Soviets ordered some equipment from American manufacturers. Consequently U.S.-Soviet trade during the first two years of the 1960s was at a higher level, as measured as a percentage of total trade with the West, than at any other time during the decade, with the exception of 1964 (see table 4).

Throughout its history, the Soviet Union has had chronic agricultural problems. Twice during this century, in 1921-1922 and 1932-1933, famines in the Soviet Union caused the deaths of more than a million Russians. In 1963 the Soviet crop was far smaller than expected, and Soviet leaders were faced with a dilemma; they could ignore the crop failure and continue to purchase Western technology, or they could divert resources from buying foreign machinery to the purchase of grain. The first alternative would result in food shortages and a reduction in the standard of living. The second would maintain the standard of living but slow Khrushchev's economic development plans. Khrushchev chose the second alternative and imported about 10 million tons of grain, including 1.8 million tons from the United States.

Within the United States, the 1963-1964 grain deal was a very controversial issue. President Kennedy portrayed the sale as simply a commercial undertaking that would benefit American taxpayers since the grain sold to the Soviet Union would no longer be stored in granaries subsidized by the U.S government. Kennedy was careful to note that the decision to sell wheat to the Soviet Union "did not represent a new Soviet-American trade policy. That must await the settlement of many matters."[19] The grain deal was opposed by U.S. shipping interests and, in order to gain acceptance of the sale, Kennedy had to require that at least 50 percent of all U.S. grain sold to the Soviet Union be shipped in American vessels. There were other opponents to the proposed sale. Former Vice-President Richard Nixon said that it would be "harming the cause of freedom" and asked rhetorically, "Why should we pull them out of their trouble and make Communism look better?"[20] The grain sale was not concluded until after the assassination of President Kennedy. President Johnson supported the sale, although some analysts contend that his support was not so much a result of his conviction that the sale was advantageous as a belief that approval of it constituted a test of his control over Congress.[21]

In order to increase East-West trade, Johnson first had to request from the Congress certain revisions in the existing trade laws. To strengthen the case for the expansion of U.S.-Soviet trade, Johnson appointed a blue-ribbon panel of business, labor, and academic leaders headed by J. William Miller, chairman of the board of Cummins Engine Company. The Miller Committee issued its recommendations in April 1965 and reported, "the time is ripe to make more active use of trade arrangements as political instruments in relations with Communist countries. Trade should be brought into the policy arena. It should be offered or withheld purposefully and systematically, as opportunities and circumstances warrant."[22] The Miller Committee also noted that the expansion of East-West trade would require from the communist states "a growing commitment to international rules and adherence to international standards for responsible behavior."[23] In short, expanded East-West trade would result in the creation of an economic regime.

In his 1966 State of the Union address, President Johnson reiterated his support of "building bridges" to Eastern Europe. In support of this objective he noted that he would propose new legislation concerning East-West trade. Secretary of State Rusk summarized the intended effect of the new legislation:

The Soviet Union and other nations of Eastern Europe are increasingly conscious of their stake in stability and in improving peaceful relations with the outside world. Progress toward normal trade relations will increase that stake.

Under the terms of the proposed legislation, each agreement would be only one step in the process of reducing tensions.[24]

The new East-West trade legislation was thus designed to reduce tensions and to provide the Eastern European countries and the Soviet Union with a greater stake in the Western international economic system.

At about the same time that President Johnson sent the East-West Trade Relations Act to the Congress, Premier Kosygin and Secretary-General Brezhnev began to show an interest in increasing

East-West trade. Soviet imports of Western technology were curtailed in the aftermath of the disastrous 1963 Soviet wheat harvest. These curtailments concerned the Soviet leadership, and internal reforms were instituted that were designed to promote the modernization of Soviet industry. For instance, in 1965 the State Committee for the Coordination of Scientific Research was reorganized and upgraded and became the State Committee on Science and Technology, which was headed by V.A. Kirillin, who eventually became a deputy chairman of the Soviet Council of Ministers, and Gherman Gvishiani, the son-in-law of Premier Kosygin.[25]

At the Twenty-Third Party Congress held in April 1966, Kosygin emphasized the need for expanded East-West interaction in order to gain access to Western technology: "In our time it is becoming more and more evident that the scientific and technical revolution underway in the modern world calls for freer international contacts and creates conditions for broad economic exchanges between Socialist and Capitalist countries."[26] Kosygin's speech was quickly followed by action designed to stimulate East-West trade. In May 1966, Soviet trade officials began to negotiate with Italy's Fiat. Three months later, the Soviet Union announced that it had concluded an agreement for Fiat to build a $1.5 billion automobile plant. The huge Fiat plant was only the beginning of the Soviet Union's turn to the West. From 1965 through 1968, Soviet trade with the West increased dramatically, going from a little over $3 billion in 1965 to over $4 billion by 1968. Throughout this same period, total U.S.-Soviet trade remained at a stable level of about $100 million per year. As a percentage of total Soviet trade with the West, the U.S. share declined from 3.3 percent in 1965 to 2.4 percent in 1968. What had happened to the U.S. policy of building bridges?

Two major obstacles prevented the Johnson administration from increasing cultural and economic relations with Eastern Europe and the Soviet Union. First, the Congress failed to approve the East-West Trade Relations Act of 1966, the legislation that provided for the revision of restrictive U.S. cold war trade policies. Second, U.S. trade with the East did not increase as a result of American involvement in Vietnam. These two obstacles were integrally related. As U.S. involvement in Vietnam became more intense, congressmen grew increasingly uneasy about providing economic benefits for some of the same countries that were supplying weapons and other war material to North Vietnam. Within the executive branch, Vietnam became the dominant item on the foreign policy agenda from 1965 on, and little attention was devoted to issues not related to Vietnam. Thus, the nascent Soviet-American economic regime, marked by the 1963-1964 grain deal, did not develop during the limited détente period.

## The Maintenance of the Crisis Management Regime

During the Cuban missile crisis, President Kennedy and Secretary Khrushchev found that there were no means to communicate quickly and effectively with one another. At several points in the crisis, a direct, secret, and rapid communications channel would have been very useful. For instance, clarifications concerning movements of military units could have been issued and alternative proposals for ending the crisis proposed and discussed. Instead Kennedy and Khrushchev had to rely on a variety of cumbersome modes of communication, ranging from personal emissaries to public press releases. In the aftermath of the crisis, the United States and the Soviet Union agreed to install a direct communications link, the so-called hot line, between their capitals. This was the first major amendment to the U.S.-Soviet crisis management regime developed during the acute cold war.

The second major change in this regime was made possible by the hot line. While Soviet and American leaders developed rules and procedures for crisis management during the acute cold war, the hot line provided a means for crisis prevention. For example, when the *U.S.S Liberty* was sunk by Israeli planes during the June War in 1967, President Johnson dispatched U.S. aircraft to the area to search for survivors. Johnson notified the Soviet leaders of this mission by the hot line so that they would be aware of the actual purpose of U.S. aircraft.[27] Although the use of the hot line is classified information, its use during the June War was reportedly the first.[28]

The third major change in the crisis management regime developed during the acute cold war concerned the use of nuclear threats.

Several times between 1947 and 1962, the United States and the Soviet Union threatened to use nuclear weapons. Following the Cuban missile crisis, neither superpower used nuclear threats to gain political-diplomatic advantages.

The fourth change in this regime concerned the control of the United States and the Soviet Union over their respective allies. During the acute cold war, both nations had been able to exert fairly effective control over allies; however, during the limited détente period, this control decreased substantially, as Alexander Dubcek's Czechoslovakia and Charles de Gaulle's France demonstrated.

There were a number of crises during the limited détente period (Cyprus, 1964; Indo-Pakistani War, 1965; Dominican Republic, 1965; Jordan, 1968); however, in only two areas of the world did the United States and the Soviet Union, albeit indirectly through their respective clients, confront one another—in the Middle East and in Vietnam.

On the morning of June 5, 1967, Israel launched a preemptive attack on Egyptian and other Arab air bases, an action that catalyzed the third Arab-Israeli war. Because of their interest and involvement in the Middle East, the United States and the Soviet Union rapidly became involved in the negotiations concerning the war. On the same morning that the fighting broke out, Kosygin communicated by the hot line with President Johnson and expressed hope that the United States could influence Israel to accept a cease-fire.[29] Kosygin and Johnson exchanged messages concerning the war on June 7 and 8.

By June 10, the Arabs were faced with a major military disaster, and the Soviet leadership, following Khrushchev's example in 1956, threatened to intervene. The Soviet Union sent a message to Johnson stipulating that, unless the Israelis halted military operations within a short period of time, the Soviet Union would take "necessary action, including military." Johnson replied that progress toward a cease-fire was being made. He also ordered ships from the U.S. Sixth Fleet to move from one hundred miles to within fifty miles of the Syrian coast. According to Johnson, this action was designed to signal to the Soviets that "the United States was prepared to resist Soviet intrusion in the Middle East."[30] Behind the scenes, the United States pressured Israel to terminate hostilities, and on June 12 a cease-fire was accepted.

Although the Soviet threat to intervene in the Six Day War indicates that the Soviets were willing to escalate the conflict, there are several reasons to believe that they were not willing to confront the United States. First, the threat was made very late in the war, just two days before the cease-fire went into effect. Second, following the war, Egypt's President Gamal Abdel Nasser complained that after the Israeli attacked on June 5 the Russians had been "frozen into immobility by their fear of a confrontation with America."[31] Third, the Soviets refused to resupply the Arabs with badly needed replacement aircraft and other military equipment throughout the war. In fact, the Soviet resupply of its Arab client states did not begin until almost two weeks after the war ended.[32] The United States also followed a restrained policy in its support to Israel and applied pressure on Israel to agree to a cease-fire. Thus by communicating with one another and applying pressure on their respective allies, the United States and the Soviet Union avoided a direct confrontation, and the crisis management regime remained intact following the June War.

Vietnam presented the United States, the Soviet Union, and China with major foreign policy challenges, which each of these states defined in a different manner. To Chinese leaders, the Vietnam War represented an important test case of their liberation war strategy, which was designed to foment a series of guerrilla conflicts throughout the developing world and thereby challenge U.S. involvement in Asia. Because of its proximity to China and because it was viewed by Chinese decision makers as a test case, Vietnam was ranked very high on the Chinese foreign policy agenda.

Soviet policy in Southeast Asia during the 1960s was motivated by two conflicting concerns: the desire to lessen tensions and improve relations with the United States and the equally important perceived need to maintain Soviet influence in the international communist movement.[33] As early as 1960, the repercussions of the Sino-Soviet conflict were manifested in Southeast Asia. As a means of demonstrating solidarity with "fraternal socialist states," the Soviet Union provided the Pathet Lao and North Vietnam with substantial quantities of arms and ammunition during 1960-1961 in order to retain their allegiance so that these groups would not turn to China for support. At the same time, Soviet leaders did not want to risk a conflict with the United States over its involvement in Southeast Asia. When President Kennedy came into office, he was anxious to avoid a Pathet Lao (communist) takeover of Laos and through a sophisticated use of "coercive diplomacy" was able to convince Khrushchev to agree to the neutralization of Laos.[34] In the aftermath of the Soviet-American understanding, the Chinese charged that the Soviets had given up their support of wars of national liberation in favor of détente with the United States. According to the Chinese, "When the struggle of the Vietnamese and the Laotian people grew acute, [the Soviet Union's] policy on the question of Indochina was one of the disengagement. . . . when the U.S. imperialist engineered the Boc Bo [Tonkin Gulf] incident, Khrushchev went so far as to concoct the slander that the incident was provoked by China."[35]

Between 1963 and 1965, Soviet commentators on international relations emphasized the desirability of reducing tensions and improving relations with the United States.[36] Just prior to Khrushchev's ouster in the fall of 1964, the Soviet Union went as far as to assist and encourage an attempt to negotiate an end to the Vietnam War; however, the United States refused to participate in private talks with Hanoi. The Chinese publicized this event as Soviet-American collusion, and the Soviet Union was forced to respond to North Vietnam's needs in a tangible manner. At about the same time, Khrushchev was forced out of office and the United States began bombing North Vietnam.

In early 1965 the Soviet Union asked China to allow passage through its territory of several thousand Soviet troops and to allow the construction of several Soviet air bases on Chinese territory.[37] Both requests were turned down. However, in February, Kosygin traveled to Hanoi to assure the North Vietnamese of Soviet support. His visit corresponded with the beginning of the U.S. bombing of North Vietnam, hardly an accommodating act by the United States toward the Soviet Union.[38] In 1965-1966, the Soviet position on Vietnam and American foreign policy in general hardened, and according to William Zimmerman, "it appeared that the trend in Soviet commentary [on U.S. foreign policy] of the latter years of

Khrushchev's tenure in power had been reversed.''[39] Soviet leaders reversed their policy again in late 1966 when the pro-Soviet faction of the Chinese leadership was purged during the Cultural Revolution and as President Johnson stressed his bridge-building policy to the East in his 1966 State of the Union message. By 1967-1968, the United States and the Soviet Union were cooperating in a number of different issue areas.

Soviet policy in Vietnam throughout the 1960s was a product of several policy changes. Nevertheless, the United States and the Soviet Union by and large continued to observe the rules of the crisis management regime. Vietnam, or more specifically the Soviet Union's need to demonstrate its commitment to international communism in relation to China's, was the major obstacle standing in the way of the improvement of U.S.-Soviet relations throughout the 1963-1968 period.

## Conclusion

In the aftermath of the Cuban missile crisis, several steps dramatically improved Soviet-American relations, and many people believed that a new era in American foreign policy had begun. The Limited Test Ban Treaty and the hot line marked positive steps toward the establishment of an arms control regime. These measures were supplemented by the Outer Space Treaty (1967) and the Non-Proliferation Treaty (1968). By 1968 the Soviet Union had even agreed to discuss the limitation of strategic weapons. In the economic issue area, a precedent for Soviet-American trade was established with the conclusion of a major grain trading agreement; however, further trade failed to develop, largely due to residual U.S. cold war economic policies. Throughout the limited détente period, the United States and the Soviet Union continued to observe the crisis management rules that had been developed during the acute cold war. These rules were tested in the Middle East and in Vietnam, and although the rules were generally observed, Vietnam precluded any dramatic improvement of Soviet-American relations. The limited détente regimes in the arms control, economic, and crisis management issue areas are summarized in table 5.

**Table 5**

**LIMITED DÉTENTE POLICIES AND REGIMES**

| Strategic Military Issue Area | Economic Issue Area | Crisis Management Issue Area |
|---|---|---|
| Nuclear deterrence regime maintained Disarmament—nonregime Arms control—regime established<br><br>Rapid, direct communication established with the hot line (1963)<br><br>Nuclear tests should not be conducted in the atmosphere or in the ocean (Limited Test Ban Treaty, 1963)<br><br>Weapons of mass destruction prohibited from outer space (1967)<br><br>The spread of nuclear weapons should be halted; nuclear states should assist non-nuclear states with peaceful nuclear programs (Non-Proliferation Treaty, 1968)<br><br>U.S. and USSR agree in principle that strategic arms limitation negotiations should be held (1968) | Weak, limited regime established with U.S.-Soviet grain trade of 1963-1964<br><br>U.S. attempted unsuccessfully to establish trade relations with Eastern Europe and Soviet Union in 1965-1966<br><br>USSR imports Western technology, 1966-1968 | Cold war crisis management regime maintained with some changes<br><br>Direct communication<br><br>After the Cuban missile crisis, neither U.S. nor USSR used nuclear threats<br><br>Bargaining is more explicit<br><br>U.S. and USSR experience less control over allies<br><br>The hot line provided the means for crisis prevention |

# Notes

1. John F. Kennedy to Nikita Khrushchev, October 27, 1962, *Department of State Bulletin* (November 12, 1962): 743.
2. Marshall Shulman, *Beyond the Cold War* (New Haven: Yale University Press, 1966).
3. "Press Conference of the President of France, May 15, 1962," in U.S. Department of State, *American Foreign Policy: Current Documents* (Washington, D.C.: Government Printing Office, 1962), pp. 544-45.
4. Institute for Strategic Studies, *The Communist Bloc and the Western Alliance: The Military Balance, 1962-63* (London: Institute for Strategic Studies, 1963).
5. William Zimmerman, *Soviet Perspectives on International Relations, 1956-1967* (Princeton: Princeton University Press, 1969), pp. 221-22.
6. *Pravda*, June 19, 1965, quoted in Vernon V. Aspaturian, "Foreign Policy Perspectives in the Sixties," in Alexander Dallin and Thomas B. Larson, eds., *Soviet Politics since Khrushchev* (Englewood Cliffs, N.J.: Prentice-Hall, 1968), p. 147.
7. Alexander Dallin, "The USSR and World Communism," in John W. Strong, ed., *The Soviet Union under Brezhnev and Kosygin: The Transition Years* (New York: Van Nostrand Reinhold, 1971), p. 203.
8. Donald S. Zagoria, *Vietnam Triangle: Moscow, Peking, Hanoi* (New York: Pegasus, 1967), pp. 67-74.
9. Thomas C. Schelling and Morton Halperin, *Strategy and Arms Control* (New York: Twentieth-Century Fund, 1961); see also Donald G. Brennan, ed., *Arms Control, Disarmament, and National Security* (New York: George Braziller, 1961).
10. N. S. Khrushchev, "The Present International Situation and the Foreign Policy of the Soviet Union," report to the December 12, 1962, session of the Supreme Soviet, in *Current Digest of the Soviet Press* (January 16, 1963): 4-8, (January 23, 1963): 3-10.
11. Ibid.
12. John F. Kennedy, "What Kind of Peace Do We Want?" Address delivered to American University, June 10, 1963, in *Public Papers of the Presidents of the United States: John F. Kennedy, 1963* (Washington, D.C.: Government Printing Office, 1964), pp. 459-63.
13. Elizabeth Young, *A Farewell to Arms Control?* (Baltimore: Penguin Books, 1972), p. 86.
14. Press Conference, March 13, 1963 in *Public Papers of John F. Kennedy, 1963*, p. 273.
15. Speech by President Lyndon B. Johnson, National Reactor Testing

Section, Arco, Idaho, August 26, 1966, in *Public Papers of the Presidents of the United States: Lyndon B. Johnson, 1966* (Washington, D.C.: Government Printing Office, 1967), p. 900.

16. Raymond Garthoff, "Negotiating with the Russians: Some Lessons from SALT," *International Security* 1-4 (Spring 1977).

17. See table 11 in Jozef Wilczynski, *The Economics and Politics of East-West Trade* (New York: Praeger, 1969), p. 52.

18. "Statement of Hon. W. Averell Harriman," in U.S. Congress, Senate, Committee on Foreign Relations, *Détente*, Hearings, 93d Cong. 2d sess., 1974, p. 11.

19. "The President's News Conference of October 9, 1963," in *Public Papers of John F. Kennedy*, pp. 767-74.

20. Richard M. Nixon quoted in Theodore Draper, "Détente," *Commentary* (June 1974): 36.

21. Seyom Brown, *The Faces of Power* (New York: Columbia University Press, 1968), p. 313.

22. "Report of the Special Committee on the U.S. Trade with East European Countries and the Soviet Union," in *Department of State Bulletin* (May 30, 1966): 846.

23. Ibid., p. 846.

24. Dean Rusk, "East-West Trade Relations Act of 1966: Letter of Transmittal," *Department of State Bulletin* (May 30, 1966): 841.

25. Eugene Zaleski, "Central Planning of Research and Development in the Soviet Union," in *Science Policy in the USSR* (Paris: Organization for Economic Co-operation and Development, 1969), pp. 56-61.

26. A. Kosygin, "Report to the 23rd Party Congress," *Pravda*, April 6, 1966, cited by Kenneth Yalowitz, "U.S.S.R.—Western Industrial Cooperation," in U.S. Congress, Joint Economic Committee, *Soviet Economic Prospects for the Seventies* (Washington, D.C.: Government Printing Office, 1973), p. 718.

27. Lyndon B. Johnson, *The Vantage Point: Perspectives on the Presidency* (New York: Holt, Rinehart and Winston, 1971), pp. 300-1.

28. Phil Williams, *Crisis Management: Confrontation and Diplomacy in the Nuclear Age* (New York: John Wiley, 1976), p. 118.

29. Johnson, *Vantage Point*, p. 298.

30. Ibid., p. 302.

31. Anthony Nutting, *Nasser* (New York: E. P. Dutton, 1972), p. 419.

32. Jon D. Glassman, *Arms for the Arabs: The Soviet Union and War in the Middle East* (Baltimore: Johns Hopkins University Press, 1975), pp. 53-59.

33. Zagoria, *Vietnam Triangle*, p. 42.

34. Alexander L. George, David K. Hall, and William R. Simons, *The Limits of Coercive Diplomacy: Laos, Cuba, Vietnam* (Boston: Little, Brown, 1971), pp. 36-85.

35. *Peking Review* (November 12, 1965): 15, quoted in Adam B. Ulam, *Expansion and Coexistence: Soviet Foreign Policy, 1917-73*, 2d ed. (New York: Praeger, 1974), p. 699.

36. Zimmerman, *Soviet Perspectives*, pp. 211-41.

37. William E. Griffiths, ed., *Sino-Soviet Relations, 1964-1965* (Cambridge: MIT Press, 1967), p. 73.

38. U. Alexis Johnson, second in command at the U.S. embassy in Saigon at this time, has noted that U.S. officials in Saigon did not consider Kosygin's presence in Hanoi as reason not to bomb the city. Interview with U. Alexis Johnson, Washington, D.C., February 24, 1978. During the May 1972 summit meeting, Kosygin remarked to Nixon and Kissinger that he would never forget the bombings of Hanoi during his 1965 visit, indicating that he considered U.S. actions to have been a personal affront.

39. Zimmerman, *Soviet Perspectives*, p. 236.

CHAPTER 3

# THE NIXON-KISSINGER
# GRAND DESIGN AND
# GRAND STRATEGY

By the late 1960s American involvement in the Vietnam War and the protest within the United States to that involvement posed a more serious threat to the fabric of American society than any other situation since the Great Depression. A solution to the Vietnam War was therefore at the top of the foreign policy agenda of the members of the Nixon administration when they entered office in January 1969. Rather than attempting to end the war through a series of *ad hoc* measures, President Nixon and his adviser for national security affairs, Henry Kissinger, sought to develop a new grand design and grand strategy for American foreign policy that would enable the United States to end the Vietnam War, as well as to deal with the broader questions concerning U.S. relations with the states of Europe, Japan, China, the Soviet Union, and the developing world.

Although Nixon and Kissinger often wrote and spoke of a "new structure of peace," they never fully delineated the desired end state of the new structure. Furthermore, given the growing opposition to international commitments as a result of U.S. involvement in Vietnam, it was not clear how the Nixon administration would gain congressional and public acceptance for a new American foreign policy.

## The International and Domestic Contexts

Eight years after his 1960 defeat, Richard Nixon assumed the presidency under the very different domestic and international environments of 1969. The Vietnam War stretched American society to the breaking point and shattered the cold war foreign policy consensus that had evolved since Truman first announced the doctrine of containment in 1947. During his campaign, Nixon ran on a platform promising peace in Vietnam, much as Eisenhower had done in 1952 with regard to Korea. The paramount issue facing Nixon when he became president was Vietnam. How could he end the war without doing irreparable harm to the credibility of American commitments to other countries?

Nixon believed that U.S. policy concerning Vietnam should be formulated with explicit attention given to the role of the United States in Asia. In 1967 he had written, "Any American policy toward Asia must come urgently to grips with the reality of China . . . we simply cannot afford to leave China forever outside the family of nations."[1] Other parts of this article presaged many of Nixon's other perspectives, which became evident only after his election to the presidency. For instance, Nixon characterized Soviet-American relations as having reached "some measure of accommodation" but not a "full-détente."[2] The task of American foreign policy, Nixon asserted, was to bring China within the community of nations, just as the United States had done with the Soviet Union. This objective could be accomplished through the use of a mixed strategy employing both positive and negative sanctions.

When they entered office in January 1969, Nixon and Kissinger viewed the international system similarly. Both saw Vietnam as an important test of American will and credibility. Nixon believed that "to abandon South Vietnam to the Communists . . . would cost us inestimably in our search for a stable, structured, and lasting peace."[3] For Kissinger, "the commitment of 500,000 Americans has settled the importance of Viet Nam. For what is involved now is confidence in American promises."[4] Both Nixon and Kissinger believed that stability in other parts of the world depended upon events in Vietnam. Although they had been archetypal cold warriors, by 1969 Nixon and Kissinger viewed negotiations with the Soviet Union and China favorably.

In March 1969, a major conflict between the Soviet Union and the People's Republic of China broke out in the Ussuri River border region. Military forces of the two countries directly engaged one another, and there were casualties on both sides. This incident contributed to a marked worsening of the Sino-Soviet rift. In fact, in 1969 the Soviets reportedly seriously considered the possibility of launching a preemptive nuclear attack against the Chinese nuclear weapons installations.[5] Soon after the Ussuri incidents, the Soviet ambassador to the United States, Anatoly Dobrynin, gave Kissinger an extended, unsolicited briefing on the conflict, and when Kissinger tried to change the subject by suggesting that it was a Sino-Soviet problem, Dobrynin, according to Kissinger, "insisted passionately that China was everybody's problem."[6] The Sino-Soviet border clash sensitized Nixon and Kissinger to the insecurity and hostility of the Chinese and the Soviets toward one another and the role of the United States in this emerging strategic triangle.

The Sino-Soviet split was only one change—albeit one of the most important—in the international system that occurred in the 1960s. Japan and the states of Western Europe had fully recovered from World War II, causing President Nixon in his first foreign policy report to the Congress to declare, "The postwar period in international relations has ended." This political, economic, and social recovery enabled the Western allies to demonstrate greater independence from the United States. Although military power remained important in international relations, economic power was of increasing salience by the early 1970s. Paradoxically, the two most militarily powerful states in the world, the United States and the Soviet Union, were deterred from using their most powerful weapons, strategic nuclear arms, for fear of escalation. Thus the international environment that Nixon and Kissinger faced when they entered office was undergoing great change, and they were confronted with the question of how best to cope. While the characteristics of the international system obviously did not determine American and Soviet foreign policy behavior, they influenced policymakers' decisions by bounding and constraining possible choices.

Domestic environments also constrained and limited policymakers' alternatives. In the United States, the Vietnam War politicized and polarized American public opinion. In the last half of 1968, 200 Americans per week were being killed in action in Vietnam, and 14,592 Americans died in combat in 1968.[7] These losses had an effect on the American public's attitude toward the war. In August 1968, the Gallup Organization found that 51 percent of those questioned thought that Vietnam was the most important problem facing the United States.[8] In January 1969, the month that President Nixon was inaugurated, 57 percent of those questioned responded that it was time "to begin to reduce month by month the number of U.S. soldiers in Vietnam."[9]

The Vietnam War caused many Americans to reexamine the premises of U.S. foreign policy concerning the entire world, not just Vietnam. Louis Harris conducted a poll in April 1969 that indicated strong opposition to the use of U.S. military forces overseas. Harris had asked, "What should the United States do if country X is invaded by outside Communist military forces?"[10] If West Berlin were attacked, 64 percent responded that they would want the United States to help, but only 26 percent would be willing to use force, and 24 percent would do nothing. Forty-two percent would be willing to help Italy (27 percent with forces) and 37 percent wanted the United States to remain uninvolved. South Korea was the only Asian state for which a majority of those questioned (51 percent) were willing to provide military assistance short of sending U.S. troops; 41 percent were willing to help Taiwan, and 40 percent were willing to assist Thailand. If Israel were attacked, only 9 percent were willing to intervene with American troops. In a review of American public opinion on the use of military force, Bruce Russett and Miroslav Nincic concluded that the unwillingness of the U.S. public to use American armed forces for the defense of other states was lower during the 1969-1975 period than at any other time during the cold war period.[11] More broadly, the general U.S. public support for executive defense policies markedly declined, and by the late 1960s the percentage of the public favoring less defense spending varied between 40 and 50 percent.[12]

A growing percentage of Americans from the mid-1960s on felt that the United States should concentrate on domestic priorities. The Institute for International Social Research and Potomac Associates asked if people agreed or disagreed with the following statement: "We shouldn't think so much in international terms but concentrate more on our own national problems and building our strength and prosperity here at home." The results for six different surveys, displayed in table 6, demonstrate the increasing support for domestic policies by the American public in 1969.

**Table 6**

**PUBLIC SUPPORT FOR DOMESTIC PROGRAMS, 1964-1976
(IN PERCENTAGES)**

|  | 1964 | 1968 | 1972 | 1974 | 1975 | 1976 |
|---|---|---|---|---|---|---|
| Agree | 55 | 60 | 73 | 77 | 71 | 73 |
| Disagree | 32 | 31 | 20 | 14 | 18 | 22 |
| Don't know | 13 | 9 | 7 | 9 | 11 | 5 |

*Source:* William Watts and Lloyd A. Free, "Nationalism, Not Isolationism," *Foreign Policy* 24 (Fall 1976): 17.

In addition to the changes in public attitudes toward U.S. foreign policy, there were also changes in the role of Congress in defense and foreign policymaking in 1968 and 1969.[13] The effects of these changes could be seen in several different areas. Perhaps most obvious was the significant opposition in Congress in 1969 to the Nixon administration's Safeguard Anti-Ballistic Missile system, which was approved by Vice-President Spiro Agnew's tie-breaking vote in the Senate. Also a substantial number of amendments called for drastic changes in military programs, such as the Cheyenne helicopter, the manned orbiting laboratory, the C-5A transport plane and the Main Battle Tank (MBT-70). Congress instituted many procedural changes that increased the congressional role in defense policymaking. For instance, it passed an amendment requiring the Department of Defense to file quarterly weapons systems reports, a procedure that substantially increased the amount of information available to the Congress.

In 1969, the Senate passed by a vote of seventy to sixteen the National Commitments Resolution, which stipulated that "a national commitment by the United States results only from affirmative action taken by the executive and legislative branches of the United States government by means of a treaty, statute, or concurrent resolution of both Houses of Congress specifically providing for such commitment." In the same year, the Senate also passed an amendment by a vote of eighty to nine that no funds in the defense appropriations bill could be used to finance the introduction of U.S. ground forces into Laos or Thailand.

When Nixon and Kissinger entered office in January 1969, they were confronted by ongoing changes in both the international system and domestic politics. The worsening of Sino-Soviet relations increased the importance of both countries' relations with the United States. At the same time, however, American involvement in Vietnam limited the development of friendlier relations between the United States and the Soviet Union and the United States and the People's Republic of China. Vietnam also contributed to substantial opposition to U.S. foreign policy within the United States. among both the Congress and the public. Nixon and Kissinger faced the difficult task of maintaining existing U.S. international commitments and having to reduce defense expenditures in the face of widespread domestic protest and an assertive Congress.

## The Grand Design and Grand Strategy

In 1969 Nixon and Kissinger were acutely aware of the demands on U.S. foreign policy and the limited and declining resources available to meet these demands. Rather than responding to each foreign policy event and crisis individually, Nixon and Kissinger sought to develop a grand design of long-range objectives and a grand strategy, or means, for achieving these objectives.

Nixon and Kissinger sought to present their grand design and grand strategy for American foreign policy in four comprehensive reports to the Congress published between 1970 and 1973.[14] The reports were patterned after the Department of Defense's annual posture statement and in addition to describing the administration's foreign policy were also designed to serve as rough guides to the bureaucracy. In the first of the reports, President Nixon stated that their purpose was to present the administration's "statement of a new approach to foreign policy, to match a new approach to foreign policy, to match a new era of international relations."[15] In his memoirs, Kissinger noted, "Once the President's annual review became established, it produced some of the most thoughtful governmental statements of foreign policy."[16]

Former members of the National Security Council staff told me that both Nixon and Kissinger considered the reports to be very important, and General Brent Scowcroft noted that "the reports went through ten to twelve drafts under the personal guidance of the Assistant to the President for National Security Affairs."[17] A fifth foreign policy report was drafted but never released to the public.[18]

The tone and substance of each report is quite different, evolving from the tentative, cautious orientation of the first report to the very optimistic, almost euphoric outlook of the 1973 document. Despite the emphasis placed on the reports, Kissinger complained, "To our sorrow, no matter how thoughtful we sought to be, we always failed in our basic aim of getting the media to treat it as a statement of the basic philosophy of American foreign policy. Almost all that the press would cover each year was the section on Indochina."[19]

In addition to the statements published after he entered office, Henry Kissinger's academic writings provide another source of data for analyzing his thinking about the ends and means of American foreign policy.[20] On the first page of his book, *A World Restored*, Kissinger set forth his basic proposition:

Whenever peace—conceived as the avoidance of war—has been the primary objective of a power or a group of powers, the international system has been at the mercy of the most ruthless member of the international community. Whenever the international order has acknowledged that certain principles could not be compromised even for the sake of peace, stability based on an equilibrium of forces was at least conceivable.[21]

A stable international system, according to Kissinger, was the foremost objective of creative statesmen such as Metternich and Castlereagh. But stability could be achieved only if the major powers accepted the structure of an international framework and the rules and processes through which the system is maintained. Those powers that did not accept the system were, by definition, revolutionary, and, if stability was to be achieved, these powers must be brought within the system. Diplomacy, limited war, appeasement, and détente were the permissible methods of influencing other states, and it was the task of statesmen to wield these tools in constructing a stable international order. In his analysis of Bismarck's career, Kissinger argued that the "flexibility of Bismarck's tactics was the result of a well-developed conceptual framework. . . . It was animated by a clear picture of the international order that Bismarck wanted to bring about. . . . He drew his inspiration from a vision of the future."[22] As a historian, Kissinger defined Bismarck's "vision of the future" as the quintessential element of statesmanship, and Kissinger aspired to the goal of implementing his own conceptual framework in his role as a statesman.

### THE NIXON DOCTRINE

Vietnam was the issue highest on the Nixon-Kissinger foreign policy agenda of 1969, given congressional and public opposition to the war. As Nixon recalled in his memoirs, "The most pressing foreign problem I would have to deal with as soon as I became President was the war in Vietnam."[23] On July 25, 1969, Nixon gave an off-the-record press conference on the island of Guam in which he proposed that the United States, while keeping its treaty commitments and maintaining a credible nuclear umbrella for its allies, would henceforth refrain from providing American manpower for stopping aggression. The United States would, however, provide military equipment and economic assistance to any ally that was confronted with aggression. Soon this new policy was known as the Nixon (or Guam) Doctrine, and Vietnamization was the first application of this general policy. In essence, the Nixon Doctrine sought to achieve four objectives: maintain U.S. treaty commitments and credibility, reduce the number of American troops fighting overseas, decrease defense expenditures, and reduce congressional and public opposition to U.S. foreign policies. In short, the Nixon Doctrine represented an attempt to lower the cost and public profile of American involvement in Southeast Asia while maintaining the predominant post-World War II position of the United States within the international system.

Although Nixon and Kissinger often spoke and wrote of "a stable structure of peace," they never described fully and explicitly the grand design of this structure. Instead they made vague references and sometimes contradictory descriptions of the new system in their speeches, press conferences, interviews, and foreign policy reports. For instance, the first foreign policy report made clear that the Nixon administration wanted to pursue closer relations with both the Soviet Union and the People's Republic of China. In discussing the future of Asia, Nixon commented, "The success of our Asia policy depends not only on the strength of our partnership with our Asian friends, but also on our relations with Mainland China and the Soviet Union."[24] Thus the aim of U.S. policy in Asia was to create a kind of regional balance among the great powers, which, because of their status, had interests in this area. In several other parts of the report, Nixon implicitly recognized the existence of a great power triangle and at one point somewhat ingenuously pointed out that the U.S. "desire for improved relations [with the People's Republic of China] is not a tactical means of exploiting the clash between China and the Soviet Union."[25]

Both Nixon and Kissinger were concerned with the problem of how a revolutionary state (one that did not accept the prevailing order) could be brought into the system. "Peace," they contended, "will endure only when every nation has a greater stake in preserving than in breaking it."[26] By developing bilateral mutual interests between the United States and the Soviet Union and the United States and the People's Republic of China, the United States could provide a stake in the system for both the USSR and China. By the beginning of 1970, the two most important themes of the Nixon-Kissinger grand design and grand strategy were clear:

only by developing a comprehensive conceptual framework could American foreign policy successfully meet the challenges of the contemporary international system; and through the development of mutual interests with the other two great powers, the United States could mold a consensus for a new international system. In his address to the UN General Assembly on October 23, 1970, Nixon summarized the administration's new approach to foreign policy: "We look forward to working together with all nations represented here in going beyond the mere containment of crises to building a structure of peace that promotes justice as well as assuring stability, and that will last because all have a stake in its lasting."[27]

After the publication of the first two foreign policy reports, the contours of the desired end of the grand design remained illusive, but the grand strategy, the means for achieving the new international system, was much clearer. Nixon and Kissinger ranked the major tasks for achieving their objectives as follows: the improvement in Soviet-American relations; the improvement of Sino-American relations; the maintenance of strong alliances with the Western European states and Japan; the encouragement of regional balances of power; and the maintenance of good relations with developing countries and their representatives in various international forums.

Perhaps because of his writings on the nineteenth-century international system, many observers assumed that Kissinger was trying to reintroduce the classical multipolar balance-of-power system into contemporary world politics. This view was given credence on July 6, 1971, in a speech in Kansas City, when President Nixon noted that there were five great concentrations of economic power in the world.[28] Five months later in an interview with *Time* magazine, Nixon stated, "I think it would be a safer world and a better world if we have a strong, healthy United States, Europe, Soviet Union, China, Japan, each balancing the other, not playing one against the other, an even balance."[29] Critics were quick to challenge the president's observation. Zbigniew Brzezinski noted that, rather than a triangular or multipolar world composed of equal powers, the international system was composed of "$2\frac{1}{2} + y + z$": the "$\frac{1}{2}$" representing China and the algebraic uncertainties,

$y$ and $z$ representing Europe and Japan.[30] Stanley Hoffmann attacked the idea of a pentagonal world, contending that the United States and the Soviet Union were the only "actual world powers," that China was "still mainly a regional power," and that "both Japan and Western Europe are military dependents of the United States."[31]

A high-ranking former member of the National Security Council contended that the five polar world concept "was invested with theoretical importance that was not really there."[32] Nevertheless, Nixon and Kissinger attempted to qualify Nixon's earlier comparisons of the contemporary configuration of world power with the nineteenth-century balance of power. When asked to comment on Nixon's "five-power" speech in an interview with CBS News, Kissinger first denied that there were similarities between the two periods due to the revolutionary changes in world politics brought about by the development and deployment of nuclear weapons. However, he qualified his statement by stating that stability requires "a certain equilibrium of strength," and he concluded with the observation:

Now, what this administration has attempted to do is not so much to play a complicated nineteenth century game of balance of power, but to try to eliminate those hostilities that were vestiges of a particular perception at the end of the war and to deal with the root fact of the contemporary situation—that we and the Soviet Union, and we and the Chinese, are ideological adversaries, but we are bound together by one basic fact: that none of us can survive a nuclear war and therefore it is in our mutual interest to try to reduce these hostilities.[33]

In his fourth foreign policy report, Nixon attempted to clarify his earlier comparison: "We seek a stable structure, not a classical balance of power. Undeniably, national security must rest upon a certain equilibrium between potential adversaries."[34] "A certain balance of power is inherent in any international system," Nixon contended, "and has its place in the one we envision." In an address in October 1973, Henry Kissinger once again denied the parallel between the nineteenth century and the contemporary systems. Kissinger stated that the following factors characterized the nineteenth century: the great powers shared a common conception of legitimacy; the great powers accepted the structure of the international order; adjustments within the system were made incrementally; and the balance operated in a relatively confined geographic area. In Kissinger's view, "none of these factors pertain today."[35]

Later critics of the Nixon-Kissinger grand design have compared it to the Concert of Europe system rather than the balance-of-power system. The Concert system, a product of the Congress of Vienna, resulted in "great power tutelage" over the rest of Europe, and any territorial changes in Europe were subject to review by the great power members of the Concert. In his analysis of the Nixon-Kissinger grand design, Stephen Garrett concludes, "It was at least a modest revival of this Concert system that was the central concern of American policy during the first Nixon Administration."[36]

### DÉTENTE WITH THE SOVIET UNION

Nixon and Kissinger considered the improvement of Soviet-American relations essential to their grand design and grand strategy. As Nixon recalled in his memoirs, "In January, 1969, I felt the relationship between the United States and the Soviet Union would probably be the single most important factor in determining whether the world would live at peace during and after my administration."[37] In dealing with the Soviet Union, Nixon and Kissinger stressed three important concepts: linkage, mutual interests, and concreteness.

In his inaugural address, Nixon stated that negotiation and not confrontation would be the hallmark of his administration. The Soviets notified Nixon almost immediately that they were interested in negotiating with the United States on the limitation of defensive strategic nuclear weapons systems—antiballistic missiles (ABMs). Nixon and Kissinger, however, viewed SALT as a basic element, if not the most basic element, of Soviet-American relations and would not agree to negotiations unless the Soviet Union agreed to discuss the whole range of strategic nuclear weapons, including offensive systems, as well as a number of other areas of concern to the United States, including Vietnam and the Middle East.[38] The Soviet Union initially balked at the American insistence of broadly based negotiations but eventually accepted the American condition when they concluded that Nixon and Kissinger would not capitulate on their linkage of SALT to other issues.

According to Kissinger, there were two types of linkage: that inherent in an increasingly interdependent world and that created by diplomats in order to gain increased leverage in negotiations.[39] Nixon and Kissinger used linkage in both positive and negative modes. For instance, when the Indo-Pakistani war broke out in December 1971 and the Soviet Union continued to supply India with weapons, Kissinger informed the Soviets that unless they exercised restraint the United States would have to reconsider the proposed Moscow Summit.[40] On other occasions, the United States would offer the Soviet Union positive incentives—increased trade, for example—in return for something that the United States wanted from the USSR.

The second element in the Nixon-Kissinger approach to the Soviet Union was the concept of mutual interests. By concluding mutually beneficial agreements in the limitation of strategic arms and in trade, the United States, Kissinger and Nixon believed, could encourage the voluntary entry of the Soviet Union into the international system. With a greater stake in the system, the Soviet Union would be less likely to support destabilizing revolutionary activities. Through a complex form of behavior modification in which the United States would reward approved Soviet behavior with positive incentives and react to illegitimate activity with negative sanctions, the United States would transform the Soviet position within the international system. In essence, the goal of the administration was to create new regimes and to strengthen and expand existing regimes. By encouraging the development and expansion of regimes in different issue areas, the United States would, according to Kissinger's aide, Helmut Sonnenfeldt, "create a pattern of responsible conduct and an interlocking framework of agreements and understanding with the Soviet Union, enforced by incentives to encourage responsible behavior and disincentives to discourage confrontation."[41] In essence, the Nixon and Kissinger conception of détente with the Soviet Union was part of an international system-developing process in contrast to the classical diplomatic function of détente of system maintenance.

The third principle that Nixon and Kissinger stressed in dealing with the Soviet Union was concreteness. According to Nixon, "The disillusionment that quickly dissipated the euphoric spirits of Geneva in 1955, Camp David in 1959, Vienna in 1961, and Glassboro in 1967 is stark testimony that charm and conciliatory rhetoric have no lasting effect on the tough, pragmatic Soviet leaders."[42] The transformation of the U.S.-Soviet relationship could not be achieved through high-sounding communiqués or "spirits of goodwill"; rather, Nixon and Kissinger sought concrete agreements between the United States and the USSR in different issue areas such as arms control, trade, crisis management, and science and technology.

One of Nixon's and Kissinger's greatest motivations in improving relations with the Soviet Union was their hope that they would be able to convince the Soviet Union to pressure their North Vietnamese allies into negotiating a settlement with the United States and South Vietnam. In April 1969, Kissinger told Dobrynin that American-Soviet relations were at stake in Vietnam because "while we might talk about progress in other areas, a settlement in Vietnam was the key to everything."[43] Initial Soviet behavior in Vietnam was discouraging; as Nixon pointed out in his 1970 report, "To the detriment of the cause of peace, the Soviet leadership has failed to exert a helpful influence on the North Vietnamese in Paris."[44] Nixon went on to warn that Soviet intransigence on this issue "cannot but cloud the rest of our relationship with the Soviet Union." Throughout 1969-1970 the Soviet Union continued to supply North Vietnam with materiel to carry on the war. From a strictly economic point of view, the Soviet investment made sense; during the height of the war, the USSR was shipping approximately $1 billion worth of equipment annually to the North Vietnamese, and the United States was spending from $20 billion to $25 billion per year in support of the war. It was not until mid-1971 following the U.S. diplomatic breakthrough to China that the Soviet Union began to exert restraining pressure on its North Vietnamese allies.[45]

Clearly two very important goals for both superpowers were to lessen the possibility of nuclear war and to lessen the cost of maintaining the "delicate balance of terror." Control of strategic nuclear weapons offered the means to achieve both of these fundamental objectives. Although some arms control proponents argued that SALT was so important that it should not be linked to other issues, Nixon and Kissinger did not accept this line of reasoning. Due to their insistent linking of SALT with other issues and to an extensive review of the U.S.-Soviet military balance, it was almost a year after the president's inauguration that the SALT negotiations officially opened in Helsinki. SALT became the cornerstone of the Nixon administration's policy toward the Soviet Union. Nixon and Kissinger were guided in the SALT negotiations by the basic elements of their new approach to foreign policy. Reflecting their commitment to negotiations with adversaries as well as friends, Nixon and Kissinger welcomed the opening of the SALT talks. As they pointed out in their first report, "There is no area in which we and the Soviet Union—as well as others—have a greater common interest than in reaching agreement with regard to arms control."[46] The existence of this preeminent common interest emerged as the dominant theme in the writings and speeches of Nixon and Kissinger concerning SALT and détente during this period.

Despite Nixon's and Kissinger's acceptance of the concept of linkage, they were unwilling to link the opening of negotiations concerning Berlin to progress in other areas. In 1970 Nixon pointed out, "Even if progress on the broader issues cannot be made, the elimination of recurrent crises around Berlin would be desirable."[47] Nixon had placed the settlement of the Berlin question, a perennial problem since 1945, high on the foreign policy agenda of his administration when he came into office. Just five weeks after his inauguration, Nixon visited the major capitals of Europe and Berlin. On March 26, 1970, Great Britain, France, the Soviet Union, and the United States opened negotiations, which, after eighteen months, resulted in the Quadripartite Agreement on Berlin. From the American point of view, the agreement was designed to stabilize an area where some of the most intense American interactions of the cold war had occurred. The USSR, most likely, sought a recognition of the status quo and for that reason signed the agreement. President Nixon characterized the Berlin agreement as "a milestone achievement" and stated that "it could smooth the way toward possible accommodations on other European security issues."[48] Nixon and Kissinger later noted that the convening of the Conference on Security and Cooperation in

Europe was linked to the conclusion of a Berlin agreement and to the Soviet acceptance of the Mutual Balanced Force Reduction (MBFR) talks.[49]

### TRIPOLAR POLITICS

Although Nixon and Kissinger stressed the importance of the Soviet Union in their grand design and grand strategy for American foreign policy, they attached great significance to U.S. relations with China. In 1967, Nixon published an article in *Foreign Affairs* advocating opening discussions concerning the normalization of relations with the People's Republic of China.[50] The following year in a magazine interview conducted immediately after his nomination for president, Nixon commented, "We must not forget China. We must always seek opportunities to talk with her, as with the U.S.S.R. . . . We must not only watch for changes. We must seek to make changes."[51] Soon after his inauguration, Nixon wrote a memorandum to Kissinger suggesting that the possibilities of a rapprochement with China should be explored, and in his first foreign policy report, published in February 1970, Nixon stated that "it is certainly in our interest, and in the interest of peace and stability in Asia and the world, that we take what steps we can toward improved practical relations with Peking."[52] In March the State Department announced an easing of travel restrictions to China, and the following month trade controls were loosened. In October, Nixon met with Yahya Khan of Pakistan and Nicolae Ceausescu of Rumania, whose countries had ties to China, and asked them to tell the Chinese that the United States considered a Sino-American rapprochement "essential."[53]

Following these actions and a number of communications between the United States and China via Yahya Khan, Kissinger made a secret visit to Peking, July 9-11, 1971, and on July 15, Nixon publicly announced that the Chinese leaders had invited him to visit their country. Following the Chinese invitation, Kissinger told the president that "the tide was turning; we were beginning to see the outline of a new international order."[54] The announcement of the China trip apparently took the Soviets by surprise and caused them to move forward in several negotiations with the United States. In addition, on August 10, 1971, the worried Soviets invited Nixon to visit the Soviet Union.

Nixon's visit to China from February 21 to 28, 1972, undoubtedly concerned the Soviet leaders greatly and increased American diplomatic leverage with them. At the conclusion of Nixon's stay, a joint Sino-American communiqué was issued in which China disavowed superpower ambitions and cited Taiwan as the central obstacle to the normalization of U.S.-Chinese relations. The United States acknowledged that Taiwan was part of China, that the peaceful settlement of the Taiwan issue was for the Chinese to work out, and that the United States eventually would withdraw completely from Taiwan. During the final banquet at the end of his trip to China, Nixon proclaimed that his visit was "the week that changed the world."[55] Kissinger's assessment of the trip was almost as euphoric: "What we are doing now in China is so great, so historic that the word 'Vietnam' will be only a footnote when it is written in history."[56] With the opening to China, the triangular configuration of power that formed the structural foundation of the Nixon-Kissinger grand design was in place. Through negotiations with the Soviet Union and China perhaps even that "footnote," Vietnam, could be settled.

On March 30, 1972, however, the North Vietnamese launched a major attack on the provinces around the demilitarized zone. During the next month the situation worsened for the South Vietnamese, and on May 8, President Nixon announced the mining of Haiphong and six other North Vietnamese ports and the bombing of Hanoi and supply routes from China. Kissinger, the National Security Council staff, and State Department and CIA experts predicted that the Soviet Union would cancel the Moscow Summit in response to these American actions; however, to their surprise the Moscow Summit took place as scheduled, from May 22 to 30, 1972. After a hectic series of last-minute negotiations, President Nixon and Soviet Party Chairman Brezhnev signed two major arms control agreements, an agreement concerning the basic principles governing Soviet-American relations, and several scientific and cultural exchange agreements. The Moscow Summit marked a significant improvement in Soviet-American relations and a step toward the realization of the Nixon-Kissinger new international system.

In his 1973 foreign policy report, Nixon noted that "through the gathering momentum of individual accords we would seek to create vested interests on both sides in restraint and the strengthening of peace." In short, Nixon believed that the character and nature of Soviet-American relations could be changed through the signing of a number of agreements in different issue areas. The underlying logic of Nixon's and Kissinger's thinking was similar to that of the neofunctionalists of the European integration movement: that agreements in the economic and commercial areas would spill over (to use Ernst Haas's phrase) and affect political relations. By transforming relations with the Soviet Union and the People's Republic of China, "a new structure of peace" would be established; the grand design would be achieved. In assessing the progress to that goal, Nixon ended his report by pointing out that, as a result of the agreements concluded in 1972, "a changed world has moved closer to a lasting peace."[57] In the year following the Moscow Summit, Soviet-American relations improved dramatically; in July the grain deal was concluded, and the Trade Agreement followed in October.

The "new era," however, did not last long, for on October 6, 1973, Egypt and Syria launched a surprise attack against Israel. Within a short time, President Nixon, Secretary of State Kissinger, and Secretary of Defense James Schlesinger compared the Middle Eastern situation to the environment in which World War I began in the Balkan states. Because of the volatility of the situation, the United States sought to restrain the Arabs and their Soviet ally and the Israelis. At one point in the war, the Soviet Union threatened to intervene unilaterally, and the United States issued a worldwide alert of its military forces to deter it. The Soviet Union did not intervene, and the crisis was resolved, but in the aftermath, Secretary Kissinger was more circumspect in his assessment of détente than he had been prior to the war: "The relationship between the Soviet Union and the United States is an inherently ambiguous one . . . Our view has been that détente is made necessary because as the two great nuclear superpowers, we have a special responsibility to spare mankind the dangers of a nuclear holocaust."[58] Kissinger still emphasized the familiar theme of mutual interests but stressed the most important mutual interest, avoiding nuclear war. In this sense Nixon and Kissinger retrenched from their earlier claim that the United States could transform Soviet-American relations by weaving a complex web of agreements concerning a number of different issues. At the same time, however, following the October War, Kissinger developed the theme of global interdependence, a theme that was obviously closely related to the concepts of mutual interest and functionalism.

Initially Nixon and Kissinger conceptualized interdependence in strictly bipolar terms. The 1973 foreign policy report stated that economic and commercial "ventures do not create a one-sided dependence by the United States upon Soviet resources; they establish an interdependence between our economies which provides a continuing incentive to maintain a constructive relationship."[59] According to this view, agreements on issues of mutual interest would lead to Soviet-American interdependence, which would contribute to the building of a stable foundation for ongoing relations.

Following the Arab-Israeli war of October 1973 and the ensuing Arab oil embargo, Kissinger began to think of interdependence in multilateral terms: "As technology expands man's reach, the planet continues to shrink. Global communications make us acutely aware of each other. Human aspirations and destinies increasingly are intertwined."[60] Critics had charged that Nixon and Kissinger had paid inadequate attention to the developing states of the world. The October War made clear the latent power of the developing states that were richly endowed with natural resources; it also made clear the distinction between different kinds of developing states: those that were self-sufficient and those with inadequate resources (or even potential resources) to cope with the future.

THE NIXON RESIGNATION AND THE FORD SUCCESSION

Watergate dominated 1973 and 1974. Although Brezhnev visited the United States in June 1973 and Nixon visited the Soviet Union a year later, no agreements as significant as the SALT I agreements signed at the first summit in 1972 were concluded. After months of congressional hearings and shocking disclosures, Richard Nixon resigned as president on August 9, 1974.

As soon as Vice-President Gerald Ford returned to his office following the conversation in which Nixon informed him of his intention to resign, Ford called Kissinger and told him: "I need

you. The country needs you. I want you to stay. I'll do everything
I can to work with you."[61] Kissinger agreed to stay in the new administration, and after a short period of time Ford and Kissinger
developed a close working relationship. Although there were some
changes in the foreign policy decision-making process in the Ford
adminstration, few were substantive, Indeed, Kissinger, who had
served as the co-architect of the Nixon administration's foreign
policy initiatives, played a very similar role in the new administration. It is therefore accurate to write of the Nixon-Ford-Kissinger
policies in the period August 1974 to January 1977.

In late 1974, Kissinger noted, "We are stranded between old
conceptions of political conduct and a wholly new environment,
between the inadequacy of the nation-state and the emerging imperative of global community."[62] Throughout the Ford administration, Kissinger referred to the "fact of global interdependence"
and concluded that "interdependence has become a physical and
moral imperative."[63] He argued for the acceptance of new development plans and increased aid for developing countries, measures
that appeared to be genuine policy initiatives.[64] In his speech to the
UN Conference on Trade and Development (UNCTAD) in Nairobi
in 1976, Secretary Kissinger proposed a complex and comprehensive
American plan for reducing the increasing gap between rich and
poor states. The plan envisioned, among other things, the creation
of an international resources bank that would, Kissinger stated,
"promote more rational, systematic and equitable development
of resources in developing nations."[65] Kissinger's new emphasis on
developing states differed significantly from his tripolar great
power approach to world politics characteristic of the 1969-1973
period.

Following the October War, little progress was made in the
improvement of Soviet-American relations. As President Ford
recalled in his memoirs, "Relations with the Soviet Union were
strained; we had moved from the more glamorous phase of détente
into a time of testing."[66] Soviet testing of the United States occurred in 1975 in Angola, where the Soviets sent military aid to the
pro-communist factions seeking to gain control of the government
following the departure of Portugal from its former colony. During
the same year, the Soviets sent aid to the Portuguese communist

party, which was vying for control. Soviet support of pro-communist factions in Angola and Portugal made the limits of détente very clear, and in the 1976 presidential campaign, candidates from both parties—Ronald Reagan, George Wallace, Henry Jackson, and Jimmy Carter—criticized the Nixon-Ford-Kissinger conception and implementation of détente. Reacting to these criticisms, President Ford banned the use of the word "détente" by members of his administration. But this cosmetic change was not enough and at the Republican Convention Ford was forced to accept a Reagan-backed foreign policy platform that was, according to Ford, "nothing less than a slick denunciation of Administration foreign policy."[67]

Following Soviet actions in the October War, Angola, and Portugal, the Nixon-Ford-Kissinger characterization of the Soviet Union underwent substantial revision. No longer did they and other foreign policy officials speak and write of "weaving a complex web of Soviet-American relations;" rather Administration spokespersons such as Helmut Sonnenfeldt, counselor for the Department of State, spoke of the Soviet Union as "beginning its truly 'imperial' phase."[68] Referring to "the Russian sense of unique national destiny," Sonnenfeldt admonished Americans to "grasp the reality of the Soviet Union as a permanent competitor— an adversary—and yet also sometimes a partner."[69] In a series of speeches delivered during early 1976, Secretary Kissinger emphasized the same major point: that the Soviet Union had begun to define its interests and objectives in global terms and that "this condition will not go away" and "will have to be faced by every Administration in the foreseeable future."[70]

American policies toward the Soviet Union in the eight-year period from January 1969 through January 1977 can be divided into three relatively distinct periods: January 1969 through April 1972, May 1972 through September 1973, and October 1973 through January 1977. There is little doubt that much was accomplished in this eight-year period; the ABM Treaty and the Quadripartite Agreement on Berlin stand out as the most notable accomplishments. There were also a number of setbacks in Soviet-American relationships, and most observers were relatively pessimistic by the end of 1976 concerning the possibility of improving Soviet-American relations. Ironically the Republican administration that was defeated in 1976 left a legacy to its democratic successors that was in many ways as uncertain as the one it had faced in 1969. What had happened to the Nixon-Kissinger grand design and grand strategy?

## The Legitimation of the Nixon-Kissinger Grand Design and Grand Strategy

When President Nixon entered office in 1969, he faced a situation similar to that confronting Truman in 1945.[71] Substantial changes has occurred in the international system, and the cold war grand design and grand strategy of U.S. foreign policy was not supported domestically and seemed inadequate to the realities of international life. Both Nixon and Kissinger believed that their public statements and actions could significantly influence international events and, therefore, to some extent, create a new reality. On Kissinger's part, this belief derived from his study of the influence of Castlereagh, Metternich, and Bismarck on the course of nineteenth-century European history.

Just as Truman had to develop a structure in which to fit new facts, Nixon and Kissinger were forced to provide a structure, or in Kissinger's words, a "conceptual framework," appropriate to the 1970s. The Nixon-Kissinger attempt to legitimate their grand design and grand strategy can be divided into three phases, the first two of which correspond to the phases described by B. Thomas Trout.[72] Nixon and Kissinger recognized the need to legitimate their new policy vision. In their 1971 foreign policy report, they rhetorically asked, "Where do we want to go in the long run? What are our purposes?"[73] Between 1969 and 1971, the attentive phase, Nixon and Kissinger introduced legitimizing symbols such as "a new structure of peace" and the proclamation that "the postwar period in international relations has ended."[74] They sought to gain public and congressional acceptance of the Soviet Union and the People's Republic of China as limited adversaries of the United States. This view required greater sophistication and differentiation from the public than the dichotomous categorization of the cold war of countries as either friends or foes. Under the conditions of détente, the United States could engage in both conflictual and cooperative behavior with the Soviet Union and the People's Republic. In essence, Nixon and Kissinger sought to deemphasize ideology as a component of American foreign policy; however, in doing this, they lost a powerful means of legitimation, for as Trout has noted, "Ideologies tend to be potent sources for legitimation."[75]

Whereas Truman and Dean Acheson had used ideology to legitimate the doctrine of containment, Nixon and Kissinger attempted to legitimate their grand design and grand strategy through several other means. The publication of the annual foreign policy reports from 1970 through 1973 was one component of their tactics. Nixon and Kissinger also sought to use drama as a legitimation device, such as Nixon's visits to Peking and Moscow, so as to gain acceptance for the new foreign policy initiatives. And his report to the Congress immediately upon his return to Washington from Moscow was a good example of Nixon's manipulation of a dramatic event.

During the second phase—the assertive phase—of the legitimation process, Nixon and Kissinger sought to operationalize some of the concepts presented during the earlier attentive phase, and during the 1972-1973 period, they were able to conclude a number of agreements that called for the implementation of elements of the grand design and grand strategy. In February 1972, Nixon visited Peking and signed a statement of principles concerning Sino-American relations, the Shanghai communiqué, and shortly after he visited the Soviet Union. Reflecting on his handling of these meetings with the benefit of hindsight, Nixon concluded in 1980:

Creation of a willowy euphoria is one of the dangers of summitry. During my administration excessive euphoria built up around the 1972 Peking and Moscow Summit meetings. I must assume a substantial part of the responsibility for this. It was an election year and I wanted the political credit for what I believed were genuinely major advances toward a stable peace.[76]

Soon after the Moscow Summit, SALT and détente became inextricably intertwined. As one observer has noted: "SALT, when criticized, is defended in terms of the blessings of detente; detente, when viewed skeptically, is supported by the accomplishments of SALT."[77] In short, détente became a hostage to the SALT process. In linking these two developments so closely, Nixon and Kissinger lost the ability to criticize one development independently of the other. They apparently believed that the linkage of SALT and détente was necessary to legitimate the new U.S. approach to the Soviet Union. In doing this, however, Nixon and Kissinger made a fundamental error. In order to legitimate policy, leaders must structure policy so that it reflects the essential cognitive beliefs and normative values of society. In seeking to legitimate détente with SALT and vice-versa, Nixon and Kissinger sought a kind of boot-straps legitimation that was not directly linked to the underlying beliefs and values of American society. In place of the complicated process of long-term legitimation, Nixon and Kissinger substituted *ad hoc* legitimation through the use of dramatic events and announcements. For example, Kissinger hailed the signing of the Agreement on the Prevention of Nuclear War as the end of the cold war.

But the cold war was not over, as Soviet-American interactions during the Arab-Israeli October 1973 war clearly demonstrated. Critics of détente pointed to Soviet actions during the war as aggressive and as a violation of détente agreements. Because Nixon and Kissinger had failed to relate the policy of détente to important American beliefs and values, they had to defend their policies from a weak position. Kissinger, for example, claimed that the United States was confronted with a choice of détente or cold war and that the latter alternative could lead to nuclear war. Many observers noted that this was a false dichotomy and that the possible conditions of Soviet-American relations constituted a spectrum rather than a dichotomy.

Following the October War, Nixon and Kissinger retrenched from their earlier claims concerning the new international system. For instance, by mid-1975, Kissinger recognized, "While the cold war structure of international relations has come apart, a new stable international order has yet to be found."[78] Domestically Nixon, Ford, and Kissinger had failed to legitimate their vision for a new American foreign policy, and by 1975 members of the Ford administration spoke of the emerging global power of the Soviet Union and the need for the United States to oppose Soviet expansionism, a kind of détente-plus-containment policy.[79]

Kissinger was certainly not unaware of the potential dilemmas of continuity in maintaining grand policy visions. In fact, in *A World Restored* Kissinger's major criticism of Metternich and Castlereagh was that they failed to gain long-term support for their policies. Similarly in his assessment of Bismarck's grand design and grand strategy, Kissinger criticized the German statesman on two major grounds. First, Bismarck's grand design for a European international order reduced the flexibility that had allowed the system to adjust to changes throughout the eighteenth and first half of the nineteenth centuries. Second, Kissinger criticized Bismarck for establishing a network of relations so intricate that his successors could not maintain them. Interestingly, in his analyses of Meternich, Castlereagh, and Bismarck, Kissinger did not emphasize their failure to recognize the increasing importance of domestic interest groups in the making and sustaining of foreign policy.

Ironically Nixon and Kissinger repeated the errors of Metternich, Castlereagh, and Bismarck; they failed to legitimate their grand design and grand strategy of foreign policy. For a short time (1972-1973), they were able to gain public and congressional acceptance through the use of drama and clever public relations, but in the long run they were unable to maintain support for their policy vision because of their failure to link the components of their grand design and grand strategy to underlying American beliefs and values.

## Notes

1. Richard Nixon, "Asia After Viet Nam," *Foreign Affairs* 46-1 (October 1967): 121.

2. Ibid., p. 122.

3. Richard Nixon, *RN: The Memoirs of Richard Nixon* (New York: Grosset and Dunlap, 1978), p. 349.

4. Henry A. Kissinger, "The Viet Nam Negotiations," *Foreign Affairs* 47 (January 1969): 218-19.

5. Joseph Alsop, "Will Russia Attack China?" *Reader's Digest* (August 1973): 77-82; H. R. Haldeman with Joseph DiMona, *The Ends of Power* (New York: Times Books, 1978), pp. 90-94.

6. Henry Kissinger, *White House Years* (Boston: Little, Brown, 1979), p. 172.

7. Ibid., p. 235.

8. *Gallup Opinion Index* 39 (September 1968): 8.

9. Ibid. 44 (February 1969): 3.

10. Louis Harris, "The Limits of Commitment," *Time*, May 2, 1969, pp. 16-17.

11. Bruce Russett and Miroslav Nincic, "American Opinion on the Use of Military Force Abroad," *Political Science Quarterly* 91-3 (Fall 1976): 429-30.

12. Bruce Russett, "The Revolt of the Masses," in Bruce Russett, ed., *Peace, War, and Numbers* (Beverly Hills, Calif.: Sage, 1972), pp. 299-335.

13. Edward J. Laurance, "The Changing Role of Congress in Defense Policy-Making," *Journal of Conflict Resolution* 20-2 (June 1976): 213-54.

14. The title of the foreign policy report series is *U.S. Foreign Policy for the 1970's* and the individual reports are entitled: *A New Strategy for Peace* (February 18, 1970); *Building for Peace* (February 25, 1971); *The Emerging Structure of Peace* (February 9, 1972); and *Shaping a Durable Peace* (May 3, 1973). The reports were published by the U.S. Government Printing Office and the *Department of State Bulletin*. Quotations and references from the 1970 and 1971 reports are from the GPO-published documents, and quotations from the 1972 and 1973 reports are from the *Department of State Bulletin* versions.

15. Nixon, *New Strategy*, p. 2.

16. Kissinger, *White House Years*, p. 159.

17. General Brent Scowcroft to Dan Caldwell, January 14, 1977.

18. I attempted to obtain a copy of this report under the provisions of the Freedom of Information Act (5 U.S.C. 552), by my request and appeal were denied.

19. Kissinger, *White House Years*, p. 1053.

20. For a comprehensive bibliography of Kissinger's publications, see U.S. Congress, Senate, Committee of Foreign Relations, *Hearings on the Nomination of Henry A. Kissinger* (Washington, D.C.: Government Printing Office, 1973), pp. 2-3. A detailed and interesting analysis of Kissinger's underlying philosophy of history is Peter Dickson's *Kissinger and the Meaning of History* (New York: Cambridge University Press, 1978). For an excellent review of Kissinger's major writings, see Stephen R. Graubard, *Kissinger: Portrait of a Mind* (New York: W. W. Norton, 1973).

21. Henry A. Kissinger, *A World Restored: The Politics of Conservatism in a Revolutionary Age* (New York: Grosset and Dunlap, 1964), p. 1.

22. Henry A. Kissinger, "The White Revolutionary: Reflections on Bismarck," *Daedalus* 3 (Summer 1968): 910.

23. Nixon, *Memoirs*, p. 347.

24. Nixon, *New Strategy*, p. 60.
25. Ibid., p. 142.
26. Ibid., p. 156.
27. Nixon, *Building for Peace*, p. 200.
28. *Department of State Bulletin* (July 26, 1971): 94-95.
29. *Time* (January 3, 1972): 11.
30. Zbigniew Brzezinski, "The Balance of Power Delusion," *Foreign Policy* 7 (Summer 1972): 57.
31. Stanley Hoffmann, "Weighing the Balance of Power," *Foreign Affairs* 50 (July 1972): 620.
32. Interview with former National Security Council official.
33. CBS News interview with Henry A. Kissinger, February 1, 1973, in *Department of State Bulletin* (April 2, 1973).
34. Nixon, *Shaping a Durable Peace*, p. 232.
35. Henry A. Kissinger, "Address to Pacem in Terris III Conference," *Department of State Bulletin* (October 29, 1973).
36. Stephen A. Garrett, "Nixonian Foreign Policy: A New Balance of Power—or a Revived Concert?" *Polity* 8-3 (Spring 1976).
37. Nixon, *Memoirs*, p. 344.
38. Ibid., p. 349.
39. Kissinger, *White House Years*, p. 129.
40. Nixon, *Memoirs*, p. 529.
41. Helmut Sonnenfeldt, "The Meaning of 'Détente'," *Naval War College Review* 28-1 (Summer 1975): 7-8.
42. Richard Nixon, *The Real War* (New York: Warner Books, 1980), p. 293.
43. Nixon, *Memoirs*, p. 391.
44. Nixon, *New Strategy*, p. 137.
45. Nixon, *Memoirs*, p. 413.
46. Nixon, *New Strategy*, p. 142.
47. Ibid., p. 36.
48. Nixon, *Emerging Structure*, p. 337.
49. Henry A. Kissinger, "Press Conference of July 25, 1975" (Washington, D.C.: Office of Media Services, Department of State, 1975), p. 3; and Nixon, *Shaping a Durable Peace*, p. 761.
50. Nixon, "Asia After Viet Nam."
51. *U.S. News and World Report* (September 16, 1968): 48.
52. Nixon, *Memoirs*, p. 545.
53. Kissinger, *White House Years*, p. 699.
54. Ibid., p. 716.
55. Nixon, *Memoirs*, p. 580.

56. Quoted by John G. Stoessinger, *Henry Kissinger: The Anguish of Power* (New York: W. W. Norton, 1976), p. 131.

57. Nixon, *Shaping a Durable Peace*, p. 724.

58. Kissinger news conference of November 21, 1973, in *Department of State Bulletin* 69 (December 10, 1973): 706.

59. Nixon, *Shaping a Durable Peace*, p. 734.

60. Henry A. Kissinger, "The Challenge of Peace," address to the St. Louis World Affairs Council, May 12, 1975 (Washington, D.C.: Office of Media Services, Department of State), p. 3.

61. Gerald R. Ford, *A Time to Heal* (New York: Berkely Books, 1980), p. 29.

62. Henry A. Kissinger, "The Global Community and the Struggle Against Famine," address to the World Food Conference, November 5, 1974 (Washington, D.C.: Office of Media Services, Department of State).

63. Henry A. Kissinger, "The Americas in a Changing World," speech delivered in Caracas, Venezuela (Washington, D.C.: Office of the Media Services, Department of State), p. 5.

64. Clyde H. Farnsworth, "Kissinger Inches toward a 'Rich-Poor' Policy," *New York Times*, May 9, 1976, sec. 4, p. 1.

65. Quoted in Michael T. Kaufman, "Kissinger Offers Program to Help Poor Lands Grow," *New York Times*, May 7, 1976, p. 1.

66. Ford, *Time to Heal*, p. 122.

67. Ibid., p. 385.

68. Quoted in Leslie H. Gelb, "Detente's Supporters under Fire in the U.S.," *New York Times*, December 29, 1975, p. 1.

69. Helmut Sonnenfeldt, "The United States and the Soviet Union in the Nuclear Age," speech given to the U.S. Naval Academy, James Forrestal Lecture Series (Washington, D.C.: Office of Media Services, Department of State, April 6, 1976), p. 7.

70. Henry A. Kissinger, "The Permanent Challenge of Peace: U.S. Policy toward the Soviet Union," address to the World Affairs Council of Northern California, San Francisco, February 3, 1976 (Washington, D.C.: Office of Media Services, Department of State), p. 3.

71. B. Thomas Trout, "Legitimating Containment and Detente: A Comparative Analysis" (paper presented to the Midwest Political Science Association, April 19-21, 1979).

72. B. Thomas Trout, "Rhetoric Revisited: Political Legitimation and the Cold War," *International Studies Quarterly* 19 (September 1975): 263.

73. Nixon, *Building for Peace*, p. 227.

74. Nixon, *New Strategy*, p. 2.

75. Trout, "Rhetoric Revisited," pp. 251-84.

76. Nixon, *The Real War*, p. 266.

77. Henry S. Rowen, "Testimony before the House Committee on International Relations," reprinted in *Aviation Week and Space Technology* (September 15, 1975): 53.

78. Henry A. Kissinger, "The Challenge of Peace," speech delivered to the St. Louis World Affairs Council, May 12, 1975 (Washington, D.C.: Office of Media Services, Department of State, 1975), p. 2.

79. Henry A. Kissinger, "The Permanent Challenge of Peace."

# CHAPTER 4

# THE DÉTENTE REGIMES

## The Détente Strategic Arms Control Regime

Regimes may be implicit or explicit. The former are far more difficult to identify and analyze than the latter. The willingness of governments to create explicit regimes indicates a seriousness about a particular issue area that may or may not be indicated by an implicit regime. During the cold war the United States and the Soviet Union established a largely implicit strategic deterrence regime for the management of nuclear weapons. During the limited détente period a partial arms control regime was established. Between 1969 and 1976, the United States and the Soviet Union signed a number of confidence-building and more substantive agreements designed to control, reduce, and limit nuclear weapons and to eliminate biological weapons. In effect, the partial arms control regime that was established during the limited détente period was explicated and expanded. Table 7 shows the type of agreement (bilateral or multilateral), the date signed, procedures and rules established, and organizations charged with oversight and/or implementation.

Although many of the détente arms control agreements had antecedents in the limited détente period, the number and quality of these agreements concluded during the détente period were unprecedented in post-World War II international relations. These

**Table 7**

## STRATEGIC-ARMS CONTROL AGREEMENTS, 1971-1976

| Agreement | Type | Date Signed | Procedures and Rules Established | Organizations Charged with Oversight and/or Implementation |
|---|---|---|---|---|
| Seabed Treaty | Multilateral | Feb. 11, 1971 | Prohibits weapons of mass destruction beyond 3 miles; Each signatory allowed to verify (article III) | If questions arise, states may investigate and if not satisfied go to the UN Security Council; Review Conference called for |
| "Accidents Measures" Agreement | Bilateral | Sept. 30, 1971 | U.S. and USSR pledge to maintain and improve organizational and technical safeguards against accidental or unauthorized use of nuclear weapons. Immediate notification of the other party in cases of accidental, unauthorized, or unexplained incidents. Advance notification of any planned missile launches outside of territory of launching party. Hot line should be used "in situations requiring prompt clarification" | |

| Agreement | Type | Date Signed | Procedures and Rules Established | Organizations Charged with Oversight and/or Implementation |
|---|---|---|---|---|
| Hot Line Modernization Agreement | Bilateral | Sept. 30, 1971 | Established two satellite communication circuits—one Soviet, one American | Consultation within framework of UN |
| Biological Weapons Convention | Multilateral | April 10, 1972 | Each signatory pledges not to develop, produce, or stockpile biological toxins used as weapons<br>Destroy existing biological weapons | |
| Interim Agreement on Offensive Arms | Bilateral | May 26, 1972 | Freezes existing numbers of ICBMs<br>Permits an increase in the number of SLBMs<br>Verification by "national technical means"<br>Five-year agreement unless extended or replaced | Standing Consultative Commission (established by ABM Treaty) |
| ABM Treaty | Bilateral | May 26, 1972 | Limits U.S. and USSR to two ABM sites with no more than 100 missiles at each site<br>Bans "exotic" ABM systems<br>Verification by "national technical means"<br>Unlimited duration | Standing Consultative Commission established<br>Review conference every five years |

*—Continued*

**Table 7**—*Continued*

| Agreement | Type | Date Signed | Procedures and Rules Established | Organizations Charged with Oversight and/or Implementation |
|---|---|---|---|---|
| Protocol to ABM Treaty | Bilateral | July 3, 1974 | Reduces the number of ABM sites to one | |
| Threshold Test Ban Treaty | Bilateral | July 3, 1974 | Prohibits underground nuclear tests of greater than 150 kilotons<br>Protocol to treaty calls for an exchange of technical information | |
| Vladivostok Accord | Bilateral | Nov. 24, 1974 | Statement of intention by US and USSR to: limit strategic arsenals to 2400 launch vehicles for each side; limit of 1320 MIRVs for each side | |
| Peaceful Nuclear Explosions Treaty | Bilateral | May 26, 1976 | U.S. and USSR promise not to carry out peaceful nuclear explosions with yield greater than 150 kilotons | |

agreements contained provisions ranging from the confidence-building measures contained in the "accident measures" and hot-line modernization agreements to the total renunciation of biological weapons.[1] Significantly nine of the eleven agreements signed between 1971 and 1976 were bilateral agreements between the United States and the USSR. The most important ones were the two SALT I agreements: the Anti-Ballistic Missile (ABM) Treaty and the Interim Agreement on Offensive Weapons. The ABM Treaty was modified by a protocol signed in 1974, and President Ford and General Secretary Brezhnev during their summit meeting at Vladivostok signed an *aide-memoire* in the same year designed to supplement the Interim Agreement. The Threshold Test Ban Treaty and the Peaceful Nuclear Explosions Treaty extended the rules concerning nuclear testing.

Most of these agreements called for consultation within the framework of the UN should questions arise about the implementation of the agreements; however, the ABM Treaty called for the establishment of a new bilateral organization, the Standing Consultative Commission (SCC), which was specifically charged with resolving questions arising from the implementation of the provisions of the Interim Agreement and the ABM Treaty. Article 13 of the ABM Treaty established the SCC and called for a minimum of two meetings per year. During the two sessions in 1973, its representatives were primarily concerned with questions arising from the provision of the Interim Agreement, which allowed for the expansion of the sea-based strategic missile force provided that land-based ICBMs were dismantled (the so-called one-way freedom to mix provision). Some of the ambiguities in this trade-off were resolved by two protocols signed during the Moscow Summit of June 1974. During 1974-1975 the SCC discussed the procedures required for the replacement of ABM systems and components permitted by the ABM Treaty, as well as proposals related to the improved implementation of the "accidents measures" agreement of 1971.[2] The SCC also investigated questions concerning the implementation of the agreements by both signatories, and on at least one occasion the Soviet representative acknowledged a technical violation of the agreements when the Soviet Union failed to dismantle a number of older ICBMs according to schedule.[3] The SCC is an important precedent in the process of the development of an explicit regime concerning strategic arms control since it provides a forum for the discussion and possible resolution of outstanding issues related to the implementation of procedures and rules.

The issue of verification precluded the negotiation of any control of nuclear weapons during the acute cold war period. The SALT agreements call for verification by "national technical means," a euphemism for satellite reconnaissance and the monitoring of electronic signals. Therefore the development of an effective technological means of verification, according to the U.S. commissioner on the SCC, "made the SALT I agreements possible."[4] In the case of the Biological Weapons Convention, effective verification of the implementation of the agreement is impossible, and it is significant that this obstacle nevertheless did not preclude agreement.

Thus by the mid-1970s, the United States and the Soviet Union had concluded a number of important agreements explicitly stipulating rules and procedures for the control and, in the case of biological agents, the elimination of certain weapons. The SCC was created to oversee the implementation of the SALT agreements. In contrast to the acute cold war when the United States and the Soviet Union developed strategies for the use of nuclear weapons, the two superpowers developed, in addition to employment strategies, a strategic arms control regime for the control of nuclear arms and the elimination of biological weapons. Table 8 presents a summary of the regimes in the strategic military issue area for the acute cold war, limited détente, and détente periods. It shows that when the two superpowers failed to reach an agreement on disarmament, they developed the nuclear deterrence regime. Although the United States and the Soviet Union agreed implicitly during the acute cold war to control the proliferation of nuclear weapons, an explicit arms control regime was not created until the limited détente period. This regime was then explicated and expanded in the détente era.

## The American-Soviet Economic Regime

Having grown impressively throughout the 1960s, the Soviet economy slowed somewhat in the early 1970s. During the 1960s,

**Table 8**

**POLICIES AND REGIMES IN THE STRATEGIC MILITARY ISSUE AREA**

| Acute Cold War | Limited Détente | Détente |
|---|---|---|
| Disarmament | | Weak, limited regime |
| Nonregime | Nonregime | Biological weapons prohibited (1972) |
| U.S. presented the Baruch Plan, calling for international control of nuclear power, provided on-site inspections were permitted | | |
| USSR presented the Gromyko Plan, calling for the destruction of all nuclear weapons and then inspection | | |
| Nuclear deterrence | | |
| Regime established | Regime maintained | Regime maintained |
| Each superpower should be able to attack the other with nuclear weapons sufficient to inflict unacceptable damage | Same | Same |
| The military forces of one superpower should not be deployed against the military forces or territory of the other superpower | Same | Same |
| It is permissible to threaten the use of nuclear weapons in order to gain political-military advantage | After Cuban missile crisis, neither U.S. nor USSR used nuclear threats | Same |

*—Continued*

**Table 8** —*Continued*

| Acute Cold War | Limited Détente | Détente |
|---|---|---|
| Arms control | | |
| Implicit, weak regime | Explicit regime created | Regime expanded and explicated |
| Control of nuclear weapons should not be turned over to the allies of the superpowers | Same | Same |
| The superpowers should discourage the proliferation of nuclear weapons and provide non-nuclear states with technical assistance in the development of nuclear power for peaceful purposes | U.S. and USSR unilaterally reduce the amount of fissile material produced for nuclear weapons | Same |
| | The spread of nuclear weapons should be halted; nuclear states should assist non-nuclear states with peaceful nuclear programs (Non-Proliferation Treaty, 1968) | Same |
| Deployment of weapons to Antarctica prohibited (1959) | Same | Same |
| Nuclear testing should be halted (moratorium, 1958-1961) | Nuclear tests should not be conducted in the atmosphere or in the ocean (Limited Test Ban Treaty, 1963) | Underground nuclear tests having a yield greater than 150 kilotons prohibited (1974) |
| | | Peaceful nuclear explosives are limited (1976) |
| | U.S. and USSR should communicate directly in situations that threaten the maintenance of crisis stability. | Improved organizational and technological safeguards against accidental and unauthorized use of nuclear weapons Hot line modernized; two satellite circuits established (1971) |

| Acute Cold War | Limited Détente | Détente |
|---|---|---|
| | | If threatening situation arises, the situation should be explained to the other party via the hot line |
| | | Same |
| | Weapons of mass destruction prohibited from outer space (1967) | Antiballistic missile systems limited (ABM Treaty, 1972) |
| | U.S. and USSR agree in principle that strategic arms limitation negotiations should be held (1968) | Strategic nuclear offensive missiles limited (1972) |
| | | Satellite and electronic reconnaissance recognized and protected by ABM Treaty (1972) |
| | | SCC created to oversee implementation of SALT agreements (1972) |
| | | Weapons of mass destruction prohibited from emplacement on the seabed and the ocean floor (Seabed Treaty, 1971) |

the Soviet GNP grew at an average annual rate of 5.5 percent compared to 4.0 percent for the United States, 5.5 percent for Italy, and 11.1 percent for Japan.[5] The Soviets achieved this respectable level of growth by emphasizing the production of industrial and agricultural machinery and deemphasizing the manufacture of consumer goods. The resulting demand for consumer goods led to the creation of illegal but widespread black markets. By the late 1960s, the Soviet economy was suffering from a shortage of investment capital and a declining rate of growth in labor productivity. Additionally the Soviet Union had balance-of-payments problems caused partially by a shortage of hard (Western) currency. Relative to the United States, the Soviet economy faced some major problems. With a population 18 percent larger than that of the United States, the Soviet Union in the late 1960s produced less than half of the goods and services, invested as much (in real terms), and employed 45 percent more labor than the United States.[6]

By the early 1970s, it was clear that the leaders of the Soviet Union needed to make important decisions about the future direction of Soviet domestic and international economic policies. One alternative, and probably the riskiest for the leadership due to the uncertainties involved, would be to embark on a far-reaching economic reform. Far less risky would be a turn to the West, which could provide the credits and advanced technology needed to rejuvenate the stagnating Soviet economy. For various reasons, the Soviets chose the latter alternative, and at the Twenty-Fourth Party Congress (held from March 30 through April 9, 1971) Brezhnev strongly supported the expansion of trade with the United States and other Western advanced industrial states. In his words, "There can be no doubt that the expansion of international exchanges will have a favorable effect on the improvement of all our industry."[7] The Ninth Five-Year Plan, which was presented at the Congress, called for an annual rate of growth of 8 percent, industrial modernization, and the production of more consumer goods.[8]

Like the Soviet Union, the United States faced major economic problems in the late 1960s and early 1970s. Among the most serious problems were the domestic recession, a large and growing balance-of-payments deficit, and increasing competition, particularly from Japanese and Western European companies, for foreign markets.

In an attempt to improve the international position of the dollar and to stimulate the domestic economy, on August 15, 1971, Secretary of the Treasury John Connally announced a "new economic policy," which in effect marked the end of the Bretton Woods international monetary system that had been established at the end of World War II. Thus economic relations among the members of the Western alliance were undergoing great change by the early 1970s.

During the first two and a half years of the Nixon administration, little was done to improve East-West economic relations, for several reasons. First, the United States faced significant economic problems both domestically and within the Western international economic system. Second, Nixon and Kissinger chose to link the expansion of Soviet-American economic relations with the improvement of political relations. In his 1973 foreign policy report, Nixon noted, "In the earlier years of this Administration I linked the expansion of economic relations with improved political relations."[9] In congressional testimony in 1974, Kissinger recalled:

The first time we approved a commercial deal, which was on the order of some $30 million, was in May of 1971, following the first break-through in the SALT negotiations. . . . In other words, for a period of more than two years, we told the Soviet Union that restraint in its foreign policy conduct would lead to an expansion of trade relations with the United States.[10]

On June 1, 1971, the Department of Commerce approved export licenses for $85 million worth of vehicle manufacturing equipment to the Soviet Union, and nine days later President Nixon removed grain from the list of U.S. exports requiring licenses. In retrospect, it seems that the timing of the first U.S. approval of a commercial deal was related to the announcement by Brezhnev at the Twenty-Fourth Party Congress that the Soviet Union would be seeking expanded trade with the West. During the latter half of 1971, Nixon and Kissinger began to view trade as an important component of their grand strategy for achieving a new Soviet-American relationship.

American and Soviet governmental representatives negotiated throughout 1971 and the first part of 1972 hoping to reach a comprehensive trade agreement prior to the Moscow Summit of May

1972; however, negotiations stalled on questions concerning shipping and the Lend-Lease settlement. Nevertheless the summit provided an important impetus to the expansion of Soviet-American trade. The seventh point of the Basic Principles stated:

The USA and the USSR regard commercial and economic ties as an important and necessary element in the strengthening of their bilateral relations and thus will actively promote the growth of such ties. They will facilitate cooperation between the relevant organizations and enterprises of the two countries and the conclusion of appropriate agreements and contracts, including long-term ones.[11]

Although this agreement was not legally binding, it provided an indication of the future intentions of the United States and the Soviet Union.

On May 26, the United States and the Soviet Union agreed to establish a joint commercial commission for the purposes of resolving outstanding differences on economic issues such as Lend-Lease, most-favored-nation status for the Soviet Union, and credits and the supervision of large-scale, long-term trade. The inaugural meeting of the commission was scheduled for July. The first and most important item on the agenda was to conclude a comprehensive trade agreement. The commission was also charged with the responsibility for arranging credit procedures, setting up trade offices in Moscow and Washington, and establishing arbitration procedures for any future trade disputes. In short, the Joint Commercial Commission was supposed to resolve the residual cold war economic issues and to provide a framework for trade between two very different economic systems. This was no small task. Several days after the commission was created, a Soviet planning official indicated that the Soviet government hoped to enter into "large-scale arrangements in which the United States would provide plants and equipment and we would pay with raw materials and the end products of such plants."[12]

Prior to the Moscow Summit, U.S. companies successfully concluded several relatively small deals with the Soviet Trade Ministry, but the proposal to build a massive truck plant near the Kama River faced considerable difficulties. Within two months of the

Moscow Summit, U.S. companies and Soviet trade organizations signed contracts worth hundreds of millions of dollars, including several deals to provide manufacturing equipment for the Kama River factory. Apparently the summit helped to legitimate Soviet-American trade both within the U.S. government and within the American business community.

These agreements signed in the aftermath of the summit were basically of three types. In commercial transactions, the Soviets would either make an outright purchase of goods with a convertible currency or they would arrange for a loan through the exporting company or another Western financial institution. Second, a number of American companies concluded barter arrangements with the Soviets whereby the U.S. corporation would assist in the development of a new product and would be compensated with that product or another. For instance, Occidental Petroleum and El Paso Natural Gas signed a twenty-five-year, $10 billion agreement to assist with the exploration and development of Siberian natural gas in return for payment in natural gas in the future. Pepsi-Cola signed an agreement to assist in the construction of several soft drink factories in return for Soviet-produced vodka. The third type of agreement called for an exchange of information and technology. Although most Americans often think of U.S. industry as superior to that of the Soviet Union, there were a number of products (such as heavy castings, hydro- and steam-turbines, long-distance power transmitters, and equipment operated at very cold temperatures) in which the Soviets had made significant advances.[13]

During the winter of 1971-1972 the prolonged cold temperatures in Eastern Europe and the Soviet Union destroyed one-third of the Soviet winter wheat crop, a serious loss considering the fact that direct per-capita consumption of wheat in the Soviet Union then was about twice that of the United States. The 1972 Soviet harvest was not atypical; serious shortfalls had occurred on three occasions in the previous decade: in 1963, 1965, and 1968. In 1963-1964, the Soviets had purchased 1.8 million tons of grain from the United States for $250 million. Grain sales to foreign countries represented a solution to a chronic problem of American agriculture, over-production. In 1972 alone the U.S. government paid farmers over $3 billion not to grow crops. Thus Soviet Foreign Trade Minister

Nikolai Patolichev was enthusiastically welcomed by U.S. officials when he came to Washington in May 1972 to inquire about the possibility of purchasing American grain. Nixon and Brezhnev briefly discussed this subject at the end of the month at the Moscow Summit, and in July 1972, the United States extended $750 million credit to the Soviet Union for the purchase of grain over a three-year period. During the summer of 1972, Soviet trade officials arranged to import approximately 28 million tons of grain, 19 million tons of which came from the United States. This represented about one-fourth of the entire 1972 U.S. wheat harvest.

Because the grain deal quickly reduced U.S. grain surpluses, it was initially hailed as a boon to American farmers and consumers. However, in 1972 late monsoons caused severe crop damage throughout South Asia and China, and parts of Africa suffered from drought conditions. As a result of these developments, the world demand for wheat increased dramatically and caused the price of wheat to double between 1972 and 1974. In January 1973, the U.S. consumer price index, an indicator of the cost of food items, increased 2.3 percent over the level of the previous month. This was the largest one-month increase in twenty-two years, and it was followed by increases of 2.4 percent in February and 3.1 percent in March. At this rate, food prices would increase 30 percent in one year. Irate consumers blamed these increases on the "wheat deal," and Senator Henry Jackson characterized the sale as "one of the most notorious Government foul-ups in American history."[14] Kissinger denied that the grain deal was part of the Nixon administration's détente policy:

The Soviet grain deal, whatever criticism may be made of it, had next to nothing to do with detente. To be sure, it followed the Moscow summit by about a month. But as it turned out, at the Moscow summit there was next to no discussion of the grain deal because the assumption at that time was that the amount of purchases would be so low as to not justify the attention of the two national leaders.[15]

In his memoirs, however, Kissinger admitted that the Soviets outwitted the United States and that the wheat deal was a mistake for the United States.[16]

The Moscow Summit and the grain agreement helped to resolve the obstacles blocking the expansion of Soviet-American trade. On October 14, 1972, the United States and USSR signed a three-year maritime agreement that established premium rates for U.S. vessels that were carrying Soviet grain purchases. The agreement also increased the number of ports in each country that were open to ships of the other country. While sometimes considered a minor agreement, the maritime agreement was of major significance. In 1964, disagreement over shipping rates had almost prevented the conclusion of a Soviet-American grain deal.

On October 18, the United States and the Soviet Union signed a three-year, comprehensive trade agreement designed, according to Helmut Sonnenfeldt, to provide "a good framework with which to build our commercial relationships."[17] The agreement had four major provisions. First, the Soviet Union agreed to a settlement of its Lend-Lease debts in return for a U.S. promise to ask Congress for MFN treatment for Soviet imports. Second, the agreement provided that each country could request that the other not ship goods that "cause, threaten or contribute to a disruption of its domestic market" through unfair low pricing. (This was the so-called anti-dumping provision.) Third, each country agreed to establish a trade office in the capital of the other, and the Soviets agreed to construct a trade center complex in Moscow. Fourth, the agreement called for commercial disputes to be settled under the arbitration rules of a UN agency, the Economic Commission of Europe, in a third country. In an action related to the agreement, President Nixon signed an official determination stating that it was in the national interest for the U.S. Export-Import Bank to extend credits and guarantees for sales to the Soviet Union. Soviet and American representatives stated that they expected that during the three years covered by the agreement trade would increase to approximately $1.5 billion, a figure roughly triple the rate of trade during the 1969-1971 period.

Just two weeks prior to the signing of the 1972 trade agreement, Senator Henry Jackson introduced an amendment to the trade reform bill that would block the extension of credits or MFN status to nonmarket economies that restricted or taxed the emigration of their citizens. Cosponsored by seventy-seven other senators, the

Jackson Amendment explicitly linked the extension of economic advantages by the United States to the Soviet Union to liberalized Soviet emigration policies. In the past, the Soviets had strongly resisted any attempts by foreign powers to influence their domestic politics. Support for the Jackson Amendment increased in the Congress, and in January 1973, Congressman Charles Vanik with 238 consponsors introduced an amendment very similar to the Jackson Amendment into the House of Representatives. Soviet leaders were unwilling to agree publicly to a specific number of emigrations in return for the granting of most-favored-nation status by the Congress. In December 1974, the Congress passed the trade reform bill, which incorporated the provisions of the Jackson-Vanik Amendment. The Soviets denied that they had agreed to any compromise on the extension of trade benefits in exchange for freer Soviet emigration. Concurrent with the debate over the trade bill, the Congress passed an amendment introduced by Senator Adlai Stevenson that set a $300 million ceiling on U.S. credits to the Soviet Union without congressional approval. As a result of the adoption of the Jackson-Vanik and Stevenson amendments, the Soviet Union informed the United States on January 10, 1975, that it would not implement the provisions of the trade agreement. In an interview shortly after this event, Kissinger stated, "I think detente has had a setback."[18]

The United States and the Soviet Union in the period from 1971 through 1974 made a significant attempt to develop an economic regime. A list of the trade-related agreements and their provisions is contained in table 9, which shows, strikingly, the number and the quality of agreements concluded during this period.

By the early 1970s trade had grown substantially, and eleven agreements relating to the expansion of Soviet-American trade had been signed. These agreements removed many of the obstacles that had blocked the development of U.S.-USSR relations during the cold war. The two countries concluded three shipping agreements that removed one of the most contentious issues. The 1972 grain agreement was the largest single grain transaction and was financed by U.S. credits. MFN and Lend-Lease were the two residual cold war issues, and the 1972 Trade Agreement called for the resolution of these obstacles.

**Table 9**

**SOVIET-AMERICAN TRADE AGREEMENTS, 1971-1974**

| Agreement | Date | Major Provisions |
|---|---|---|
| Shipping agreement | April 21, 1971 | Understanding relating to port access, cargo carriage, and other maritime matters |
| US-USSR Commercial Commission | May 26, 1972 | Created to resolve outstanding obstacles to the development of US-USSR trade |
| Basic Principles | May 29, 1972 | Seventh point calls for the expansion of US-USSR commercial relations |
| Grain agreement | July 8, 1972 | USSR agreed to buy at least $750 million worth of U.S. grain, and U.S. agreed to provide $750 million credit through the Commodity Credit Corporation |
| Maritime agreement | Oct. 14, 1972 | Established premium rates for U.S. vessels and increased the number of ports open to ships of the other country |

—*Continued*

**Table 9** —*Continued*

| Agreement | Date | Major Provisions |
|---|---|---|
| Trade agreement | Oct. 18, 1972 | Settlement of Soviet Lend-Lease debt<br>Anti-dumping provision<br>Trade offices in each capital<br>Arbitration of disputes by third party<br>Credits extended by U.S.<br>MFN status extended by U.S. |
| Shipping agreement | June 5, 1973 | Premium rates for U.S. shipping |
| Tax treaty | June 20, 1973 | Elimination of double taxation of citizens and companies of one country living or working in the other |
| Trade protocols | June 22, 1973 | Establishment of a US-USSR Chamber of Commerce<br>Space in capitals provided for trade centers; embassies' commercial staffs expanded |
| Trade agreement | June 29, 1974 | Ten-year economic agreement supplementing the 1972 Trade Agreement |

The development of a Soviet-American trade regime was neither smooth nor coherent. The development of a strategic arms control regime was a government-to-government matter between the United States and the Soviet Union. Since only governmental authorities controlled biological and nuclear weapons, the efforts to control these weapons could be, and in fact were, centralized. In contrast to superpower strategic relations, Soviet-American trade involves a great many private as well as public actors. A number of scholars have noted the increasing importance of transnational and transgovernmental relations in world politics, but these analysts have generally limited their focus to relations among Western industrial states.[19] Given the Soviet government's control over individuals and organizations within the Soviet Union, a transnational approach, which posits significant activity with foreign actors by nongovernmental organizations and individuals, may not be as important in the analysis of Soviet-American relations. However, a transgovernmental approach may help to provide insights into Soviet-American relations that otherwise would be overlooked by a state-as-unitary-actor approach.

In the process of developing regimes in different issue areas, Soviet and American governmental officials and agencies worked very closely. In addition, in the economic issue area, a large number of private U.S. corporations directly negotiated and reached agreements with Soviet governmental agencies. For example, a group of American businessmen representing a number of U.S. corporations founded an organization with the representatives from the Soviet Trade Ministry for promoting Soviet-American trade. This organization, the U.S.-Soviet Trade and Economic Council, along with the National Association of Manufacturers, lobbied in favor of the Trade Reform Act and against the Jackson-Vanik Amendment.

Several intergovernmental organizations were created in the 1971-1974 period to manage and promote trade. The Joint Commercial Commission was created at the 1972 Moscow Summit to resolve the problems that existed at the time for the expansion of Soviet-American trade. The discussions by the members of the commission contributed to the conclusion of the 1972 Trade Agreement. The United States and the Soviet Union also established a Joint Chamber of Commerce at the 1973 summit meeting. In addition, the Joint Commission on Science and Technology was created in 1972 to facilitate the exchange of information and technology.

The Soviet and American governments each established organizations within their respective governmental structures to analyze and facilitate Soviet-American trade. Even as early as 1934, the Export-Import Bank was created, primarily to finance Soviet exports to the United States. The Bureau of East-West Trade was created within the Department of Commerce in 1972 to assist American corporations interested in pursuing East-West trade. Information concerning Soviet governmental officials and organizations who support Soviet-American trade is somewhat sketchy, but several observations can be made. Premier Kosygin was very interested in developing expanded U.S.-Soviet trade and apparently provided important support for the pro-trade forces within the Soviet Union. The minister of foreign trade, Nikolai Patolichev, and the deputy minster, Vladimir Alkhimov, represented the Soviet Union at the major negotiations over trade and at the meetings of the Trade and Economic Council. The chairman of the State Committee on Science and Technology, V. A. Kirillin, and the deputy chairman, Gherman Gvishiani, played important roles in negotiating various technology exchange agreements between the Soviet Union and U.S. governmental organizations, as well as American corporations. Because of the paucity of information about the internal structure and operation of the Soviet government, it is difficult to identify new organizations created for the purpose of foreign trade. The Institute for the Study of the U.S.A. and Canada, created in 1967 and headed by Georgi Arbatov, generally adopted a favorable position regarding the expansion of Soviet-American trade.

The 1971-1974 period witnessed a substantial expansion of Soviet-American trade. Not only did trade increase, but the Soviet and American governments reached a number of agreements to establish common procedures and rules to govern trade relations. Additionally several governmental and transgovernmental organizations were created for the promotion of Soviet-American trade. The creation of a Soviet-American economic regime in the 1971-1974 period markedly contrasts with the acute cold war and limited détente periods, as table 10 clearly demonstrates. During the acute

**Table 10**

**POLICIES AND REGIMES IN THE ECONOMIC ISSUE AREA**

| Acute Cold War | Limited Détente | Détente |
|---|---|---|
| Nonregime | Weak, limited regime established with the U.S.-Soviet grain deal of 1963-1964 | Regime established |
| Soviet policies:<br>  Stalin: autarky<br>  Krushchev: turn to the West | | U.S. government permitted U.S. corporations to conclude commercial contracts with Soviet trade organizations |
| U.S. policies:<br>  Marshall Plan aid offered and refused; U.S. then sought to isolate the USSR and Eastern Europe from Western international system by restricting exports and credits to USSR and imports from USSR | | Premium shipping rates for U.S. vessels agreed to (Maritime Agreement, 1972)<br><br>Trade Agreement signed, Oct. 1972, called for:<br>  Settlement of Soviet Lend-Lease debt,<br>  Anti-dumping provisions,<br>  Trade officials in each capital,<br>  Arbitration of disputes by third party, |

—*Continued*

Table 10 *—Continued*

| Acute Cold War | Limited Détente | Détente |
|---|---|---|
| | | Credits extended by U.S., Most-favored-nation status extended by U.S. |
| | | Organizations created: Joint Commercial Commission (1972) Joint Chamber of Commerce (1973) U.S.-Soviet Trade and Economic Council (1972) |
| | | Double taxation of citizens and companies located in the other country prohibited (Tax Treaty, 1973) |
| | | Long-term (ten-year) trade agreement called for (1974) |

cold war, there was no significant economic interaction between the superpowers. The wheat deal of 1963-1964 was the only major trade transaction of the limited détente period. The economic regime created in the 1971-1974 period, if implemented, would have resolved the major stumbling blocks to the development of Soviet-American trade; however, the Jackson and Stevenson amendments caused the Soviets to refrain from implementing the provision of the 1972 Trade Agreement.

## Continued Maintenance of the Crisis Management Regime

During the acute cold war, the United States and the Soviet Union developed a set of rules for managing crises, and the crisis management regime was maintained throughout the limited détente period. During the 1969-1976 period, this regime was explicated, expanded, and tested.

The major American-Soviet crises that Presidents Nixon and Ford faced concerned U.S. involvement in Vietnam, the Soviet attempt to establish a submarine base at Cienfuegos, Cuba, in the fall of 1970, the Jordanian crisis of September-October 1970, the Indo-Pakistani War of December 1971, the Arab-Israeli war of October 1973, and the Angolan civil war of late 1975 and early 1976. The memoirs of Nixon, Ford, and particularly Kissinger contain detailed descriptions of the major events and negotiations concerning these crises.[20]

An overall comparison of Soviet-American crisis management during the acute cold war, limited détente, and détente periods reveals several important differences. First, during the détente crises, the superpowers emphasized even more than earlier the practice of communicating directly with one another in addition to engaging in signaling maneuvers. The hot line (updated by a 1971 agreement) provided the physical means for communication between Moscow and Washington. In addition, direct communications between Soviet and American leaders took place in other forms. Ambassador Dobrynin, who had played a key role in the resolution of the Cuban missile crisis, often consulted with Henry Kissinger and, less often, with President Nixon. The vital importance of the Dobrynin-Kissinger back-channel negotiations in reaching the SALT I agreements has been described in detail.[21] Less publicized but probably as important in the development of improved Soviet-American relations were the Dobrynin-Kissinger discussions about political-military crises. The Cienfuegos crisis was a case in point. One of the most dramatic instances of Soviet-American communication occurred during the October War when, at the height of the crisis, Brezhnev invited Kissinger to Moscow to discuss the course of the war. This action was unprecedented in both the acute cold war and limited détente periods.

The second major difference in the management of crises by the superpowers during the three periods was the attempt in the détente period to explicate the rules of crisis interaction. As indicated in table 11, five major agreements were signed during a four-year period. The Hot Line Modernization Agreement updated the 1963 agreement and called for the establishment of two satellite circuits. This agreement provided an indication that the 1963 agreement had proved its worth during the eight years of its existence.

A body of rules and regulations concerning navigation on the high seas evolved over centuries of traditional practice. These "rules of the road," as they were called, were codified in 1958 at Geneva in the International Regulations for Preventing Collisions at Sea. These rules regulate the lighting and maneuvering of ships on the high seas and in territorial and inland waters. The rules also established common signaling and communication procedures. The advantages of an internationally accepted set of navigation rules is clear; nevertheless Soviet and American naval vessels frequently violated the rules throughout the acute cold war and limited détente periods, engaging in games of "chicken." Typically a vessel of one superpower would maneuver in the vicinity of the vessels of the other superpower, and one or the other would refuse to yield the right of way to the other vessel. Some of these encounters ended in collisions between the Soviet and American naval vessels. One might discount the importance of such incidents; however there have been a number of collisions between large combatant vessels armed with nuclear weapons. The final report of the House Intelligence Committee noted that in the 1966-1976 period U.S. nuclear submarines in Soviet territorial waters collided with nine hostile vessels.[22] The possibility of escalation in the event of a major collision is a distinct and ominous possibility.

**Table 11**

**CRISIS MANAGEMENT AND CRISIS PREVENTION AGREEMENTS, 1971-1975**

| Agreement | Date Signed | Procedures and Rules Established | Organizations |
|---|---|---|---|
| Hot Line Modernization | Sept. 30, 1971 | Updated 1963 Agreement Established two satellite communication circuits—one Soviet, one American | Consultation within the framework of the UN |
| Agreement for the Prevention of Naval Incidents | May 25, 1972 | Recognized that naval operations are subject to regulation by the 1958 Geneva Convention on the High Seas Prohibits simulated attacks on ships | |
| Basic Principles | May 29, 1972 | Agreed to avoid military confrontations and prevent the | Summit meeting reaffirmed |

—Continued

Table 11 —Continued

| Agreement | Date Signed | Procedures and Rules Established | Organizations |
|---|---|---|---|
| | | outbreak of nuclear war Signed agreements should be "faithfully implemented" Efforts at arms control should continue | Two sides welcomed contact between the legislative bodies |
| Agreement on the Prevention of Nuclear War | June 22, 1973 | Prevent the development of situations that threaten an exacerbation of tensions If a situation appears to involve the risk of nuclear war, both sides shall consult with one another | UN shall be informed of such consultations |
| Conference on Security and Cooperation in Europe: Final Act | August 1, 1975 | Agreed to notify all signatories of the agreement of major military maneuvers and movements Called for observers to attend military maneuvers | Resolved to organize follow-on meetings Review conference scheduled for 1977 |

In the fall of 1970, the Soviet Union proposed negotiations on incidents at sea.[23] The United States agreed to negotiations in June 1971, and talks began in October 1971. After eight months, an agreement was signed at the Moscow Summit that called for joint recognition of the Geneva Convention rules of the road. Although the agreement did not eliminate all U.S.-Soviet naval incidents, it substantially reduced deliberate provocations and the number of collisions. Perhaps due at least in part to the Incidents at Sea Agreement and noted by a number of observers, Soviet-American naval interaction during the 1973 October war was noticeably restrained on both sides.

In addition to the SALT and other agreements concluded at the Moscow Summit, Nixon and Brezhnev signed the Basic Principles of Relations between the United States of America and the Union of Soviet Socialist Republics. This document was unnoticed by most American observers and dismissed by others as mere "atmospherics"; yet according to Kissinger, the Basic Principles marked the opening of a new era of "restraint" and "creativity" in Soviet-American relations. In a press conference in Moscow after the signing of the Basic Principles, Kissinger noted, "We have laid out a road map. Will we follow this road? I don't know. Is it automatic? Absolutely not. But it lays down a general rule of conduct, which, if both sides act with wisdom, they can, perhaps, over a period of time make a contribution. At this point, it is an aspiration."[24] Despite the fact that the Basic Principles were not legally binding, they established a set of guidelines for evaluating the legitimacy of the foreign policy behavior of each superpower. In a sense, therefore, the Basic Principles and a similar document signed a year later constitute the most concise statements of the Soviet-American theory of détente.

In the second point of this document, the two powers agreed to "do their utmost to avoid military confrontations and to prevent the outbreak of nuclear war."[25] They agreed to "always exercise restraint in their mutual relations" and to this end to conduct negotiations "in a spirit of reciprocity, mutual accommodation and mutual benefit." Furthermore, both sides recognized "that efforts to obtain unilateral advantage at the expense of the other, directly or indirectly, are inconsistent with these objectives." In the third point, U.S. and Soviet leaders agreed "to do everything in their power so that conflicts or situations will not arise which would serve to increase international tensions.'' In the remaining points of the document, the two signatories called for the implementation of the Soviet-American treaties and agreements already concluded, the continuation of periodic summit meetings, the continuation of arms control and disarmament negotiations, and the facilitation of increased commercial, economic, scientific, and cultural cooperation. The final point stated, "The basic principles . . . do not affect any obligations with respect to other countries earlier assumed by the U.S.A. and the U.S.S.R." In other words, the principles did not apply in situations where long-time Soviet or American allies were involved.

Former members of Kissinger's National Security Council staff indicated that Kissinger was more favorable toward this document than was any other American official.[26] Seen by most American officials at the time as a cosmetic agreement, the draft of the Basic Principles was not given to the Central Intelligence Agency for analysis, a standard procedure with other agreements under negotiation. The Soviet Union clearly valued the Basic Principles and pushed for its acceptance. In fact, at the Moscow Summit, Brezhnev, according to Kissinger, commented that "he considered the 'Basic Principles of U.S.-Soviet Relations' even more important than the projected SALT agreement."[27] The Soviet Union insisted that the Basic Principles be typed on special paper normally used only for treaties. Soviet commentators gave a great deal of publicity to the Basic Principles and when listing the achievements of Soviet-American relations consistently mentioned the Basic Principles at the top of the list. One writer in *Pravda* noted, "Above all, the document entitled 'The Basic Principles . . .' deserves special attention. This is the first document between the U.S.S.R. and the U.S.A. to give international legal form to relations between the two sides on the basis of the principles of peaceful coexistence."[28] Thus for the Soviet Union, the Basic Principles represented the formal status and acceptance of the Soviet concept of peaceful coexistence.

In his 1973 foreign policy report, Nixon referred to the Basic Principles as "a code of conduct" and in discussing the Middle East noted, "The danger of immediate U.S.-Soviet confrontation, a source of grave concern in 1970 and 1971, is at the moment reduced. The Moscow Summit and the agreement on the Basic Principles of our relations contributed to this, not only for the present but also for the longer term."[29] Assistant Secretary of State Joseph Sisco stated in early 1973 that the Basic Principles were understood to mean that the Middle East "should not be an area over which there should be a confrontation between us [the United States and Soviet Union]."[30] In his memoirs, Kissinger claimed that he and Nixon interpreted the Basic Principles as a repudiation of the Brezhnev Doctrine.[31]

Stemming from a proposal made by the Soviets at the 1972 Moscow Summit, the Agreement of the Prevention of Nuclear War was signed on June 22, 1973, during Secretary Brezhnev's visit to the United States.[32] The signatories agreed to "act in such a manner as to prevent the development of situations capable of causing a dangerous exacerbation of their relations" (article 1) and to "refrain from the threat or use of force against the other party, against the allies of the other party and against other countries, which may endanger international peace and security" (article 2). Should a situation develop involving the risk of nuclear war, the parties agreed to "immediately enter into urgent consultations with each other and make every effort to avert this risk" (article 4). In article 6, the signatories noted that nothing in the agreement "shall affect or impair the obligations undertaken by either party towards its allies or other countries in treaties, agreements, and other appropriate documents."

The Soviet draft of what became the Agreement on the Prevention of Nuclear War contained a provision calling for joint Soviet-American intervention into a conflict if it threatened world peace.[33] Since this proposal, if accepted, would result in a condominium of the superpowers and therefore probably the worsening of relations with the People's Republic of China, the United States rejected it. Kissinger met with the head of Peking's liaison office in Washington to lessen Chinese fears that the final agreement marked a superpower condominium.[34] *Pravda* and *Izvestia* hailed the agreement as a major accomplishment: "The permanent 'Agreement on the Prevention of Nuclear War' . . . is an important step on the path to lessening and eventually eliminating the threat of the outbreak of nuclear war and to creating a system of real guarantees of international security."[35] NATO members were very critical of the agreement, believing that it marked a weakening of the U.S. commitment to European defense. One senior West German military officer went as far as to term the agreement "a worse betrayal than Munich."[36] Several years after the signing of the agreement, a former member of the U.S. SALT delegation, Raymond Garthoff, criticized the Nixon administration for failing to use the Prevention of Nuclear War Agreement as a bargaining chip in the negotiations, for although this agreement was viewed as unimportant and harmless in Washington, it was regarded as very important by the Soviet Union.[37]

The Basic Principles and the Agreement on the Prevention of Nuclear War, Nixon and Kissinger claimed, marked the end of the cold war. Indeed, for the period May 1972 through September 1973, U.S.-Soviet relations seemed to be marked by a new cordiality. However, the outbreak of the October War and the ensuing Soviet-American crisis called the operational significance of the détente crisis management agreements into question. Nevertheless, at the Conference on Security and Cooperation in Europe, the United States and the Soviet Union, as well as the European participants, signed an agreement containing a number of wide-ranging provisions, including several confidence-building measures that could contribute to the prevention of future crises. The signatories agreed to notify one another of their major military maneuvers (defined as those operations involving greater than 25,000 troops) twenty-one days or more in advance of the maneuver.[38] The signatories also agreed on a voluntary basis to exchange observers for military movements. These provisions could contribute to reduced fears and anxieties.

During the acute cold war, the United States and the Soviet Union developed a number of rules for the management of crises. Taken together these rules constituted an implicit regime. Table 12 presents a summary of this regime and the changes that were instituted during the limited détente and détente periods. The basic rules for crisis management were developed during the acute cold war and were strengthened during the limited détente and détente periods. Importantly, beginning with the Hot-Line Agreement and

**Table 12**

**THE SOVIET-AMERICAN CRISIS MANAGEMENT AND CRISIS PREVENTION REGIME**

| Acute Cold War | Limited Détente | Détente |
|---|---|---|
| Implicit regime established | Implicit regime maintained | Regime made explicit |
| Rules concerning the use of force | | |
| Don't use military force against the military forces or the territory of the other superpower | Same | Same (Basic Principles) |
| Avoid escalation of conflict | Same | Same |
| Use proxy military forces | Same | Same |
| De facto spheres of influence recognized | Same | Same |
| Except in extreme situations, nuclear weapons should not be used | Same | Same (Agreement on the Prevention of Nuclear War) |
| Communication rules | | |
| Communicate by deed rather than by word | Communicate by both deed and word (Hot Line, 1963) | Use direct communication in both crisis and bargaining situations |
| Threats of the use of force, including nuclear blackmail, are permissible to accentuate signals | After Cuban missile crisis neither U.S. nor USSR used nuclear threats | Ambiguous |

—Continued

**Table 12** —*Continued*

| Acute Cold War | Limited Détente | Détente |
|---|---|---|
| **Bargaining rules** | | |
| Bargaining is largely tacit | Bargaining is more explicit | Bargaining is explicit between U.S. and Soviet leaders, although it is secret |
| Risks should be limited | Same | Same |
| **Alliance management** | | |
| U.S. and USSR exercise control over allies in order to prevent escalation of conflict | U.S. and USSR exercise less control over allies | Same |
| **Crisis prevention rules** | | |
| | Clarify ambiguous situations via hot line | Avoid confrontations; notify other party of major military maneuvers |

supplemented with a number of agreements in the 1971-1975 period, the United States and Soviet Union developed rules for crisis prevention. This was the most important difference between the first and latter two periods, although there were a number of other differences.

Rules concerning communication, bargaining, and alliance management differed in several significant respects. Soviet and American leaders relied a great deal more on direct communication during the détente period. As decision makers discovered during the acute cold war, communication by deed and tacit bargaining often result in ambiguous situations in which the positions and objectives of each side are unclear. To remove some of the ambiguity, Soviet and American leaders increasingly communicated directly with one another and attempted to reach explicit agreements on specific issues.

In the 1963-1976 period, the superpowers were far less able to exercise control over allies than during the acute cold war. Strains in both the Eastern and Western alliance systems were obvious from the mid-1960s on; as evidenced by France's exit from the military organization of NATO in 1966 and Czechoslovakia's Prague spring of 1968. By the early 1970s, the leaders of European states recognized that they could exercise some freedom from their superpower sponsors. For the West, the European option to exercise this freedom was clearest in the actions of the European states (with the exception of the Netherlands) to abide by the Arab demands during the October War. Food riots in Poland in 1970 and the independent foreign policies espoused by Ceausescu in Rumania brought the same point home for the Soviet Union.

## Conclusion

It is a commonly held view that American and Soviet post-1945 foreign policy can be characterized according to the period in which it occurred. Thus journalists and foreign policy analysts refer to Soviet cold war foreign policy or to American détente foreign policy. The findings of the previous four chapters suggest that Soviet and American foreign policy behavior did indeed differ by period but that their behaviors also differed by issue area. The United States and the Soviet Union developed rules and procedures for managing crises during the acute cold war, and these rules were further developed and expanded in the ensuing two periods. The development of the crisis management regime suggests that, even in circumstances of intense latent conflict, the United States and the Soviet Union share certain common interests, in this case the avoidance of situations that could escalate into a major super-power conflict.

The crisis management regime did not, however, preclude the development of major Soviet-American confrontations over Berlin in 1948 and 1961 and over Cuba in 1962. In the aftermath of the Cuban missile crisis, the superpowers reached a number of agreements in the arms control issue area. In fact, the number and the quality of agreements reached during the 1963-1968 period constituted an arms control regime.

These findings challenge the Nixon-Kissinger assertion that a new international system was developed during their administration, for there were important antecedents to their initiatives in both the crisis management and arms control issue areas. Nixon and Kissinger did, however, pursue several new initiatives. The opening to China was perhaps the most striking of these. Nixon and Kissinger also sought a more cooperative, less conflictual relationship with the Soviet Union. In pursuit of this objective, Nixon and Kissinger attempted to develop an economic regime with the Soviet Union. By "weaving a web of economic interrelationships," Nixon and Kissinger believed that they could give the Soviet Union a greater stake in the maintenance of a stable international system and that because of this the USSR would pursue a moderate foreign policy. Nixon and Kissinger succeeded in negotiating a trade agreement that removed the major obstacles to the development of Soviet-American trade. The implementation of this regime was blocked by the passage of the Jackson and Stevenson amendments and the Soviet refusal to abide by the provisions of this legislation.

Another important contribution of Nixon and Kissinger was to interrelate policies in different issue areas into a grand design and grand strategy. In essence, Nixon and Kissinger sought to interrelate regimes in different issue areas into a broad, overarching framework. Thus the development of the Soviet-American economic regime and the explication and expansion of the crisis management and arms control regimes were all part of, just as was the opening to China, the attempt by Nixon and Kissinger to move toward a new international system.

## Notes

1. For the texts of these agreements, see U.S. Arms Control and Disarmament Agency, *Arms Control and Disarmament Agreements* (Washington, D.C.: Government Printing Office, 1977).

2. U.S. Arms Control and Disarmament Agency, *The 14th Annual Report* (Washington, D.C.: Government Printing Office, 1975), pp. 12-13.

3. Jan M. Lodal, "Verifying SALT," *Foreign Policy* 24 (Fall 1976): 46-47.

4. Interview with Sidney Graybeal, U.S. Commissioner on the SCC, January 16, 1975.

5. U.S. Congress, Joint Economic Committee, "Statement of Abram Bergson," *Soviet Economic Outlook* (Washington, D.C.: Government Printing Office, 1973), pp. 34-35.

6. Herbert Block, "Value and Burden of Soviet Defense," in U.S. Congress, Joint Economic Committee, *Soviet Economic Prospects for the Seventies* (Washington, D.C.: Government Printing Office, June 1973), p. 196.

7. Quoted by Daniel Yergin, "Great Expectations: Trade with Russia," *Yale Review* 65 (December 1975): 176-77.

8. James H. Noren and E. Douglas Whitehouse, "Soviet Industry in the 1971-75 Plan," in *Soviet Economic Prospects.*

9. Richard Nixon, *U.S. Foreign Policy for the 1970s: Shaping a Durable Peace*, reprinted in *Department of State Bulletin* 68 (June 4, 1973).

10. U.S. Congress, Senate, Committee on Finance, "Testimony of Henry A. Kissinger," *The Trade Reform Act of 1973* (Washington, D.C.: Government Printing Office, 1974), p. 468.

11. Lester A. Sobel, ed., *Kissinger and Detente* (New York: Facts on File, 1975), pp. 135-36.

12. Ibid., p. 129.

13. James C. DeHaven, *Technology Exchange: Import Possibilities from the U.S.S.R.*, Rand Report R-1414-ARPA (Santa Monica, Calif.: Rand Corporation, April 1974), pp. 33-34.

14. U.S. Congress, Senate, Committee on Government Operations, *Hearing on Sales of Grain to the Soviet Union* (Washington, D.C.: Government Printing Office, 1974), p. 1.

15. "Testimony of Henry Kissinger," in *Trade Reform Act of 1973*, p. 467.

16. Henry Kissinger, *White House Years* (Boston: Little, Brown, 1979), pp. 1269-70.

17. U.S. Congress, Senate, Committee on Finance, "Testimony of Helmut Sonnenfeldt," *Nominations of Helmut Sonnenfeldt, Donald C. Alexander, and Edward C. Schmults* (Washington, D.C.: Government Printing Office, 1973), p. 60.

18. Quoted in Sobel, *Kissinger and Detente*, p. 180.

19. Keohane and Nye point out that Soviet-American relations fit the conditions of complex interdependence very little; see Robert O. Keohane and Joseph Nye, *Power and Interdependence: World Politics in Transition* (Boston: Little, Brown, 1977), p. 217. In his analysis of international interdependence, Richard Cooper analyzed only the relationships among Western industrial states; see his *The Economics of Interdependence* (New York: McGraw-Hill, 1968).

20. Richard Nixon, *RN: The Memoirs of Richard Nixon* (New York: Grosset and Dunlap, 1978); Gerald Ford, *A Time to Heal* (New York: Berkley Books, 1980); and Kissinger, *White House Years*.

21. John Newhouse, *Cold Dawn: The Story of SALT* (New York: Holt, Rinehart and Winston, 1973).

22. U.S. Congress, House, Select Committee on Intelligence, *U.S. Intelligence Agencies and Activities Hearings,* 94th Cong., 1st sess., 1975.

23. These negotiations are described in detail by Anthony F. Wolf, "Agreement at Sea: The United States-USSR Agreement on Incidents at Sea." *Korean Journal of International Studies* 9-3 (1978): 57-80.

24. Quoted in Marvin Kalb and Bernard Kalb, *Kissinger* (Boston: Little, Brown, 1974), p. 333.

25. *Department of State Bulletin* (April 23, 1973): 485.

26. This paragraph is based on information obtained from interviews conducted in September 1976 with officials from the National Security Council, CIA, and Departments of State and Defense.

27. Kissinger, *White House Years*, p. 1208.

28. Yu. Chernov, "Real Force of International Development," *Pravda*, June 15, 1972, pp. 4-5, in *Current Digest of the Soviet Press* 24 (July 12, 1972): 3.

29. Nixon, *Shaping a Durable Peace*, 1973, p. 787.

30. *Department of State Bulletin* (April 23, 1973): 485.

31. Kissinger, *White House Years*, p. 1151.

32. *New York Times*, June 22, 1973.

33. Ibid.

34. Ibid., June 26, 1973.

35. "On the Results of Comrade L. I. Brezhnev's Visit to the United States of America," *Pravda* and *Izvestia*, June 30, 1973, p. 1, in *Current Digest of the Soviet Press* 25-4 (June 20, 1973): 13.

36. Quoted by J. I. Coffey, "SALT under the Carter Administration" (paper presented at the Annual Meeting of the International Studies Association, Washington, D.C., February 22-25, 1978), p. 41.

37. Raymond L. Garthoff, "Negotiating with the Russians: Some Lessons from SALT," *International Security* 1-4 (Spring 1977): 21.

38. "Conference on Security and Cooperation in Europe: Final Act," *Department of State Bulletin* (September 1, 1975): 328.

_____PART II

# COMPARATIVE CASE STUDIES

# CHAPTER 5

# THE UNITED NATIONS DISARMAMENT SUBCOMMITTEE NEGOTIATIONS AND THE STRATEGIC ARMS LIMITATION TALKS

"The chief feature of the Cold War in the 1950s," as Louis Halle has pointed out, "was to be the arms race. Both sides appeared to be advancing toward a final clash."[1] In 1962 the two superpowers went to the brink of nuclear war and, following the resolution of the Cuban missile crisis, concluded a number of arms control agreements that, taken together, constituted an arms control regime. By the late 1960s, Soviet and American decision makers were ready to open negotiations on the control of strategic nuclear weapons, and in November 1969, the Strategic Arms Limitation Talks (SALT) opened in Helsinki. The SALT negotiations were not without historical precedent. From 1955 through 1957, representatives from the United States, the Soviet Union, Great Britain, France, and Canada constituted the United Nations Disarmament Subcommittee. This group discussed a number of significant arms control proposals but failed to reach an agreement. Fifteen years later, the United States and the Soviet Union signed two important agreements limiting strategic nuclear weapons.

## The UN Disarmament Subcommittee Negotiations, 1955-1957

In January 1952, the UN General Assembly passed a resolution calling for the establishment of a disarmament commission. According to Jerome Wiesner, "The Commission did not succeed in initiating serious discussions during its 1952 and 1953 meetings and was essentially moribund from 1953 until mid-1954."[2] In 1953 the General Assembly established the Disarmament Subcommittee consisting of the United States, the Soviet Union, Great Britain, France, and Canada. From 1954 through 1957, five formal negotiating sessions were held, and a number of substantive proposals were presented and debated.[3] Although these negotiations were constructive and important in some respects, they failed to produce any agreements.

Throughout the cold war, the United States was undoubtedly the world's most powerful state in economic terms, yet U.S. and Soviet decision makers considered military power to be the *sine qua non* of a state's power. If power is measured in strategic military terms, then the international system of the mid-1950s was unambiguously bipolar since the United States and the Soviet Union possessed a greater number of and a greater capability to deliver nuclear weapons than any other state. There were, however, significant asymmetries in American and Soviet force structures. Although the United States in fact possessed more nuclear weapons than did the Soviet Union in the mid-1950s, American decision makers were fearful that Soviet strategic forces were equal to or even superior to U.S. forces. This fear became acute in 1957 when the Soviets launched the first intercontinental ballistic missile (ICBM) and earth-orbiting satellite.[4] Soviet leaders undoubtedly were aware of their strategic inferiority relative to the United States but did nothing to dispel, and even encouraged, the American misperception. Adding to the image of Soviet strength were Soviet conventional forces; in 1955 the Soviets had 5.7 million troops, while the United States had only half that number.

American policymakers viewed this asymmetry as particularly serious in the European context, and this concern eventually was manifested in the doctrine of massive retaliation, which, as John Foster Dulles explained in 1954, meant that the United States would "depend primarily upon a great [nuclear] capacity to retaliate, instantly, by means and at places of our own choosing."[5] Massive retaliation was the result of Dulles's and other U.S. policymakers' belief in what Robert Jervis has described as the central tenet of deterrence theory: "that great dangers arise if an aggressor believes that the status quo powers are weak in capability or resolve."[6] According to this view, the status quo powers must be willing to display the willingness and capacity to go to war in order to deter potential aggressors from seeking expansionist goals. Throughout his tenure as secretary of state, Dulles based his policy prescriptions on this central assumption.

In contrast to deterrence theory, "spiral theory," according to Jervis, posits that a reduction in tensions and an increase in diplomatic and commercial contacts lead to an ever-increasing improvement of relations, or conversely, that an increase in tensions leads to an ever-worsening of relations.[7] Arms races are perhaps the most obvious manifestation of this dynamic. According to the cooperative spiral model, a reduction in U.S.-Soviet tensions should lead to greater and greater improvement in overall relations.

On March 19, 1955, President Eisenhower created the position of special assistant to the president for disarmament and appointed Harold Stassen to fill the post. Stassen analyzed Soviet-American strategic relations from a very different point of view—more akin to the spiral theory perspective—than had Dulles.[8] While Dulles believed that the political environment in general must improve and that German reunification, in particular, must be achieved prior to the beginning of any serious Soviet-American negotiations on arms control and disarmament, Stassen and apparently Eisehower believed that overall political settlements and arms control negotiations could proceed concurrently. An official publication from Stassen's office stated, "World tensions and world armaments tend to reinforce one another. Each serves as a breeding ground for the other."[9]

By 1955, Khrushchev had consolidated his power within the Soviet Union, moderated the more severe Stalinist policies, and embarked on a new policy toward the West. As Adam Ulam has noted, "The year 1955 appeared the most hopeful of the post-war era insofar as the relaxation of international tensions and prospects for an East-West settlement were concerned."[10] Soviet moderation in foreign policy matters was marked by several accommodating gestures: an obsolete naval base in Finland was abandoned and, more importantly, in May the Austrian State Treaty was concluded, and all Soviet forces were withdrawn from Austria.

Despite these significant gestures, there were a number of unresolved issues in Soviet-American relations in 1955. During and immediately following World War II, the most important foreign policy objectives of both American and Soviet decision makers concerned the future of the European states, Germany in particular. Integrally related to "the German problem" was Berlin, which became a perennial flashpoint in Soviet-American relations throughout the cold war. A second major problem concerned the control of nuclear weapons. By the mid-1950s both Soviet and American decision makers realized that it was physically impossible to account for all of the fissionable material in the world. Additionally the tremendous power of nuclear weapons was understood and appreciated. In President Eisenhower's view, "The monumental question of what steps the world's major powers might take toward divesting themselves of the massive weaponry built up . . . was the topic of highest priority. Was there a chance that we might take a step forward? We hoped so."[11] In May 1954, the UN Disarmament Subcommittee negotiations opened. Not until a year later was significant progress in the negotiations made.

On May 10, 1955, the Soviet Union presented a proposal that according to Soviet representative Yakov Malik reflected "all the most important and fundamental wishes of the Western Powers." Indeed the Soviet proposal incorporated many of the provisions of the 1954 Anglo-French proposal.[13] The Soviet proposal consisted of three parts: the reduction of tensions through the liquidation of overseas bases and the numerical reduction and eventual elimination of the armed forces of major world powers, the reduction and eventual elimination of nuclear weapons, and the establishment of an international control organ.

The French delegate, Jules Moch, remarked that the proposal "looks too good to be true," and the British representative, Anthony Nutting, characterized the Soviet presentation as "an encouraging development and a significant advance."[14] The proposal was significant for several reasons. First, it was a notable shift of policy toward the Western position and appeared to indicate that the Khrushchev-Zhukov view that nuclear weapons would destroy all civilization had, at least for the moment, triumphed over Molotov's long-held Stalinist view that the use of nuclear weapons would result in the destruction of only capitalist states. Second, the Soviets admitted in the third part of their proposal that, given the amount of fissionable material in the world, hidden stockpiles were a very real possibility and that some kind of inspection system was needed. Third, the May 10, 1955, proposal indicated a real Soviet concern about the problem of surprise attack and a desire to do something about this problem, a concern shared by Western delegates. Fourth, for the first time the Soviet Union revealed a willingness to discuss partial arms control and disarmament measures as opposed to the comprehensive proposals for general and complete disarmament that had been presented up to that time. At a minimum the Soviet proposal suggested that the Soviets recognize the value of a strategy of limited collaboration with the United States.[15]

Although all four Western delegations at the negotiations recognized that the Soviet proposal differed significantly from the previous ones, the U.S. government did not formally respond to it. In fact, on September 6, 1955, Stassen placed a "reservation" on all previous U.S. proposals, which in effect withdrew them from consideration. There were several plausible reasons for these actions. Stassen had been in his position only seven weeks when the Soviet Union made its proposal, and he probably did not understand the significance of it. Furthermore Stassen and Eisenhower both believed that there should be a complete review of existing American positions prior to embarking on new negotiations. In addition to these factors, powerful interests—notably Dulles, the Joint Chiefs of Staff, and the Atomic Energy Agency—opposed substantive arms control and disarmament negotiations with the USSR. As a result of the preoccupation of Stassen and his colleagues and the opposition of Dulles and his bureaucratic allies, "the moment of hope" for achieving meaningful arms control in 1955 was rejected by the United States.[16]

Probably the major concern of both American and Soviet decisionmakers in the mid-1950s was the possibility of a surprise attack by one superpower against the other.[17] Leaders of both superpowers realized that each of their countries was vulnerable to attack. In July 1955 at the Geneva summit meeting among the heads of government of the United States, the United Kingdom, and the Soviet Union, President Eisenhower presented the Open

Skies proposal, which called for the exchange of the blueprints of Soviet and American military bases and the reciprocal aerial inspection of both countries. From the American point of view, Open Skies had two significant advantages: it would decrease the probability of a Soviet surprise attack and would also enable the United States to gain valuable intelligence on Soviet military capabilities. Khrushchev was quick to recognize the latter aspect of the proposal. On the same day that the plan was presented, he told Eisenhower that the proposal was nothing more than an espionage plot against the Soviet Union.[18] One month after Eisenhower's presentation, Bulganin denied the feasibility of aerial reconnaissance: "During unofficial talks with the leaders of the United States Government we straightforwardly declared that aerophotography cannot give the expected results, because both countries stretch over vast territories in which, if desired, one can conceal anything."[19]

The Soviets had little reason to accept the Open Skies proposal since it would open the Soviet Union to inspection. Because of the democratic nature of American society, the Soviets most likely had a fairly easy time in gaining intelligence about American military forces. Thus the asymmetrical advantages flowing to the United States from the Open Skies proposal doomed it, like the Baruch Plan before it, to failure.

Despite the failure of the Soviet May 10 proposal and the Eisenhower Open Skies plan, arms control negotiations remained active throughout 1956. In March, Eisenhower wrote to Bulganin and proposed a mutual cut-off in the production of fissionable materials used to make nuclear weapons and the transfer of agreed amounts of fissionable materials from military to peaceful purposes. Because this proposal, if accepted, would freeze the Soviets into an inferior position vis-à-vis the United States and because it required on-site inspection, the Soviet Union rejected it outright.[20]

The same month that Eisenhower wrote to Bulganin, Gromyko proposed to the subcommittee negotiations in London that debate concerning nuclear disarmament be shelved temporarily and that a treaty concerning conventional military forces should be concluded.[21] During 1956 the Soviets also proposed the creation of denuclearized zones in East and West Germany, the reduction of military budgets, and the cessation of nuclear weapons tests. The United States rejected all of these proposals. On the positive side, the USSR agreed for the first time to consider aerial photoreconnaissance of its territory, and proposed inspection zones of 800 kilometers on each side of the demarcation line between the eastern and western sectors of Germany.[22] The official U.S. State Department history of this period points out, "The U.S. could under no circumstances agree to a proposal which by its terms would tend to perpetuate the unnatural division of Germany."[23] Thus the German problem, a product of conflicting foreign policy objectives of American and Soviet decision makers, doomed the negotiations on establishing aerial inspection zones, and try as they might, the negotiators could not reach agreement as long as important problems related to the structure of the international system remained unresolved.

In addition to structural factors of the international system, situational variables can affect the conduct of arms control negotiations in three different ways. First, international crises can hinder negotiations. For example, in 1960 the Soviets shot down an American U-2 spy plane, an action that led to the break-up of the Paris summit. Second, crises may have a positive (or catalytic) effect upon negotiations, as the Cuban missile crisis had upon the negotiations of the Hot-Line and Limited Test Ban agreements of 1963. Third, in some cases crises have no apparent effect upon potential or actual negotiations. This appeared to be the case in November 1956 when the United States and the Soviet Union prepared for the upcoming UN Disarmament Subcommittee negotiations even though the Hungarian and Suez crises were unresolved. The reasons that both superpowers maintained the schedule of the planned negotiations are undoubtedly complex and multifaceted; however, one can conclude that an important reason for the Soviet Union's favoring the negotiations was a change in the structure of the international system—the emergence of China as a power. As China demonstrated more and more independence from Moscow, Soviet foreign policy was increasingly concerned with the triangular relationship among the United States, China, and the USSR.[24]

For whatever reasons, the Disarmament Subcommittee opened "the longest and most intensive series of negotiations in its history."[25] The agenda included far more detailed measures than did the 1955 negotiations, and though the formal negotiations were multilateral, there were extensive bilateral meetings between the American and Soviet delegations. The subcommittee discussions were serious and wide-ranging. For instance, the United States presented a package proposal that included halting the production of fissionable materials for military purposes, limiting nuclear tests (coupled with provisions for an inspection system), installing inspection systems to guard against surprise attack, and cutting 10 percent from armaments and military budgets.[26]

In April Khrushchev and Bulganin attended several sessions of the London subcommittee meetings. In retrospect, Khrushchev assessed the state of the negotiations in the following terms: "The main issues were still Germany, disarmament, and peaceful coexistence. We had already seen that the West wasn't yet ready to deal seriously with these very important issues. The Western powers were still trying to coax us into an accommodation on their terms."[27] Furthermore, Khrushchev believed that "if we had given the West a chance, war [against the Soviet Union] would have been declared while Dulles was alive.[28]

Despite these post hoc statements (made perhaps to defend his earlier espousal of arms control and disarmament), during 1957 it appeared that Khrushchev was a strong supporter of the objectives of the conference. Interestingly although Dulles perceived Soviet policies as consistently hostile toward the United States, in late 1957 he thought that the Soviets might be willing to accept the Atoms for Peace plan, the Open Skies proposal, and gradual, reciprocal arms control measures.[29] Although it is impossible to determine what factors contributed to the apparent seriousness of the negotiations, the positive attitudes concerning the discussions held by Eisenhower, Dulles, and Khrushchev undoubtedly played an important role.

The adoption of a number of procedural techniques facilitated communication among various delegations. First, the subcommittee accepted an item-by-item agenda in contrast to the plan-against-plan approach that had been used previously; the former approach permitted negotiators to isolate controversial issues for discussion. A second procedural technique that facilitated serious discussion of the issues was the cultivation of informal sessions between Soviet and Western representatives.[30] Since the secret verbatim proceedings of the formal subcommittee sessions were often leaked to the press, delegates were very restrained and guarded. The cultivation of informal communications channels enabled delegates to communicate their positions clearly and to clarify any unintended ambiguities in another delegation's position. For the first time in the post-World War II period, Soviet negotiators were allowed to meet with Western delegates on an individual basis. This resulted in the development of personal relationships between Western and Soviet negotiators that at the very least increased the contact between delegates and the civility of the negotiating sessions. Former participants in the London subcommittee negotiations point to these developments as marking significant changes in the negotiating style of the Soviets and as contributing to progress on substantive issues.[31]

On April 30 the Soviet delegate, who had just returned from Moscow with new instructions, presented a sequence of proposals that were designed to achieve a partial agreement with the West. When the subcommittee recessed, Stassen returned to Washington to report to the president on the discussions. Evidently both the president and Stassen were pleased with the progress of the negotiations;[32] however, Dulles was hesitant to agree to more than first-stage reductions prior to achieving some progress on German reunification.

Stassen returned to London on May 27 and several days later submitted a discussion paper to the Soviet delegation at the same time that he sent it to U.S. allies. The memorandum brought the American and Soviet positions close together, and early Soviet responses to the note brought the two superpowers even closer. However, the governments of U.S. allies immediately protested Stassen's unusual procedures.[33] Four heads of government wrote to President Eisenhower to protest; Great Britain's Harold Macmillan was particularly disturbed about the likely reaction of French and German opinion. President Eisenhower recalled Stassen to Washington and privately withdrew the memorandum. Stassen's mistake was particularly ironic in light of the effective consultation with allies that had taken place prior to May.

During the next several months, the NATO governments worked to achieve a unified position. As they prepared to present their proposal, the Soviet representative, Valerian Zorin, attacked the Western countries on August 27, singling out the German political situation as an obstacle to continued negotiations.[34] When the Western governments presented their proposal on August 29, it was substantially different from the Stassen memorandum that the Soviet representatives had seen; there was a general hardening of positions throughout the proposal. For instance, part of the proposal stipulated that the "paper is offered for negotiation on the understanding that its provisions are inseparable."[35] This all-or-nothing approach appeared to be a rejection of the previous acceptance of the point-by-point negotiating technique. Zorin's August 27 speech marked the beginning of the end for the subcommittee. What were the reasons for the break-up?

In May, Konrad Adenauer had visited Washington presumably for the purpose of ensuring that no arms control agreement would set back the eventual reunification of Germany. Although Dulles favored a resolution of the German question prior to the conclusion of any disarmament measure,[36] Eisenhower indicated his willingness to move forward on disarmament: "If a beginning could be made toward effective measures of disarmament, this would create a degree of confidence which would facilitate further progress in the field of disarmament and in the settlement of outstanding major political problems, such as the major reunification of Germany."[37] Eisenhower apparently wanted to conclude the negotiations with some kind of agreement; however, the withdrawal of Stassen's informal memorandum closely followed Adenauer's visit, and the Soviet Union may have interpreted this action as a consequence of the visit.

Other US and NATO actions were undoubtedly upsetting to the Soviets. The United States began a new series of nuclear tests on May 15, the same day that the British exploded their first thermonuclear device. On May 19, Admiral Arthur Radford, chairman of the Joint Chiefs of Staff, declared that the United States "cannot trust the Russians on a disarmament agreement or anything. They have broken their word too many times."[38] To make matters worse, in June General Lauris Norstad, who was supreme allied commander in Europe, testified to the Congress that NATO forces had the power to destroy "anything that is of military significance in the Soviet Union."[39] Because of these factors, the negotiations lost the momentum characteristic of the period from March through May. Furthermore the Soviet Union objected to "unequal representation" (four Western governments and only one communist government) on the subcommittee. In seeking to explain the disintegration of the subcommittee's negotiations, President Eisenhower pointed to the Soviet launchings of the first ICBM on August 26 and Sputnik on October 2. Because of these developments, according to Eisenhower, the Soviet Union was no longer interested in achieving arms control and disarmament.[40]

In the fall of 1957 the subcommittee was expanded to include representatives from all of the countries that were members of the UN, and in November the Soviet Union announced its refusal to participate in the enlarged subcommittee. Thus ended the UN-sponsored negotiations on disarmament that had been carried on since 1945. In assessing his administration's progress on arms control and disarmament, Eisenhower singled out the establishment of the International Atomic Energy Agency (IAEA) as the most notable achievement. Overall, however, Eisenhower concluded, "In the end our accomplishments were meager, almost negligible."[41]

In this case a general lessening of tensions in the 1953-1955 period led to a willingness by both the United States and the Soviet Union to participate in substantive arms control negotiations. Although significant political issues, particularly Germany, remained important throughout the 1955-1957 period, the governments of the two superpowers presented serious proposals for the control of nuclear arms. The Soviet proposal of May 10, 1955, one of the most important of the period, differed in some significant respects from previous Soviet proposals but was not addressed by the United States in any detail. Stassen's information memorandum elicited a positive Soviet response but was withdrawn due to pressure from U.S. allies and bureaucratic opposition.

On one level, the breakdown of the negotiations in the fall of 1957 can be explained by the withdrawal of the Stassen memorandum, the beginning of a new U.S. nuclear weapons testing program, the British explosion of its first hydrogen bomb, and the Soviet testing of its first ICBM. All of these events were filtered through the perceptions of decision makers, and there are several social-psychological reasons for the collapse of the negotiations. Dulles believed that the United States should maintain a strong defense posture and not agree to more than first-stage reductions prior to achieving progress toward German reunification. Stassen, on the other hand, believed that arms reductions would lead to an overall reduction of tensions. His tactical error of submitting his memorandum to the Soviet Union without first clearing it with U.S. allies was one of the major causes of the demise of negotiations. Once Stassen had lost his standing with Eisenhower, Dulles was able to make his view prevail. There may have been a similar schism within the Soviet government; in his memoirs, Khrushchev indicated substantial debate within the Politburo over the Austrian State Treaty.[42] Although this observation is suggestive, there are not enough data to conclude whether and/or to what extent differing policy factions concerning the 1955-1957 arms control negotiations existed within the Soviet government.

## The Strategic Arms Limitation Talks, 1969-1972

In the years following the demise of the UN Disarmament Subcommittee negotiations, the United States and the Soviet Union embarked on massive programs to develop and deploy sophisticated intercontinental and submarine-launched ballistic missile systems. The Soviet launchings of the first ICBM and, shortly thereafter, Sputnik caused many American policymakers to conclude that the Soviet Union was ahead of the United States in missile technology.

In the 1960 presidential campaign, John Kennedy attacked the Eisenhower administration's defense policies on two counts. First, Kennedy criticized the Eisenhower-Dulles doctrine of massive retaliation and emphasized the need for increased conventional forces to provide a "flexible response." After his election, Kennedy expanded the number of combat divisions from eleven to fifteen, enlarged airlift and tactical air capabilities, increased the number of military personnel, and increased the number of naval vessels. During the campaign, Kennedy also attacked the Republican administration for allowing a dangerous "missile gap" between the United States and Soviet Union to develop. In order to close this gap, in his first defense budget Kennedy tripled the rate of construction of Polaris submarines (from three to nine) and doubled the production capacity of Minuteman ICBMs. He also ordered Secretary of Defense Robert McNamara to assess the magnitude of the missile gap.

Reconnaissance flights over the Soviet Union by U-2 spy planes had been suspended since mid-1960 following the downing of the U-2 plane piloted by Gary Powers. Lacking the U-2 capability, American policymakers could not verify the number of missile launchers in the Soviet Union until early 1961 when the U.S. SAMOS reconnaissance satellite system became operational, and McNamara found that a missile gap did, in fact, exist—but in favor of the United States. This discovery came too late to affect the momentum of U.S. research and development and deployment schedules. By the end of 1962, the United States had deployed 294 ICBMs, 155 submarine-launched ballistic missiles (SLBMs), and 600 long-range bombers, and the Soviet Union had deployed 75 ICBMs, 75 SLBMs, and 190 long-range bombers.[43] The number of U.S. strategic nuclear launch vehicles continued to grow until 1967 when the number of ICBMs and SLBMs was stabilized; thereafter the number of long-range bombers in the U.S. inventory decreased. The total number of Soviet strategic nuclear launch vehicles grew continously until 1975.

In a message to the Eighteen-Nation Disarmament Committee in January 1964, President Lyndon Johnson proposed a "verified freeze of the number and characteristics of strategic nuclear offensive and defensive vehicles." The Soviet Union rejected this proposal because it called for on-site inspection, and, if accepted, it would have frozen the USSR into a position of strategic inferiority. During 1965 and 1966, Johnson made several other unsuccessful overtures to the Soviet Union to begin talks on limiting strategic nuclear weapons. In early 1967, he requested authorization to begin deployment of an ABM unless the Soviets indicated a genuine desire to begin negotiations on arms limitations. In March 1967, Premier Kosygin wrote to Johnson and agreed to open bilateral discussions on "means of limiting the arms race in of-

fensive and defensive nuclear missiles." The Soviet Union insisted
that prior to opening negotiations it must receive specific assurance
that West Germany would not have independent access to nuclear
weapons. When, in July 1968, the United States and Soviet Union
as well as sixty other countries signed the Non-Proliferation Treaty,
West Germany moved to accept the treaty in principle in 1968 and
signed it in November 1969. This action opened the door to SALT,
and on August 19, 1968, Soviet Ambassador Anatoly Dobrynin
announced that his government had agreed to a meeting to discuss
the control of strategic arms scheduled for the next month. The
following day, however, Soviet forces invaded Czechoslovakia and,
in protest of Soviet actions, the United States cancelled the meeting
indefinitely.

The apparent willingness of Soviet decision makers to discuss
limitations on strategic nuclear arms was due to four major forces.
First, Sino-Soviet relations took a turn for the worse in the late
1960s. Second, by 1968-1969, the Soviet Union had developed and
deployed almost as many strategic nuclear launch vehicles as had
the United States; thus it had achieved approximate strategic
parity with the United States. Third, defense costs were increasingly burdensome to the Soviet Union, and SALT represented an
opportunity to reduce military expenditures and free up resources
for other sectors of the Soviet economy. Fourth, Soviet policymakers were particularly interested in limiting the American ABM
program that they apparently viewed as superior to their own. The
Soviet Union took the initiative and on the day that Nixon was
inaugurated publicly announced interest in immediately com-
mencing negotiations on the limitation of strategic nuclear weapons.

During the 1968 presidential campaign, Richard Nixon had
indicated an intention "to restore our objective of clearcut military
superiority." However soon after inauguration, the newly elected
president stated that he would seek the objective of strategic
nuclear "sufficiency," a goal that differed from parity virtually in
name only. Nixon and his assistant for national security affairs,
Henry Kissinger, decided to conduct a comprehensive review of
U.S. strategic doctrine prior to beginning negotiations with the
Soviets. In addition, they decided to link the opening of SALT
with progress in other areas of importance to the United States,
including Vietnam, the Middle East, and Berlin.[44]

In mid-February 1969, Nixon and Kissinger met with Soviet Ambassador Dobrynin for the first time, and Nixon emphasized the linkage of SALT to other issues.[45] On June 11, 1969, the United States informed the Soviet Union that it was prepared to begin the SALT negotiations.[46] Curiously, the Soviets did not respond until four months later when Dobrynin informed Nixon that the USSR was ready to set a date for the negotiations to open. On November 17, 1969, official representatives from the United States and the Soviet Union met in Helsinki, Finland, in the first round of the talks. During the next thirty months the two delegations held seven formal negotiating sessions meeting alternately in Helsinki and Vienna.[47]

The task of the delegations was not easy, for while the United States and the Soviet Union held an approximately equal number of strategic nuclear launchers, the quality of these weapons differed in some significant respects. Since the build-up of the late 1950s and early 1960s, American force planners emphasized the development of technologically sophisticated, accurate missiles with a relatively small payload (1 to 2 megatons). The Soviet Union, on the other hand, developed and deployed a number of different types of missiles; some were similar in design and capability to U.S. weapons (namely, the SS-11 and SS-13) and others (the SS-9 and SS-18, for example) had a far greater "throw weight" than any U.S. missiles.[48]

During the late 1960s and 1970s, the USSR possessed four principal advantages relative to American strategic forces. First, it had a larger number and a greater variety of forces than did the United States. Second, most of the Soviet ICBMs had a greater throw-weight capability than did U.S. missiles. Third, the Soviet Union placed greater emphasis on civil defense than the United States did. Fourth, the Soviets maintained an extensive air defense system.

Throughout the 1960s and into the 1970s the United States possessed strategic forces that were superior to Soviet forces in significant respects. First, American ICBMs and SLBMs were technologically superior to Soviet strategic forces. Advances in miniaturization made during the early 1960s enabled the United States to develop and deploy multiple reentry vehicles (MRV) on submarines beginning in 1964. During the late 1960s the United States developed another category of multiple warheads—multiple independently targetable reentry vehicles (MIRV)—which were first deployed in 1970 on Minuteman III missiles. A second U.S. advantage was the technological lead that the nation possessed in ABM technology. Third, the United States had a superior bomber force with the ability to penetrate Soviet air defenses. Fourth, U.S. submarines were technologically superior (quieter and faster) than their Soviet counterparts. Fifth, the United States had access to its own and allied military bases surrounding the Soviet Union.

Despite the advantages held by each superpower, both American and Soviet decision makers realized that the populations of their countries were, in essence, hostages and that if one state launched an attack on the other, the attacked state could launch a retaliatory second strike from its remaining ICBM, submarine, and bomber forces. In the words of J. Robert Oppenheimer, the United States and Soviet Union were like two scorpions trapped in the same bottle. The two superpowers were strategically interdependent in another sense: if one power developed and deployed a new weapon, the other side would either have to develop the same weapon or a counter to it since the logic of deterrence demanded that the two superpowers possess approximately equal forces. For this reason, deployment of ABM systems was considered by some to represent a needless expansion of Soviet-American arms competition, costly to both sides and providing no greater security for either side.

In this context and with the precedents of a number of significant arms control agreements concluded by the United States and the USSR during the limited détente period, the American and Soviet SALT delegations met to discuss the control of strategic nuclear weapons.

The American SALT delegation was headed by the director of the Arms Control and Disarmament Agency (ACDA), Gerard Smith, and consisted of representatives from many different governmental bureaucracies, including (ACDA), the Departments of State and Defense, the Central Intelligence Agency, the Joint Chiefs of Staff, and the National Security Council. President Nixon and Henry Kissinger issued instructions to the American delegation, which would then present various proposals to the Soviet delegation.

The Soviet SALT delegation was headed by Deputy Foreign Minister Vladimir S. Semenov, a veteran foreign affairs official with little previous background in strategic matters, and consisted of twenty-four officials, of whom one-third were military officers, one-third Foreign Ministry personnel, and the remaining one-third with no announced affiliations were assumed to be from the Soviet intelligence agency (KGB).[49] During the negotiations, the Soviet delegation adhered to positions worked out prior to the negotiations and were uncomfortable with the informal discussions that the American delegation occasionally proposed. The civilian members of the Soviet delegation, including Semenov, often appeared uninformed about the military capabilities of both American and Soviet weapons systems.

The two delegations introduced a number of substantive issues for discussion. The Soviet Union was in favor of concentrating on limiting defensive systems, particularly ABM, while the Americans were primarily concerned about the Soviet build-up of large ICBMs such as the SS-9. Underlying the discussions of particular issues were the perennial problems of inspection and verification, issues that had blocked many earlier arms control agreements. Furthermore the Soviets repeatedly expressed a desire to discuss U.S. nuclear forces in Europe, what the Soviets termed "forward-based systems" (FBS), and the American negotiators were just as insistent that these forces not be discussed due to the negative impact that such discussions would have upon the NATO allies of the United States.

In addition to the formal negotiations, early in 1969 the United States and the Soviet Union established a secret communications channel between Kissinger and Dobrynin. This so-called back channel was unknown to most American officials, including the members of the U.S. SALT delegation. As Kissinger recalled in his memoirs, "Dobrynin and I began to conduct preliminary negotiations on almost all major issues, he on behalf of the Politburo, I as confidant to Nixon."[50] In late 1970, a stalemate in the SALT negotiations developed over a number of issues. Throughout early 1971, Kissinger and Dobrynin met secretly to discuss these issues and to exchange messages between Nixon and Kosygin.[51] After many back channel meetings, an agreement was announced on May 20, 1971. According to Kissinger, it was significant in two respects. Substantively, the agreement marked Soviet willingness to negotiate limitations on both offensive and defensive systems rather than dealing only with ABM. Procedurally, the agreement "was a mile-stone in confirming White House dominance of foreign affairs. . . . [It] was the first sustained US-Soviet negotiation on the Presidential level—the forerunner of others in the years ahead."[52] In his memoirs, Ambassador Smith strongly criticized the May 20 agreement and the back channel procedure used to negotiate it. According to Smith, "There were no building blocks, no analytical work, no strategic analysis in the agencies concerned. There were no Verification Panel or National Security Council discussions. There were no consultations with congressional committees or with allies. It was a one-man stand, a presidential aide against the resources of the Soviet leadership."[53]

The SALT negotiations were not conducted in a vacuum; domestic politics in both states affected and reflected the ongoing negotiations. At the Twenty-Fourth Party Congress in March 1971, Brezhnev, who emerged at the Congress as the most important figure in the Soviet governing troika, committed himself to a policy of lessening tensions and continuing the SALT negotiations with the United States. In his speech to the Congress, Brezhnev stated:

We proceed from the assumption that it is possible to improve relations between the USSR and the U.S.A.; our principal line with respect to the capitalist countries including the U.S.A., is consistently and fully to practice the principles of peaceful coexistence, to develop mutually advantageous ties, and to cooperate, with states prepared to do so, in strengthening peace, making our relations with them as stable as possible.[54]

Brezhnev also emphasized the need to increase the output of agricultural production and consumer goods. Probably he viewed SALT as a means to stabilize or decrease defense spending in order to reach these objectives.

A debate on the development of an ABM system in 1969 politicized the issue of strategic nuclear policy within the United States. After extensive hearings and extended floor debate, the Senate approved the Nixon administration's Safeguard ABM system by Vice-President Agnew's tie-breaking vote. The ABM debate, however, had sensitized members of the public and the Congress to the issues of nuclear strategy and, following the debate, the Congress played an increasingly larger role in the review of U.S. strategic policy.[55] Interest groups on both the Left and the Right began to call attention to Soviet-American strategic relations. For instance, the conservative American Security Council criticized "the trend toward total disarmament sweeping the country," and in September 1970, at its annual convention the American Legion called for on-site inspection and firm guarantees that the Soviet Union would comply with any agreements signed. On the Left, the Federation of American Scientists attacked the Nixon administration's SALT proposals as a "sham" because they would "legalize an accelerated arms race." Nixon and Kissinger responded to these criticisms in general terms; Nixon devoted only five pages to a discussion of SALT in his first foreign policy report to the Congress.[56] Furthermore Nixon and Kissinger refused to keep the Congress fully informed of the ongoing negotiations. Several influential members of Congress including Albert Gore, Edward Brooke, Edmund Muskie, and Henry Jackson repeatedly tried to hold hearings on the SALT negotiations with members of the U.S. SALT delegation and National Security Council but were rebuffed in their attempts.[57]

Although both the Soviet and American governments attributed a great deal of importance to the negotiations, SALT could not be conducted without consideration of other aspects of Soviet-American relations. At the end of March 1972, the North Vietnamese, supplied with military materiel by both China and the Soviet Union, unleashed a powerful offensive against their U.S.-backed South Vietnamese enemies. The situation worsened for the South Vietnamese throughout April and became critical in early May. Even though a Soviet-American summit meeting was scheduled for late May, President Nixon ordered the bombing of Hanoi and the mining of Haiphong and seven other North Vietnamese ports in order to prevent the defeat of the South Vietnamese government. Most of the American experts on the Soviet Union on the National Security Council staff and in the State Department and Central Intelligence Agency predicted that Soviet leaders would cancel the summit; however, they went ahead with the meeting, and a number of broad agreements calling for economic, scientific, and technological cooperation were concluded. Clearly the most important achievement of the summit was the signing of two SALT agreements.[58]

The Interim Agreement on Offensive Missiles placed a quantitative limit on both ICBMs and SLBMs. The United States was limited to 1054 ICBMs, the Soviet Union to 1618. Each side had the right under the agreement to deploy SLBMs in exchange for the dismantling of old ICBMs. This was the so-called one-way freedom to mix (from land to sea forces) provision of the agreement. If all older ICBMs were dismantled, the United States could build up to 710 SLBMs on 44 submarines and the Soviets could build up to 950 SLBMs on 62 submarines. The Soviet Union was limited to 313 "heavy" ICBMs. The Interim Agreement had a duration of five years (1972-1977), and both sides stated that they intended to replace it with a permanent accord or treaty. In short, this agreement placed quantitative limits on both sides without restricting qualitative improvements in offensive weapons such as MIRV.

In the ABM Treaty, the United States and the Soviet Union agreed not to deploy more than two ABM sites, one at the national capital and the other at an ICBM site at least 1300 kilometers from the first site. Each site was limited to no more than 100 interceptor missiles and launchers. To ensure its continued observance, the treaty called for "national technical means of verification," an official euphemism for satellite reconnaissance and the monitoring of electronic signals. Both signatories promised neither to interfere with satellite verification procedures nor to conceal deliberately any ABM components. Restrictions were also placed on ABM radars, and the deployment of new ABM systems relying on new technologies (such as lasers) was proscribed. An organization, the Standing Consultative Commission, was established to implement the Interim Agreement and to investigate questions from either party concerning the implementation of the agreement. The treaty was of unlimited duration although periodic reviews were scheduled for every five years with either party having the right to withdraw on six months' notice. When the treaty was signed, some American analysts contended that it marked the codification of the doctrine of assured destruction since, in effect, the signatories agreed not to defend themselves against attack.[59]

Because the ABM agreement was a treaty, the Nixon administration was required by the Constitution to submit it to the Senate for approval, which was accomplished relatively quickly by a vote of eighty-eight to two. Although it was not a treaty, the Interim Agreement also had to be submitted to Congress for approval according to the 1961 law that established the Arms Control and Disarmament Agency. During congressional debate, considerable concern was expressed over whether the Soviet Union was granted strategic superiority by the Interim Agreement. Critics of the agreement pointed out that the USSR had about 50 percent more ICBMs under the agreement and about a four-to-one superiority over the United States in deliverable payload, assuming that only ICBMs and SLBMs (excluding bombers) were counted. Supporters of the agreement pointed out that the United States, however, had four times as many long-range strategic bombers as the Soviet Union and that, if bombers were included, the two superpowers had approximately equivalent deliverable payloads. In addition, due to MRV and MIRV technologies, the United States possessed a substantially greater number of warheads than did the Soviet Union.

Raymond Garthoff, a former member of the U.S. SALT delegation, has noted that negotiations on SALT within the U.S. government were even more difficult than the interdelegation negotiations.[60] In the debate over SALT within the United States following the Moscow Summit, four different clusters of opinion emerged.

The first group consisted of Nixon, Kissinger, and until his resignation as head of the U.S. SALT delegation, Ambassador Gerard Smith. In his first foreign policy report, Nixon pointed out that there was "no area in which [the United States] and the Soviet Union . . . have a greater common interest than in reaching agreement with regard to arms control."[61] In the next year's report, Nixon claimed that agreement in the arms control area "could create a new commitment to stability and influence attitudes toward other issues."[62] When agreement was reached in May 1972, Kissinger contended that the SALT agreements were "without precedent in the nuclear age; indeed, in all relevant modern history"[63] and that "nothing that this Administration has done has seemed to it more important for the future of the world than to make an important first step in the limitation of strategic arms."[64] In his briefing of a number of congressional leaders, Nixon noted that neither side won or lost by the agreements; rather "both sides won, and the whole world won.''[65] Thus to Nixon and Kissinger, the signing of the SALT agreements marked a mutual step by the United States and the Soviet Union toward increased strategic stability and a significant improvement of Soviet-American relations. SALT was the foundation of détente, just as détente was the most important component of the administration's new grand design of American foreign policy.

Not all were satisfied with the results of SALT, however. Within the administration itself, a second opinion group consisting of Secretary of Defense Melvin Laird, Chairman of the Joint Chiefs of Staff Thomas Moorer, and others in the Department of Defense conditioned their approval of the SALT agreements on the continued development of sophisticated strategic weapons systems— namely, the Trident submarine and missile system, the B-1 bomber, the Washington, D.C., ABM site, and the submarine-launched cruise missile.[66] In his testimony to the Senate, Laird saw the advantages of the SALT agreements as "putting the brakes on Soviet strategic force momentum" and allowing the United States to maintain a strong strategic position.[67] The Laird-Moorer support of the SALT agreements in return for the administration's support of new strategic weapons systems was not unprecedented; Department of Defense officials had demanded and received similar assurances in 1963 in return for their support of the Limited Test Ban Treaty.

A third group of U.S. policymakers, including Henry Jackson, Elmo Zumwalt, and Paul Nitze, criticized the numerical advantages given to the Soviet Union by the Interim Agreement in ICBMs, SLBMs, and submarines.[68] These critics were particularly concerned that Soviet quantitative advantages in missiles would be translated into effective political value by the Soviet Union. Given the large throw weight of Soviet missiles (for example, the SS-9 was capable of delivering an 18- to 25- megaton warhead), critics feared that American land-based missiles would become vulnerable to Soviet attack. Since the Interim Agreement in no way limited qualitative improvement of offensive missiles, the Soviet Union would be free, according to the agreement, to equip its 313 heavy ICBMs with MIRVs, making a formidable first-strike force. The Jackson-Zumwalt group also criticized the Nixon administration for its secretive negotiating style. Paul Nitze, a former member of the U.S. SALT delegation, noted that Nixon often negotiated with Brezhnev with only a Soviet interpreter present, and no records of these conversations were kept. Consequently U.S. negotiators were often uninformed about their own government's position. While some advocates of the ABM Treaty contended that it marked the Soviet recognition of the doctrine of mutual assured destruction, the Jackson-Nitze-Zumwalt group strongly disagreed. According to Nitze, "In essence, Americans think in terms of deterring nuclear war almost exclusively. The Soviet leaders think much more of what might happen in such a war."[69]

Because of his concern over the deficiencies of the SALT agreements and perhaps not unrelated to partisan political reasons (he was actively seeking the 1972 Democratic presidential nomination), Senator Jackson introduced an amendment to the Interim Agreement stipulating that any future arms treaty should "not limit the U.S. to levels of intercontinental strategic forces inferior to the limits for the Soviet Union." The Senate accepted the Jackson Amendment by a vote of fifty-six to thirty-five and then approved the agreement by eighty-eight to two. Any future negotiators had to keep in mind the provisions of the Jackson Amendment since it was very unlikely that any agreement that did not conform to its guidelines would be approved by the Senate. An action that may have been linked to the amendment was the replacement of virtually all of the senior officials of ACDA following SALT I; of the 17 officials in ACDA's top positions in 1972, only 3 were left by 1974. Gerard Smith resigned as ACDA director and U.S. SALT negotiator reportedly because he felt that he had been "persistently denied the responsibility he thought he should have."[70] Dr. Fred Iklé, a strategist known to be somewhat skeptical toward both SALT and Soviet intentions, was appointed ACDA director, and U. Alexis Johnson, a career diplomat with little substantial previous arms control experience, was appointed the chief American SALT negotiator.

Following their replacement, former members of the U.S. SALT delegation formed a fourth cluster of opinion and engaged in their own assessment of the SALT I negotiations. One former negotiator criticized the emphasis on secrecy and the lack of information provided to the public and members of Congress and advocated the opening up of the negotiating process.[71] Raymond Garthoff criticized the negotiations on three counts: the Moscow Summit negotiations were hectic, confused, and not successful in gaining U.S. objectives; the ABM Treaty, although it represented a "truly significant arms limitation, . . . could have been reached in 1970, rather than 1972"; and the United States failed to extract concessions on some agreements valued by the Soviet Union, such as the 1973 Agreement on the Prevention of Nuclear War.[72] Following service in the Carter administration as the president's special representative and ambassador-at-large for nonproliferation negotiations, Gerard Smith published his detailed memoirs of SALT I. He criticized Nixon and Kissinger for failing to keep the U.S. SALT delegation and the Congress informed of their back-channel negotiations, for linking the Moscow Summit and the SALT I agreements, and for failing to ban MIRVs.[73]

Policymaking on SALT was fragmented and conflictual not only within the U.S. government; it was very likely that there were significant differences among various factions in the Politburo. In fact, there were indications of some dissatisfaction over the Brezhnev détente policies when, just prior to the Moscow Summit, Pyotr Shelest, a member of the Politburo and head of the Ukrainian Communist party, was demoted. Although this action may have been done for domestic political reasons, it seemed that Shelest, an outspoken hard-liner on foreign policy issues, probably opposed Nixon's visit and was replaced for that reason.[74] Three groups within the Soviet government can be identified: the Brezhnev pro-détente majority, the ideologues, and the military.

At the Twenty-Fourth Party Congress, Brezhnev first personally identified himself with détente and strengthened this identification with the signing of the various Moscow Summit agreements. Just as détente depended upon SALT, Nixon and Brezhnev increasingly depended upon their détente policies to provide them with popular support. Dr. Georgi Arbatov, the director of the Soviet Institute for the Study of the U.S.A. and Canada, compared the SALT agreements to the establishment of Soviet-American relations in 1933 and even praised "the positive, realistic position of the American side on many of the questions discussed . . . [which was] an important prerequisite for the success of the talks."[75]

Not all Soviet policymakers approved of the Brezhnev détente policies. Chief party ideologue Mikhail Suslov declared, "The affirmation in international affairs of the principles of peaceful coexistence does not in the slightest signify a slackening of the class struggle on a worldwide scale or a 'reconciliation' between socialism and capitalism. They are irreconcilable."[76] According to Suslov, the lessening of tensions in the world should not only not lead to reconciliation; rather,

a certain easing of international tension, the retreat of the policy of war and aggression and the failure of the "cold war" are opening up to the world's progressive forces additional possibilities for developing the struggle of the working people against the oppression of the capitalist monopolies.[77]

In addition to the ideologues, the Soviet military appeared to harbor reservations about the SALT agreements. Many members of the Soviet military view international politics as a zero-sum game, a position reflected by General of the Army S. Sokolov when in early 1973 he warned, "Despite a certain warming up of the international climate, we cannot forget that the aggressive nature of imperialism remains unchanged."[78]

The SALT negotiations have been the most important arms control negotiations of the twentieth century and resulted in several notable achievements. The ABM Treaty was a significant attempt to stabilize the strategic balance and to save money in the process. The Interim Agreement placed a quantitative limit on the strategic offensive forces of both sides and at the very least provided a basis for contingency planning for both sides. More abstractly and behind the specific value of the SALT agreements, as Gerard Smith has pointed out, "is the great worth of the [SALT] process itself."[79] For the first time Soviet civilians entered into the complexities of strategic nuclear planning. Despite the procedural and substantive criticisms of the SALT I negotiations, the agreements nevertheless marked the most important control of nuclear weapons in the post-World War II era. SALT significantly expanded the arms control regime of the limited détente period to the control of strategic nuclear weapons.

## A Comparison of the Two Cases

In comparing the histories of the UN Disarmament Subcommittee negotiations and the SALT talks, two questions will be addressed: to what extend did U.S. and Soviet actions differ in the two cases, and what are the most plausible reasons for the different outcomes of the two negotiations?

The most obvious difference in the outcome of the two cases is that the SALT negotiations resulted in several important agreements, while the UN Subcommittee negotiations did not. A number of factors at the international, domestic, and decision-making levels of analysis contribute to an understanding of the reasons for the contrasting outcomes of the two negotiations.

At the international level, a number of important and significant political-strategic obstacles stood in the way of an arms control agreement in the mid-1950s. First, the fact that the United States enjoyed an advantage of five-to-one in strategic nuclear weapons undoubtedly contributed to the Soviet reluctance to conclude any arms control agreement that would freeze the Soviet Union into a position of strategic inferiority. By the late 1960s the Soviets had achieved nuclear parity, which constituted the first of two prerequisites for the beginning of SALT. The second prerequisite concerned the place of Germany in Soviet strategic thinking. Given the substantial losses inflicted on the Soviet Union by Germany in the two world wars, Soviet leaders have an abiding fear of West Germany. A primary objective of post-1945 Soviet foreign policy has been the continued division of East and West Germany. Because of their fear and distrust, Soviet leaders have strongly opposed all measures by Germany to obtain and/or develop nuclear weapons. The signing of the Non-Proliferation Treaty by Germany, therefore was a very significant event and paved the way to the opening of the SALT negotiations. The Quadripartite Agreement on Berlin in 1971 also contributed to the decreased importance of the German problem during the détente period. Third, Soviet decision makers had a greater fear of the Chinese in the late 1960s than ten years earlier. This was due to the Chinese development of nuclear weapons and the marked worsening of Sino-Soviet relations in early 1969. Thus the achievement of parity, the lessening of tensions on their western front, and the increasing of tensions on their eastern border provided the impetus for the Soviet Union to seek the limitation of strategic arms.

The level and pace of technological development of the major states within the international system can affect the prospects for arms control. In his focused comparison study of eight arms control agreements, Joseph Kruzel found that "negotiations are more likely to be undertaken, and are more likely to succeed, in a period of stable military technology than at a time of great technological ferment."[80] In the mid-1950s at the time of the London Subcommittee negotiations, the United States and the Soviet Union each had one means, bombers, of delivering strategic nuclear weapons; a decade later each superpower had a triad of forces consisting of bombers, ICBMs, and SLBMs. These facts could lead one to conclude that an agreement to limit nuclear weapons was easier, at least from a technological perspective, to negotiate at the UN Subcommittee negotiations than at SALT; however, two technological developments actually facilitated the SALT agreements. First, the development and deployment during the 1960s by both the United States and the Soviet Union of SLBMs, which were invulnerable and therefore provided each side with a secure second-strike capability, actually stabilized the strategic balance. Second, in the mid-1950s both American and Soviet decision makers were concerned primarily with the problem of surprise attack and would not enter into an agreement that could not be verified with a high degree of confidence. Eisenhower's Open Skies proposal, presented at Geneva in 1955, provided an opportunity for each side to achieve an accurate verification capability, but the Soviet Union rejected this proposal. In the early 1960s both the United States and the Soviet Union began launching satellites that were used for high-altitude photography. By the early 1970s satellite reconnaissance was very advanced and relatively invulnerable to available countermeasures. Thus the technological development and deployment of invulnerable second-strike weapons sytems (SLBMs) and reconnaissance satellites facilitated the successful negotiation of the SALT agreements. Kruzel's proposition should therefore be modified to note that technological advances may either facilitate or hinder the progress of arms control negotiations, depending on the characteristics of the weapon being developed and deployed.

Domestic political factors did not play a very significant role in either of the cases. In the mid-1950s most members of Congress and the public considered arms control and disarmament issues to be technical areas best left to the experts, a view that was shared by American leaders (with the exception of Adlai Stevenson) at that time. President Eisenhower, for instance, refused to discuss publicly the advantages and disadvantages of a comprehensive test ban because he felt that the issues involved were too complicated for the American public. Due in part to the politicization of defense and military issues in general and because of U.S. involvement in Vietnam, by the late 1960s a number of congressmen, interest groups, and citizens closely followed defense-related issues, including arms control. Some of these organizations and individuals (among them, veterans' organizations and defense contractors' associations) objected to any substantial cutbacks or limitations of U.S. forces. The loose coalition of individuals and interest groups opposed to U.S. involvement in Vietnam partially counteracted the traditional pro-military sentiment of much of the Congress and the public. Nixon and Kissinger were extremely secretive during the SALT negotiations, and the Congress had little or no influence on the development of the SALT agreements. Once the agreements were signed, however, Nixon and Kissinger were required by law to submit them to the Congress for approval.

In gaining congressional and popular acceptance, Nixon and Kissinger justified the SALT agreements in a manner designed to satisfy hawks and doves simultaneously; they noted that the SALT agreements would result in a decrease in defense spending while at the same time restraining the growth of Soviet strategic forces. But in attempting to placate both sides, Nixon and Kissinger fully satisfied neither, and following SALT I, members of the Congress became increasingly involved in the SALT process; the passage of the Jackson Amendment was only the most visible manifestation of this increased involvement. Nixon and Kissinger also used détente to legitimate SALT and vice-versa, and it became difficult to separate the two processes for purposes of evaluation. Thus although SALT I was not influenced by domestic political factors to any great extent, it became a highly politicized issue after 1972.

The lack of evidence makes it difficult to determine to what extent domestic political factors influenced Soviet leaders to negotiate and conclude the two SALT agreements. In the Ninth Five-Year Plan (1971-1975), Brezhnev and Kosygin set out an ambitious, consumer-oriented economic course for the Soviet Union. If this plan were to succeed, as economist Gregory Grossman has pointed out, "it needed (in addition to favorable weather) large-scale economic assistance from the West."[81] It is also plausible that the Soviet leadership believed that the SALT agreements would result in substantial economic savings for their country. Public opinion, which plays an unimportant role in most issues in the Soviet Union, was not significant in the development of SALT.

Several important bureaucratic and leadership factors contributed to the success of SALT and the failure of the UN Disarmament Subcommittee. U.S. governmental planning for arms control and disarmament was fragmented during the Eisenhower administration, and this lack of coordination contributed to the failure of the UN negotiations. When Harold Stassen submitted his informal memorandum to the Soviet delegation on May 27, 1957, he had not consulted with Eisenhower, Dulles, or U.S. allies, all of whom objected to some aspects of his memorandum. Consequently the United States withdrew the memorandum from consideration, and the Soviet Union, with some justification, charged the United States with negotiating in bad faith. In contrast to the London negotiation, U.S. governmental policymaking for SALT was extremely centralized and secret; in fact, many of the agreements were worked out in the Nixon-Kissinger-Dobrynin back-channel negotiations.

In both the UN Disarmament Subcommittee and SALT negotiations, there was significant opposition to reaching an agreement, but the character of the opposition differed in the two cases. In the first case, John Foster Dulles and senior military leaders were strongly opposed to any substantive arms control measures until the German problem was resolved. Harold Stassen and the White House Disarmament Office provided a countervailing view to that of Dulles, but this pespective was downgraded by Eisenhower, at least in part because of Stassen's error in submitting his informal discussion paper to the Soviet Union without the prior consent and approval of U.S. allies. In the SALT case, Nixon and Brezhnev became identified with and committed to the progress of the SALT negotiations. In both the United States and the Soviet Union, cabinet-level officials and organizations opposed the SALT agreements, although not enough to block the agreements.

One of the most important differences in the behavior of American and Soviet decision makers concerned their evaluation of the significance of various issues. In the mid-1950s, most American policymakers believed that German reunification was more important than arms control. Consequently the progress of the London negotiations was coupled to the progress of German reunification. By the late 1960s, American and Soviet decision makers considered the limitation of strategic arms to be a top foreign policy goal and SALT, although it was occasionally linked to other issue areas for tactical bargaining reasons, was not forestalled by any other issues.

The different outcomes of the two arms control negotiations analyzed here were due to a number of factors at the international system and decision-making levels; domestic politics did not play an important role in either of these cases. The Soviet achievement of parity, the worsening of Sino-Soviet relations, and the increasing burden of defense costs contributed to the successful outcome of the SALT negotiations. Additionally Nixon and Kissinger perceived of SALT as part of a system and regime developing process, an approach that contrasted markedly with the more limited objectives of Eisenhower and Dulles who viewed arms control negotiations as *ad hoc* efforts to reduce the danger of nuclear war.

## Notes

1. Louis J. Halle, *The Cold War as History* (New York: Harper and Row, 1967), p. 236.

2. Jerome B. Wiesner, "Comprehensive Arms-Limitation Systems," in Donald G. Brennan, ed., *Arms Control, Disarmament, and National Security* (New York: George Braziller, 1961), p. 198.

3. The dates that the UN Disarmament Subcommittee met were: May

13-June 22, 1954; February 25-May 18, 1955; August 29-October 7, 1955; March 19-May 4, 1956; and March 18-September 6, 1957; see Philip Noel-Baker, *The Arms Race: A Programme for World Disarmament* (New York: Oceana Publications, 1958), p. 203.

4. American fears of Soviet forces and intentions are clearly evident in the Gaither Report. See Security Resources Panel of the Science Advisory Committee, *Deterrence and Survival in the Nuclear Age* (Washington, D.C.: Office of Defense Mobilization, Executive Office of the President, 1957); declassified in January 1973.

5. John Foster Dulles, "The Evolution of Foreign Policy," *Department of State Bulletin* 30 (January 25, 1954): 108.

6. Robert Jervis, *Perception and Misperception in International Politics* (Princeton: Princeton University Press, 1976), p. 58.

7. Ibid., pp. 62-67.

8. Stassen's aide delivered a speech, later published as a journal article, in which he characterized (without specifically naming them) Stassen as an advocate of the "relaxation of tension" approach and Dulles as a proponent of an "increased pressure" approach. Robert E. Matteson, "The Disarmament Dilemma," *Orbis* 2 (Fall 1958): 292.

9. White House Disarmament Staff, *Pathway to Peace* (Washington, D.C.: Government Printing Office, 1957), p. 7.

10. Adam Ulam, *Expansion and Coexistence: Soviet Foreign Policy, 1917-73*, 2d ed. (New York: Praeger Publishers, 1974), p. 564.

11. Dwight D. Eisenhower, *Mandate for Change* (Garden City, N.Y.: Doubleday, 1963), p. 507.

12. Quoted in Noel-Baker, *Arms Race,* p. 213.

13. For the texts of both proposals, see U.S. Department of State, *Documents on Disarmament 1945-1959* (Washington, D.C.: Government Printing Office, 1961).

14. Quoted in Bernhard G. Bechhoefer, *Postwar Negotiations for Arms Control* (Washington, D.C.: Brookings Institution, 1961), pp. 295-96.

15. Alexander Dallin, *The Soviet Union, Arms Control and Disarmament* (New York: School of International Affairs, Columbia University, 1964), p. 20.

16. The material in this paragraph is based on the information derived from interviews with several members of the U.S. delegation to the UN Disarmament Subcommittee meetings and Frances Anderson Gulick, "United States Policy on Disarmament: 1955-1958" (Ph.D. diss., Fletcher School of Law and Diplomacy, 1960).

17. For an expression of American concern with the problem of surprise attack, see the declassified U.S. government study, directed by J. R. Killian

and completed in 1955, entitled "Meeting the Threat of Surprise Attack," published in Declassified Documents Reference System, *Retrospective Collection* (Arlington, Va.: Carrollton Press, 1977); see also James R. Killian, Jr., *Sputnik, Scientists, and Eisenhower* (Cambridge: MIT Press, 1977), pp. 67-93.

18. Chalmers M. Roberts, *The Nuclear Years: The Arms Race and Arms Control, 1945-1970* (New York: Praeger, 1971), p. 33.

19. Quoted in Bechhoefer, *Postwar Negotiations*, p. 373.

20. For the texts of the Eisenhower-Bulganin exchange of letters, see *Department of State Bulletin* (March 26, 1956): 514-15; (August 20, 1956): 299-301; and (January 21, 1957): 89-90.

21. Noel-Baker, *Arms Race*, p. 228.

22. Bulganin's letter to Eisenhower of November 17, 1956, in *Department of State Bulletin* (January 21, 1957): 89-90.

23. U.S. Department of State, *Disarmament: The Intensified Effort, 1955-1958*, publication 6676 (Washington, D.C.: Government Printing Office, 1958), p. 44.

24. Ulam, *Expansion and Coexistence*, p. 613.

25. Department of State, *Disarmament*, p. 31.

26. John H. Barton and Lawrence D. Weiler, eds., *International Arms Control: Issues and Agreements* (Stanford: Stanford University Press, 1976), p. 79.

27. *Khrushchev Remembers* (Boston: Little, Brown, 1970), 1: 404.

28. Ibid., p. 516.

29. Ole R. Holsti, "Cognitive Dynamics and Images of the Enemy: Dulles and Russia," in David J. Finlay, Ole R. Holsti, and Richard R. Fagan, *Enemies in Politics* (Chicago: Rand McNally, 1967), p. 59.

30. For comments on these two developments, see Department of State, *Disarmament*, pp. 35-37.

31. Interview with a former member of the U.S. delegation to the UN Disarmament Subcommittee.

32. Bechhoefer, *Postwar Negotiations*, p. 398.

33. Dwight D. Eisenhower, *Waging Peace, 1956-1961* (Garden City, N.Y.: Doubleday, 1965), pp. 472-73.

34. Bechhoefer, *Postwar Negotiations*, p. 411.

35. Ibid., p. 408.

36. "Secretary Dulles' News Conference of May 29, 1957," *Department of State Bulletin* (June 17, 1957): 956-57.

37. "Eisenhower-Adenauer Joint Declaration," in ibid., p. 956.

38. *Washington Post and Times Herald*, May 20, 1957, p. A1.

39. *New York Times*, June 23, 1957, p. 23.

40. Eisenhower, *Waging Peace*.

41. Ibid., p. 468.

42. *Khrushchev Remembers: The Last Testament* (Boston: Little, Brown, 1974), 2: 493.

43. Institute for Strategic Studies, *The Communist Bloc and the Western Alliance: The Military Balance, 1962-63* (London: Institute for Strategic Studies, 1963).

44. Richard Nixon, *RN: The Memoirs of Richard Nixon* (New York: Grosset and Dunlap, 1978), p. 346.

45. Ibid., pp. 369-70.

46. Henry Kissinger, *White House Years* (Boston: Little, Brown, 1979), p. 138.

47. For accounts of the SALT I negotiations (those that took place from November 1969 through May 1972) that emphasize the importance of the back channel negotiations, see Kissinger, *White House Years*; Nixon, *Memoirs*; John Newhouse, *Cold Dawn: The Story of SALT* (New York: Holt, Rinehart, and Winston, 1973). For accounts that stress the role of the U.S. SALT delegation, see Barton and Weiler, *International Arms Control*; Gerard Smith, *Doubletalk: The Story of the First Strategic Arms Limitation Talks* (Garden City, N.Y.: Doubleday, 1980).

48. "Throw weight" is defined as "the maximum useful weight which has been flight tested on the boost stages of the missile." U.S. Arms Control and Disarmament Agency, *SALT Lexicon*, rev. ed. (Washington, D.C.: Government Printing Office, 1975), p. 18.

49. For an excellent description of both Soviet and American organizations involved with SALT, see Thomas W. Wolfe, *The SALT Experience* (Cambridge: Ballinger Publishing Company, 1979), pp. 23-92. See also Smith, *Doubletalk*, pp. 45-50.

50. Kissinger, *White House Years*, p. 139.

51. See Kissnger's testimony of June 15, 1972, in U.S. Congress, Senate, Committee on Armed Services, *Military Implications of the Treaty on the Limitations of Anti-Ballistic Missile Systems and the Interim Agreement on Limitation of Strategic Offensive Arms*, 92d Cong., 2d sess., 1972 (hereafter cited as *Armed Services Hearings*).

52. Kissinger, *White House Years*, pp. 822-23.

53. Smith, *Doubletalk*, p. 225.

54. "TASS Summary of Brezhnev's Report to Congress," Foreign Broadcast Information Service, *Soviet Union Daily Report*, no. 61, supp. 16, March 30, 1971, p. 15.

55. Edward J. Laurance, "The Changing Role of Congress in Defense Policy-Making," *Journal of Conflict Resolution* 20 (June 1976).

56. Richard Nixon, *U.S. Foreign Policy for the 1970s: A New Strategy for Peace* (Washington, D.C.: Government Printing Office, 1970), pp. 142-47.

57. For informative accounts of congressional involvement in SALT, see Alton Frye, *A Responsible Congress: The Politics of National Security* (New York: McGraw-Hill, 1975), and Alan Platt, *The U.S. Senate and Strategic Arms Policy, 1969-1977* (Boulder, Colo.: Westview Press, 1978).

58. For the texts of the two SALT agreements, see U.S. Arms Control and Disarmament Agency, *Arms Control and Disarmament Agreements: Texts and History of Negotiations* (Washington, D.C.: Government Printing Office, 1977), pp. 130-47.

59. Barton and Weiler, *International Arms Control*, p. 202; Walter Clemens, Jr., *The Superpowers and Arms Control* (Lexington, Mass.: Lexington Books, D. C. Heath, 1973).

60. Raymond L. Garthoff, "Negotiating with the Russians: Some Lessons from SALT," *International Security* 1 (Spring 1977); also see Smith, *Doubletalk*.

61. Nixon, *U.S. Foreign Policy for the 1970s: A New Strategy for Peace*, p. 142.

62. Richard Nixon, *U.S. Foreign Policy for the 1970s: Building for Peace* (Washington, D.C.: Government Printing Office, 1971), p. 188.

63. Kissinger's briefing of congressional leaders, June 15, 1972; reprinted in U.S. Congress, Senate Committee on Foreign Relations, *Strategic Arms Limitation Agreements*, Hearings on S. J. Res. 242, 92d Cong., 2d sess., 1972, p. 294 (hereafter cited as *Foreign Relations Hearings*).

64. Kissinger press conference of May 26, 1972, in *Armed Services Hearings*, p. 392.

65. President Nixon's briefing to congressional leaders, June 15, 1972, in *Foreign Relations Hearings*, p. 392.

66. Testimony by Secretary of Defense Melvin Laird, *Armed Services Hearings*, p. 4.

67. Ibid.

68. For the views of these policymakers on SALT, see *Armed Services Hearings*; Paul Nitze, "Assuring Strategic Stability in an Era of Detente," *Foreign Affairs* (January 1976); Elmo Zumwalt, *On Watch: A Memoir* (New York: New York Times/Quadrangle, 1976).

69. Nitze, "Assuring Strategic Stability," p. 212.

70. Newhouse, *Cold Dawn*, p. 44.

71. Lawrence D. Weiler, *The Arms Race, Secret Negotiations and the Congress*, Occasional Paper 12 (Muscatine, Iowa: Stanley Foundation, 1976).

72. Garthoff, "Negotiating with the Russians."

73. Smith, *Doubletalk*, pp. 465-73.

74. Ulam, *Expansion and Coexistence*, p. 769; Dimitri Simes, "The Death of Detente?" *International Security* 5 (Summer 1980): 8.

75. G. Arbatov, "The Strength of a Policy of Realism," *Izvestia*, June 22, 1972, pp. 3-4, translated in *Current Digest of the Soviet Press* 24-25 (July 18, 1972): 4.

76. M. A. Suslov, "The Twentieth Congress of the French Communist Party: Speech by Comrade M. A. Suslov," *Pravda* and *Izvestia*, December 4, 1972, in *Current Digest of the Soviet Press* 24-50 (December 26, 1972): 14.

77. Ibid.

78. S. Sokolov, "Standing Guard over Peace and Socialism" *Pravda*, February 23, 1973, in *Current Digest of the Soviet Press* (March 14, 1972).

79. Gerard C. Smith, "Negotiating with the Soviets," *New York Times Magazine*, February 27, 1977, p. 26.

80. Joseph J. Kruzel, "The Preconditions and Consequences of Arms Control Agreements" (Ph.D. diss., Harvard University, 1975), p. 349.

81. Gregory Grossman, "The Soviet Economy Before and After the Twenty-Fifth Congress," in Alexander Dallin, ed., *The Twenty-Fifth Congress of the CPSU: Assessment and Context* (Stanford: Hoover Institution Press, 1977), p. 56.

# CHAPTER 6

# SOVIET-AMERICAN TRADE NEGOTIATIONS, 1958-1961 AND 1971-1974

The policies implemented by the Soviet government from 1947 to 1953 and the U.S. government from 1947 through 1962 did not allow for any significant amount of Soviet-American trade to take place because of the maintenance of separate Soviet and American policies in the economic area. During the mid-1960s, particularly following the American sale to the Soviet Union of 65 million bushels of grain in 1964, a significant level of trade began to develop between the United States and Soviet Union, as table 13 demonstrates, and by the early 1970s Soviet-American trade, swollen in 1973 and 1975 by massive grain sales to the Soviet Union, had grown to a substantial level.

Procedures, rules, and several Soviet-U.S. organizations were established to facilitate this new trade, in the process developing a Soviet-American economic regime. The establishment of this regime contrasted markedly with the absence of any such regime during the cold war and raised new and challenging questions for Soviet and American policymakers. How were economic regimes developed? What obstacles stood in the way of their development? What were the domestic and international consequences of the development of an economic regime? How could regimes change? How were the regimes in one issue area related to those in other issue areas?

A comparison of Soviet-American trade negotiations from 1958

Table 13
**SOVIET TRADE WITH THE UNITED STATES, 1960-1975**
**(MILLIONS OF U.S. DOLLARS)**

| Year | Exports | Imports | Turnover |
|------|---------|---------|----------|
| 1960 | 25  | 60   | 85   |
| 1961 | 24  | 51   | 74   |
| 1962 | 17  | 27   | 44   |
| 1963 | 25  | 28   | 53   |
| 1964 | 21  | 163  | 184  |
| 1965 | 34  | 65   | 99   |
| 1966 | 49  | 42   | 91   |
| 1967 | 41  | 60   | 101  |
| 1968 | 58  | 58   | 116  |
| 1969 | 52  | 106  | 158  |
| 1970 | 72  | 119  | 191  |
| 1971 | 57  | 161  | 218  |
| 1972 | 95  | 547  | 642  |
| 1973 | 214 | 1190 | 1304 |
| 1974 | 350 | 607  | 957  |
| 1975 | 255 | 1837 | 2092 |

*Sources:* For 1960-1965: U.S. Department of Commerce, cited by E. Douglas Kenna, statement prepared for hearings on the *Soviet Economic Outlook*, U.S. Congress, Joint Economic Committee (Washington, D.C.: Government Printing Office, 1973, p. 23; data for 1966-1975 from U.S. Department of Commerce, Bureau of East-West Trade, *Selected Trade and Economic Data of the Centrally Planned Economies* (Washington, D.C.: Department of Commerce, 1976), p. 8.

through 1961 and from 1971 through 1974 helps to provide answers to some of these questions. In the first case, the Soviet government sought to expand trade with the United States, but, for a number of reasons, the United States was not interested. The second case study focuses on the attempt to reach this agreement in the early 1970s.

## Soviet-American Negotiations on Trade, 1958-1961

Soviet-American trade began to increase with the death of Stalin in 1953. In 1957 Khrushchev launched a campaign to modernize

Soviet industry and to overtake the United States in per-capita production of meat and milk. Given the weaknesses and limitations of the Soviet economy, Khrushchev necessarily had to trade with the West if he intended to reach one or both of his goals. From the beginning of 1958 through the middle of 1961, Khrushchev energetically sought the expansion of trade with the West.

In the spring of 1958, Khrushchev made several significant overtures to the United States concerning the expansion of Soviet-American trade. In March he granted an interview to the American owner and publisher of the *Journal of Commerce*, presumably to signal the United States that the Soviet Union desired to expand trading relations. Khrushchev noted:

We consider that the successful development of trade between the U.S.S.R. and the U.S.A. on the basis of equality and mutual advantage would not only be in the interests of the Soviet and American peoples and of the strengthening of confidence in U.S.-Soviet relations, but would also contribute to the further relaxation of international tension and would therefore be in the interests of all countries and peoples.[1]

According to Khrushchev, trade would not only be mutually beneficial; it would contribute to the lessening of tensions between the two superpowers. Recognizing the ideological difference between the United States and the Soviet Union (as Khrushchev noted, "You have your political system and we have ours"), Khrushchev stated that this difference "should not prevent our countries living in peace, co-existing and maintaining good business ties."[2] He concluded the interview with an invitation: "We should be only too pleased if the United States of America were to become one of our big trading partners."[3]

Khrushchev's interview was not a formal government-to-government invitation for expanded Soviet-American trade; however, in June, he sent Eisenhower a letter in which he officially proposed the expansion of trade.[4] He reiterated the themes from the April interview: trade would be mutually advantageous and would generally improve Soviet-American relations. Khrushchev also specifically proposed the importation of entire ("turn-key") factories and equipment for the production of consumer goods and housing.

Responding to Khrushchev's proposal, Eisenhower noted that

"United States export and import trade is carried on by individual firms and not under government auspices" and that there was no need "to formalize [trade] relations between United States firms and Soviet trade organizations."[5] What Eisenhower did not mention, however, was that a number of U.S. government-imposed restrictions that inhibited the growth of such trade remained in force. In effect, Eisenhower's response indicated a U.S. intention to maintain its cold war policies and to show that it was not interested in formalizing and expanding the nascent Soviet-American trade regime.

Despite Eisenhower's unenthusiastic response, the Soviet government stepped up its efforts in 1959 to increase its trade with the United States. Perhaps intended as a signal that the Soviet Union was a trustworthy trading partner, $1.5 million was paid to E. I. du Pont de Nemours and Company by the Soviet government in settlement of a World War II dispute in which du Pont provided the Soviet Union with information on the commercial production of neoprene synthetic rubber. The official Soviet signatory of the settlement noted that the agreement was designed to clear the way for extensive trade possibilities between du Pont and the Soviet Union.[6]

In a speech to the opening of the Leipzig trade fair several days after the settlement, Khrushchev stated that the Soviet Union was prepared to place large commercial orders with American companies if, and only if, the United States granted his nation substantial credits.[7] Despite his support of increased Soviet-American trade, Khrushchev was aware of the possible dangers of the development of such trade for Eastern Europe and the Soviet Union. Asked if there were any theoretical or ideological objections by communist leaders to socialist countries' receiving economic aid from capitalist countries, Khrushchev answered:

Of course, there is no theoretical objection of any kind. We ourselves would be prepared to take something if it were economically beneficial. But the nature of capitalism is such that it cannot offer [aid] unfortunately without certain definite ends in view. In accepting [aid], therefore, the greatest caution must be exercised so that one does not lose something. It is like the fly around a dish of honey. First one wing gets caught, then another until the fly finds itself drowning in honey.[8]

This answer is as revealing as it is colorful. Khrushchev sought the importation of Western technology and the extension of credit in support of his consumer and industrialization policies; at the same time, however, he was very aware of the danger of importing capitalism, as well as simply importing capitalist machinery and money.

The late 1950s marked substantially increased travel by Soviet and American leaders between their two countries. In 1958, Mikoyan visited the United States, followed a year later by First Deputy Premier Kozlov. In July 1959, Vice-President Nixon traveled to Moscow to open the American exhibition, where he engaged Khrushchev in their famous kitchen debate. The following September, Khrushchev made a thirteen-day visit to seven American cities. In his memoirs, Khrushchev recalled, "I was . . . looking forward to establishing contacts with the American business world. Even Stalin had been interested in obtaining American credits. We wanted the Americans to call off the trade embargo against the Soviet Union and other socialist countries."[9] President Eisenhower raised the issue of the Soviet Lend-Lease debt when Khrushchev was in Washington, and Khrushchev proposed to repay the debt if the United States would extend $3 billion credit to the Soviet Union.[10] These terms were unacceptable to the United States, and the discussion was dropped. Whether justified or not, the maintenance of U.S. cold war economic policies blocked the development of a Soviet-American trade regime.

As table 14 indicates, trade between the Soviet Union and the Western European states in 1959 was significantly greater than that between the Soviet Union and Canada, Japan, or the United States. The United States' percentage of exports to and imports from the Soviet Union was the lowest of any NATO member, undoubtedly due to a very great extent to the American restrictions on trade. Since the United States was unwilling to relax its trade restrictions against East-West trade significantly, during the late 1950s the Soviet Union increasingly developed trading relations with Western Europe. According to Prime Minister Antonio Segni of Italy, by 1959 the Soviet Union had asked NATO members for credits worth hundreds of millions of dollars and had requested $100 million credits from Italy alone.[11] Western European govern-

Table 14

PERCENTAGE OF TRADE OF NATO MEMBERS AND JAPAN
WITH SINO-SOVIET BLOC, 1959

| Country | Share of Total Exports to Bloc | Share of Total Imports from Bloc |
| --- | --- | --- |
| Belgium-Luxembourg | 2.9 | 2.4 |
| Canada | 0.7 | 0.3 |
| Denmark | 4.6 | 5.6 |
| France | 3.6 | 3.5 |
| West Germany | 7.0 | 6.9 |
| Greece | 16.5 | 7.5 |
| Iceland | 33.7 | 30.6 |
| Italy | 5.4 | 5.0 |
| Netherlands | 1.9 | 3.4 |
| Norway | 5.6 | 3.7 |
| Japan | 1.1 | 1.9 |
| Portugal | 2.3 | 1.0 |
| Turkey | 11.5 | 9.6 |
| United Kingdom | 2.8 | 3.4 |
| United States | 0.5 | 0.5 |

Source: U.S. Department of Commerce and UN Commodity Trade Statistics, 1959,
cited by U.S. Congress, Joint Economic Committee, *A New Look at Trade
Policy toward the Communist Bloc: The Elements of a Common Strategy
for the West* (Washington, D.C.: Government Printing Office, 1961),
pp. 85-97.

ments and private financial institutions extended substantial credits
to the Soviet Union and Eastern European states for the purchase
of new equipment embodying Western technological innovations.
Even though its allies extended credits, the Johnson Act continued
to hamper U.S. trade with the East, although an exception to this
policy was made in 1960 when the United States restored MFN
status to Poland.

By 1960, Khrushchev ceased making overtures for increased
trade to the United States, for several reasons. First, the U.S.
government showed very little interest in modifying its cold war
policies. Second, the USSR was able to gain access to advanced

technology in Western Europe, sometimes even through foreign-based subsidiaries of U.S. companies. In each year from 1961 through 1963, Soviet-American trade turnover (the total value of exports plus imports) was substantially less than the 1960 level (see table 13). Only in 1964, following a disastrous harvest in the Soviet Union, did Soviet-American trade turnover increase markedly, and this was due to Soviet purchases of American grain. The worsening of political relations between the superpowers in 1960-1961 undoubtedly contributed to the deterioration of the discussions concerning trade, and by the end of 1961, U.S.-Soviet trade was essentially moribund.

## Soviet-American Negotiations on Trade, 1971-1974

In his report on the Ninth Five-Year Plan delivered to the Supreme Soviet in November 1971, Premier Alexei Kosygin noted the importance of Soviet trade with the West:

New possibilities are being opened up in our relations with the countries of the West as we undertake the conclusion of long-term agreements that insure regular orders for industry. Consideration can be given to mutually beneficial cooperation with foreign firms and banks in working out a number of very important economic questions associated with use of the Soviet Unions's natural resources, construction of industrial enterprises, and exploration for new technical solutions.[12]

Ironically this statement reflected the classical liberal theory of comparative advantage as developed by John Stuart Mill, David Ricardo, and others. Kosygin not only advocated increased trade; he predicted that the volume of Soviet agricultural production would exceed the 1970 level of agricultural production in the United States, a claim that was reminiscent of Khrushchev's campaign announced in 1957 to overtake the United States in per-capita production of meat and milk. Just as Khrushchev was forced to do in the 1958-1960 period, the Soviet Union was forced to expand significantly its trade with the West in order to meet Kosygin's goals. Important negotiations on Soviet-American trade were conducted from 1971 through January 1975, and a number of agreements were concluded between U.S. business and Soviet trade agencies. The most comprehensive and important agreement was the Trade Agreement signed in October 1972.

The Soviet Union had a number of specific reasons for wanting to conclude a long-term, comprehensive trade agreement with the United States. First, at the Twenty-Fourth Party Congress, Brezhnev and Kosygin had stressed the importance of increasing the production of consumer goods, and the easiest way to accomplish this objective was to rely upon imports from the West. Second, these imports would aid the modernization of some sectors of Soviet industry. A third reason was to obtain increased Western capital and investment. Finally, Soviet agriculture has had chronic problems, and the establishment of a stable trading relationship with the West would provide access to supplies of grain when needed. During the summer of 1972, this access had proved extremely valuable, and a trade agreement perhaps would provide assured Soviet access to Western grain.

A Soviet-American trade agreement also promised certain potential advantages for the United States. The expansion of U.S. exports to the Soviet Union would result in increased sales and, perhaps, increased employment by American corporations. Furthermore, increased exports would improve the U.S. balance of trade, a serious concern in the early 1970s. Second, the formalization of the U.S.-Soviet trade relationship would provide the United States with access to those technologies in which the Soviets were further advanced than the United States. Examples included heavy castings, concrete technology for large structures, and power transmission technology.[13] Third, an increase in trade could provide the United States with access to Soviet raw materials, such as chromium, as well as natural gas and oil. Fourth and most important in the view of Nixon and Kissinger, increased Soviet-American trade was an essential component of their grand strategy. In Kissinger's words, "We regard mutually beneficial economic contact with the U.S.S.R. as an important element in our overall effort to develop incentives for responsible and restrained international conduct."[14] Increased trade thus provided the means to promote détente within the Soviet Union by providing goods and services that the Soviet leaders wanted and within the United States by providing U.S. corporations with expanded business opportunities.

Despite the potential advantages, from increased trade to both the United States and the Soviet Union, a number of obstacles stood in the way of expanded commercial relations. Nixon and Kissinger linked trade with other issues. For instance, when Kissinger went to Moscow to make final arrangements for the 1972 summit meeting, Nixon instructed him "to make Vietnam the first order of business and to refuse to discuss anything that the Soviets wanted—particularly the trade agreements for which they were so eager—until they specifically committed themselves to help end the war."[15] Thus due to the Nixon-Kissinger policy of linkage and to the failure of Soviet and American negotiations to resolve several important issues, the trade agreement was not reached at the Moscow Summit.

After several months of negotiations following the summit and the settlement of a number of secondary issues, such as shipping rates, the United States and the Soviet Union signed a three-year comprehensive trade agreement on October 18, 1972. The agreement called for the resolution of the issues that had blocked the expansion of Soviet-American trade throughout the cold war. According to the terms of the agreement, the Soviets would pay $722 million in World War II Lend-Lease debts. In return, the United States promised to grant most-favored-nation status to the Soviet Union and to make available long-term, relatively low interest Export-Import (Exim) Bank credits. The signatories also agreed to provide space in their respective capitals for the offices of trade organizations of the other country. Importantly the Trade Agreement prohibited dumping, that is, the disruption of a domestic market through unfair low pricing. Finally, the agreement called for the arbitration of disputes according to the rules of the UN Economic Commission of Europe.

After the signing of the Trade Agreement, Soviet and American representatives stated that they expected U.S.-Soviet trade to triple during the three-year period covered by the agreement. Secretary of Commerce Maurice Stans predicted that trade would increase to $5 billion in the 1971-1975 period.[16] Despite the dramatic absolute increases envisioned in these predictions, such expansion would not significantly affect overall U.S. trade. In 1971, U.S. trade with the Soviet Union represented less than 1 percent of total

U.S. foreign trade, and an increased total trade turnover to $3 billion in the 1972-1980 period would represent less than 2 percent of total U.S. trade.[17] Despite this relatively small potential for expansion, American businessmen were generally eager to establish contacts with Soviet trade agencies. Primarily interested in the political implications of increased trade, Nixon and Kissinger nevertheless actively encouraged business to enter the new market.[18]

### THE JACKSON-VANIK AMENDMENT

In the fall of 1972, the Nixon administration delivered a legislative proposal, the East-West trade bill of 1972, to the Congress. At the beginning of October, Senator Henry Jackson adopted a bargaining tool from Nixon and Kissinger when he proposed to block the extension of MFN status and credits to nonmarket economies that restricted or taxed the emigration of their citizens. In January 1973, Congressman Charles Vanik introduced a bill similar to Jackson's into the House of Representatives.[19]

For a number of reasons, the Jackson-Vanik Amendment quickly gained support in the Congress with 77 co-sponsors in the Senate and 287 in the House. The amendment appealed to a bipartisan group of legislators ranging from Democrats Edward Kennedy and George McGovern to Republicans Barry Goldwater and John Tower. Jackson argued that the basic motivation of the amendment was humanitarian: "When people such as those who want to leave the Soviet Union ask for help, the least we can do is provide the tiniest bit more freedom for them."[20] Another motivation behind the amendment was undoubtedly political. Jackson was a presidential candidate in 1972, and his support came from the moderate and conservative wings of the Democratic party; undoubtedly part of his motivation was to solidify this support as well as support from Jewish voters and interest groups.[21]

The results of the 1972 wheat deal were just becoming apparent in the first part of 1973, and it was clear that the Soviets had outbargained the United States during their wheat-buying spree in the summer of 1972. The popular and congressional reaction to the wheat deal increased the skepticism of many over the trade agreements and contributed to the support of the Jackson-Vanik Amendment. Additionally the East-West trade bill contained a number of provisions granting the president greater power in the determination of trade policy. A number of legislators were concerned over what they saw as Nixon's usurpation of power in other areas (such as the conduct of the war in Vietnam) and sought to attach conditions to the bill calling for greater congressional involvement in the determination of trade policy.

On April 10, 1973, Nixon formally sent Congress a comprehensive trade bill, renamed the Trade Reform Act of 1973. There were no provisions in the bill concerning Soviet emigration policies. The previous month, Secretary of the Treasury George Shultz had gone to Moscow to discuss trade in general and the provisions of the Jackson-Vanik Amendment with Secretary Brezhnev. Soon after the introduction of the amendment into the Congress, the White House announced that the president had received assurances from the Soviet Union that it was suspending the emigration fees previously imposed on Soviet Jews wishing to emigrate to Israel. On April 23 during a visit to Moscow by a group of U.S. senators, Brezhnev remarked that the Soviet Union hoped for a substantial expansion of Soviet-American trade but that Jewish emigration could not be linked to trade. In an unusual move, Soviet Nobel-prize-winning physicist Andrei Sakharov wrote an open letter to the Congress expressing support for the Jackson-Vanik Amendment, which he characterized as "an attempt to protect the right of emigration of citizens in countries that are entering into new and friendlier relations with the United States."[22]

In December, the House of Representatives passed a bill containing the Jackson-Vanik Amendment, and the Nixon administration was thus forced to add the provisions of the amendment to pending trade legislation. Congress had last delegated negotiating authority in the trade area to the executive branch in 1962 in the Trade Expansion Act. In the Trade Reform Act, the Nixon administration sought five major objectives: negotiate a more open international trading system; guarantee fair treatment of U.S. products in the world market; enable the United States to manage surges of imports; provide the necessary permanent authority to manage U.S. policy effectively; and open up and take advantage of trade opportunities in all countries.[23] In short, the Trade Reform Act was a major overhaul of U.S. trade legislation, and a number of significant issues including the inequities in the General Agreement on Tariffs and Trade, what to do about future oil embargoes, and the need for flexible exchange rates were addressed. A large number and diverse group of corporations, professional associations, and unions presented testimony on the proposed act. According to Henry Kissinger, "The Trade Reform Act is one of the most important pieces of legislation that has come before the Congress in years."[24]

There were six articles to the bill, and the provisions of the Jackson-Vanik Amendment were contained in article 4. Specifically, this article proposed the granting of authority to the president to extend most-favored-nation (MFN) status to those communist countries that did not enjoy it. At that time, Poland and Yugoslavia were the only nonmarket economies that had been granted MFN. No country would be eligible to receive MFN treatment or U.S. government credits if it denied the right of emigration to its citizens or imposed more than a nominal tax for emigration.

The clear intent of article 4 was to pressure the Soviet Union to allow greater Jewish emigration by linking MFN to the number of Jews allowed to emigrate. From 1967 through 1970, fewer than 6000 Jews emigrated from the Soviet Union. In 1971, 12,900 emigrated, followed by 31,200 in 1972 and 30,600 in 1973.[25] Despite these large numbers of Jewish emigrants, in 1974 there were still another 120,000 to 140,000 Soviet Jews who had applied for exit visas but were not allowed out of the USSR.

MFN treatment is somewhat of a misnomer since it provides for nondiscriminatory rather than favored treatment. States that are not granted MFN are subject to tariffs designed to inhibit trade. The use of MFN as a political instrument of diplomacy is not unprecedented. In fact, in 1911 the United States terminated the MFN treaty that it had with Russia in order to exert pressure on the czarist government to grant more humane treatment to Russian Jews. This early attempt to influence Russian domestic politics through the instrument of trade was not particularly successful.[26] Soon after its official recognition of the Soviet government, the United States granted MFN status to the Soviet Union in 1935. This remained in force until 1951 when it was withdrawn as a result of Soviet involvement in the planning of the Korean War.

The linkage strategies pursued by the Nixon administration and Senator Jackson differed significantly. Nixon and Kissinger sought to use economic means to moderate Soviet foreign policy behavior. According to Kissinger,

The major objective that we seek in obtaining most-favored-nation status for the Soviet Union is, in addition to the economic one, political. We are trying to encourage the Soviet Union to maintain a moderate course in foreign policy, to move step by step to an attitude of real coexistence with the United States, and to create linkages between the Soviet Union and the United States such that whenever a potential crisis arises, there would be at least enough influence to put a brake on a conflicting course.[27]

In other congressional testimony, Kissinger noted that "the domestic practices of the Soviet Union are not necessarily related to détente which we primarily relate to the conduct of foreign policy."[28] Kissinger noted that, despite the foreign policy focus of the Nixon administration's détente position, he was convinced that the most effective way to increase the emigration of Soviet Jews was by "working for a broad improvement in relations and dealing with emigration by informal means."[29]

In contrast, Jackson explicitly sought to link MFN to changes in Soviet domestic policy. One of Jackson's principal advisers, Richard Pearle, argued that Jackson did not really deal with Soviet domestic politics since "we just want people to be allowed to come out."[30] Despite this semantical defense of the Jackson Amendment, however, it seems clear that the amendment had tremendous implications for Soviet domestic politics. Soviet leaders have always strongly objected to any interference in their domestic affairs by foreign countries. Since the Soviet Union is a multinational state with more than one hundred different nationalities, Soviet leaders are particularly sensitive to the implications of allowing one group unrestricted emigration. Considered from this perspective, one can understand Soviet concern over the domestic implications of the Jackson-Vanik Amendment.

In the debate over the trade reform bill, MFN became an important symbolic issue. Ironically MFN affected only about 10 percent of Soviet exports to the United States.[31] The Soviet Union, however, considered the MFN issue to be of great significance and sent a contingent of Soviet officials to the United States on two occasions—February 1973 and February 1974—to lobby in favor of MFN status.

These officials were assisted in their efforts by lobbyists from the National Association of Manufacturers (NAM). In fact, during the Senate hearings on the Trade Reform Act, a number of business organizations including NAM, the U.S. Chamber of Commerce, the National Foreign Trade Council, and the East-West Trade Council opposed title 4 of the act, which incorporated the Jackson-Vanik Amendment. Business organizations argued that title 4 should be deleted from the bill for several reasons.[32] First, business witnesses at the hearings on the act expressed support for the "quiet diplomacy" of the Nixon administration. They argued that continued denial of MFN had a negative effect on American exports since it limited the sales of products to communist countries. Furthermore, the limitation and/or elimination of Exim Bank credits and guarantees encouraged potential communist buyers to turn to Western European and Japanese sellers who could offer them liberal credit terms.

While American business overwhelmingly opposed title 4 and supported passage of the trade reform bill (with title 4 deleted), the AFL-CIO opposed passage of the bill and supported title 4. In his appearance before the Senate Committee on Finance, George Meany, president of the AFL-CIO, characterized the "administration's so-called Trade Reform Act as totally obsolete" and argued that "it is worse than no bill at all."[33] With regard to title 4, Meany argued that the Soviet Union was primarily interested in obtaining American technology and that "once the Soviet Union has that technology, the seeming advantage of the U.S. businessmen quickly can be closed off."[34]

In March 1974, Secretary of State Kissinger testified before the Senate Committee on Finance and soon afterward began meeting with Senators Jackson, Abraham Ribicoff, and Jacob Javits in order to reach a compromise on the MFN and Jewish emigration issues. Kissinger believed that the only feasible agreement with the Soviet Union on the issue of Jewish emigration would be an implicit understanding.[35] In conversations with Soviet Foreign Minister Gromyko in Geneva in April, in Cyprus in May, and in Moscow in

July, U.S. officials sought to clarify Soviet emigration policies. Following President Nixon's resignation, President Ford met with Ambassador Dobrynin on August 14 to discuss the emigration of Soviet Jews. Dobrynin told President Ford that the Soviet Union would give an oral guarantee that it would allow 55,000 Jews to emigrate each year but that this guarantee would not be made formally.[36] Ford related Dobrynin's assurances to Jackson, Javits, and Ribicoff. According to Ford, "Ribicoff and Javits were understanding and cooperative. But Jackson was adamant. He kept saying that we were being too soft on the Russians. . . . He was about to launch his Presidential campaign, and he was playing politics to the hilt."[37]

After a series of trilateral discussions among Kissinger, Jackson, and Dobrynin, Kissinger wrote a letter to Jackson describing Soviet emigration policies as conveyed by Soviet leaders to the U.S. government.[38] In essence, the understanding stipulated that there would be no interference with applications for emigration, that there would be no harassment of applicants, that there would be no obstacles to emigration except for reasons of national security, and that the emigration tax that the Soviets suspended in 1973 would remain suspended. Kissinger stated that the Soviet leaders had made assurances, but not commitments, to the U.S. government that these guidelines would be followed in the future. He also noted that "if any number was used in regard to Soviet emigration, this would be wholly our responsibility; that is, the Soviet Government could not be held accountable for or bound by any such figures."[39] Finally, Kissinger noted that Soviet leaders had indicated that the United States could informally raise the question of whether these understandings were being carried out.

Senator Jackson sent a letter to Secretary Kissinger in which he presented the conditions concerning Jewish emigration, which he considered as essential as for the United States to grant the Soviet Union MFN status. Jackson stipulated that no unreasonable impediments should be placed in the way of persons wishing to emigrate. People who had access to "genuinely sensitive classified information" should become eligible for emigration within three years of the date on which they last had access to such information. Jackson also wrote that "we understand that the actual number of emigrants would rise promptly from the 1973 level and would continue to rise to correspond to the number of applications, and may therefore exceed 60,000 per annum."[40] Jackson argued that this number was to be a "benchmark as the minimum standard of initial compliance."[41]

The Kissinger and Jackson letters were released to the public by Senator Jackson on the same day that they were exchanged, October 18, 1974. They contained several obvious discrepancies, and in testimony before the Senate Finance Committee Kissinger noted that Jackson's more explicit and rigorous criteria for judging Soviet performance on the issue of emigration would be considered by President Ford at the time that he would be required to make a determination on whether to extend MFN status and credit to the Soviet Union.[42]

Following the exchange of correspondence, members of the Ford administration and Congress worked out a set of principles according to which the president would be empowered to waive the provisions of the original Jackson-Vanik Amendment and to grant MFN and credits to the Soviet Union for a period of eighteen months. This initial approval was subject to review and the granting of additional approval for one-year periods. As part of a three-week, worldwide trip, Kissinger stopped in Moscow October 23-27 for discussions with Soviet leaders. Brezhnev reportedly reacted very strongly to the publicity that had been given to Moscow's assurances on Jewish emigration.[43] Nevertheless it appeared that a compromise had been reached with the exchange of Kissinger's and Jackson's letters.

On December 20, the Senate passed the Trade Reform Act by 72 to 4 and the House by 323 to 36. As amended, the bill granted the president power to eliminate tariffs of 5 percent or lower and to reduce by 60 percent tariffs above 5 percent. Tariffs could be eliminated on goods imported from developing countries. The bill also provided the president with the authority to grant MFN status and credit to the Soviet Union.

Concurrent with its consideration of the Trade Reform Act, Congress also voted on an amendment by Senator Adlai Stevenson that placed an annual limit on Exim Bank credit to the Soviet Union of $300 million for a four-year period. This amendment contained a $40 million sublimit on the amount of loans or credit guarantees that could be used for exploration of energy in the Soviet Union. To some observers it appeared that the Stevenson Amendment was designed to inhibit the expansion of Soviet-American trade;[44] however, this ceiling could be raised with congressional approval. Therefore, it is equally plausible that the primary intent of Senator Stevenson was to assert the power of the Congress vis-à-vis the president over questions of trade financing.[45]

The Soviet Union reacted strongly to the passage of the Stevenson Amendment and to congressional assertions that the Soviet Union had agreed to increase Jewish emigration in exchange for MFN. On December 18, the Soviet news agency Tass released an article reporting that "leading circles" in the Soviet Union "categorically reject as inadmissible any attempts, from whomever they come, to interfere in affairs which are entirely within the internal competence of the Soviet state and do not concern anybody else."[46] On the same day, the text of a letter from Gromyko to Kissinger dated October 26 and previously undisclosed by Kissinger was released. In it, Gromyko stated that the Soviet Union "resolutely" rejected any interpretation of Soviet assurances concerning emigration that mention specific numbers.[47] U.S. congressmen discounted the Tass report and Gromyko letter as face-saving measures; however, Soviet commentators writing after the passage of the trade bill consistently mentioned the unacceptability to the Soviet Union of the understandings contained in the Kissinger-Jackson exchange of letters.[48] Throughout the last part of December, the Soviet press attacked Senator Jackson and "his cold war views." One author even favorably quoted a number of U.S. businessmen who supported the expansion of Soviet-American trade and opposed the Jackson-Vanik Amendment.[49]

On January 10, 1975, the Soviet Union informed the United States that it would not enter the provisions of the 1972 Trade Agreement into force. It objected to the limitation placed on Exim credits and the linking of MFN to emigration as violations of the trade agreement and the principle of noninterference in the domestic affairs of other states. Interestingly, the Soviet Union nullified rather than cancelled the Trade Agreement, which meant that, if they decided to sign the agreement at some future date, they could do so. In response to the Soviet decision, Kissinger announced that the United States would not take the steps to expand Soviet-American trade called for in the agreement.[50]

## Conclusion

American and Soviet actions in the two cases examined in this chapter contrasted markedly. In the 1958-1961 case, U.S. and Soviet leaders correctly perceived the Eastern and Western bloc economic systems as autonomous. Khrushchev sought to increase the interactions between the two blocs. In one of his many conversations with Henry Kissinger, Dobrynin once remarked that "great opportunities had been lost in Soviet-American affairs, especially between 1959 and 1963."[51] In a 1962 interview, Khrushchev stated, "Nowhere do our interests clash directly, either on territorial or economic questions."[52] Khrushchev's actions were consistent with his rhetorical claims; he sought to increase U.S.-Soviet trade. American leaders in the late 1950s, however, rebuffed his overtures.

In contrast to the bipolar international economic system of the acute cold war period, the international economic system of the early 1970s was multipolar, and there was substantial interaction between Eastern and Western states. During the 1960s, the states of Western Europe and Japan increasingly ignored the COCOM restrictions and trade with Eastern Europe and the Soviet Union. U.S. cold war economic restrictions trade was increased with Yugoslavia, Poland, and Rumania for political reasons. American business groups pressured the U.S. government to reduce restrictions so that they could enter the Eastern market.

By the 1970s economic issues were perceived by both American and Soviet decision makers as more important than during the 1950s. The chronic problems of the Soviet economy in general and the agricultural and advanced technology sectors in particular motivated Soviet leaders more than U.S. leaders to develop a comprehensive economic regime. Additionally the United States was far ahead of the Soviet Union in the production of advanced technologies and agricultural products. Because the Soviet Union needed these products, particularly following the disastrous harvest of

1972, it allowed the Moscow Summit to proceed as scheduled, despite the U.S. bombing of Hanoi and mining of Haiphong. In the post-summit détente atmosphere, the United States extended credits to the Soviet Union to purchase grain from it. Soon after the grain deal was concluded, the magnitude of the worldwide grain shortfall of 1972 became apparent, and food prices in the United States increased dramatically, demonstrating the sensitivity of both states to economic developments in the other country. American-Soviet trade was not so important to the superpowers that they were willing to pay any price for the expansion of it, as evidenced by the U.S. passage of the Jackson-Vanik Amendment and the resulting Soviet nullification of the 1972 Trade Agreement.

Although the Soviet leaders increased trade with Western Europe and Japan during the 1960s, they nevertheless wanted to develop U.S.-Soviet trade in the early 1970s for several reasons. First, many Soviet decision makers preferred U.S. products, apparently believing that they were superior to those of other Western countries. Second, the United States in the early 1970s annually exported approximately 75 percent of the total grain exported in the world, and there were, therefore, no other grain-exporting states that could meet the Soviet demand in 1972.

In addition to Soviet decision makers' desire to increase U.S.-Soviet trade, Nixon and Kissinger viewed the development of an economic regime as an important element in their strategy for dealing with the Soviet Union. The willingness of U.S. leaders to expand U.S.-Soviet trade was an important change from the 1958-1961 period and was one of the major reasons that an incipient economic regime was developed. If the leaders of both states favored the further development and implementation of this regime, why did the regime fail to develop?

During the cold war, the executive and congressional branches of government shared a common set of beliefs on dealing with the Soviet Union. This vision had broken down by the 1970s, and the Nixon administration was unsuccessful in legitimating a new grand design acceptable to the Congress and the public. In many ways, the Jackson-Vanik Amendment reflected the traditional American moralistic approach to foreign policy and competed with the Nixon-Kissinger *realpolitik*. Because many congressmen believed in the former approach and because Nixon and Kissinger failed to consult with Congress adequately, the administration was forced to include the Jackson-Vanik Amendment in the Trade Reform Act. For domestic political reasons, American and Soviet leaders felt that they were unable to develop further and implement the economic regime established by the 1972 Trade Agreement.

The linkage of economic issues with social issues is problematic since there are neither established currencies within issue areas nor exchange rates across them. Thus, while decision makers can calculate approximately the economic advantages of a trade agreement, it is extremely difficult to determine the benefits of a trade agreement versus the social costs of agreements (such as freer emigration) in other issue areas. There are no indicators that can be applied across issue areas to reach a net assessment; therefore decision makers must make subjective evaluations. In 1974 Soviet leaders decided that the social and political costs of the Trade Agreement (a change in Soviet emigration policy) were greater than the potential economic benefits of increased U.S.-Soviet trade.

In contrast to the 1958-1961 case, both Soviet and American decision makers, undoubtedly for a variety of shared and different reasons, favored the implementation and expansion of an economic regime in the 1971-1974 case. The fact of international interdependence, as Kissinger repeatedly noted during his last two years in office, impelled cooperation among states, including the United States and the Soviet Union. Thus, while a number of international and leadership factors were conducive to the successful development of a Soviet-American economic regime, domestic factors precluded it.

## Notes

1. "Interview Given by N. S. Khrushchev to Eric Ridder, Owner and Publisher of the American *Journal of Commerce,*" *International Affairs* (Moscow) 5 (May 1958): 4.

2. Ibid., p. 11.

3. Ibid., p. 7.

4. For the texts of Khrushchev's letter and Eisenhower's response, see *Department of State Bulletin* (August 4, 1958): 200-2.

5. Ibid., p. 200.

6. *New York Times*, March 3, 1958, p. 1.

7. Samuel Pisar, *A New Look at Trade Policy toward the Communist Bloc*, Study prepared for the U.S. Congress, Joint Economic Committee (Washington, D.C.: Government Printing Office, 1961), p. 12.

8. *New York Times*, May 11, 1959.

9. *Khrushchev Remembers: The Last Testament*, trans. and ed. Strobe Talbott (Boston: Little, Brown, 1974), p. 375.

10. Ibid., p. 378.

11. *New York Times*, October 15, 1959.

12. *Pravda*, November 25, 1971, cited by Kenneth Yalowitz, "U.S.S.R.-Western Industrial Cooperation," U.S. Congress, Joint Economic Committee, *Soviet Economic Prospects for the Seventies* (Washington, D.C.: Government Printing Office, 1973), p. 717.

13. James C. DeHaven, *Technology Exchange: Import Possibilities from the U.S.S.R.*, Report R-1414-ARPA (Santa Monica, Calif.: Rand Corporation, April 1974).

14. "Statement of Henry Kissinger," in U.S. Congress, Senate, Committee on Finance, *Hearings on the Emigration Amendment to the Trade Reform Act of 1974*, 93d Cong., 2d sess., December 3, 1974, p. 53.

15. Richard Nixon, *RN: The Memoirs of Richard Nixon* (New York: Grosset and Dunlap, 1978), p. 587.

16. *Washington Post*, November 3, 1972.

17. John P. Hardt and George D. Holliday, *U.S.-Soviet Commercial Relations: The Interplay of Economics, Technology Transfer, and Diplomacy*, Report prepared for U.S. Congress, House, Committee on Foreign Affairs (Washington, D.C.: Government Printing Office, June 1973), p. 42.

18. Interview with former Secretary of the Treasury, George P. Shultz, San Francisco, October 12, 1977.

19. For a study of the domestic politics of this case, see Dan Caldwell, "The Jackson-Vanik Amendment," in John Spanier and Joseph Nogee, eds., *Congress, the Presidency and American Foreign Policy* (New York: Pergamon Press, 1981), pp. 1-21.

20. *Time* (October 1, 1973): 23.

21. The author of the most comprehensive study of the amendment concluded that Jackson was primarily motivated by domestic political reasons in presenting his bill; see Paula Stern, *Water's Edge: Domestic Politics and the Making of American Foreign Policy* (Westport, Conn.: Greenwood Press, 1979).

22. "Open letter to the Congress of the United States from Andrei

Sakharov," September 14, 1973, reprinted in U.S. Congress, Senate, Committee on Finance, *The Trade Reform Act of 1973, Hearings*, 93d Cong., 2d sess., 1974, pp. 2254-55.

23. "Statement of Peter M. Flanigan, Executive Director, Council on International Economic Policies," in *Trade Reform Act*, pp. 169-70.

24. Kissinger, in *Emigration Amendment Hearings*, p. 72.

25. The figures for 1967-1971 were compiled by the National Conference on Soviet Jewry and are cited by Stern, *Water's Edge*, p. 217. The figures for 1972 and 1973 were compiled by the Intergovernmental Committee for European Migration and cited by *Los Angeles Times*, November 3, 1979, pt. I, p. 32.

26. William W. Orbach, *The American Movement to Aid Soviet Jews* (Amherst: University of Massachusetts Press, 1979).

27. Kissinger, *Trade Reform Act of 1973, Hearings*, p. 486.

28. Kissinger, in *Emigration Amendment Hearings*, p. 94.

29. Ibid., p. 52.

30. *Time* (October 1, 1973): 23.

31. George Shultz in *Trade Reform Act of 1973, Hearings*, p. 9.

32. See, in particular, the statement of William R. Hewlett, in *Trade Reform Act of 1973, Hearings*, pp. 2262-86.

33. George Meany, in *Trade Reform Act of 1973, Hearings*, p. 1136.

34. Ibid.

35. Kissinger, in *Emigration Amendment Hearings*, p. 53.

36. Gerald R. Ford, *A Time to Heal* (New York: Berkley Books, 1980), p. 135.

37. Ibid., pp. 135-36. October 18, 1974," in *Emigration Amendment Hearings*, pp. 36-39.

38. "Exchange of letters between Secretary Kissinger and Senator Jackson, October 18, 1974," in *Emigration Amendment Hearings*, pp. 36-39.

39. Kissinger statement in ibid., p. 53.

40. Henry Jackson to Henry Kissinger, October 18, 1974, in ibid., p. 38.

41. Ibid.

42. Kissinger statement, in *Emigration Amendment Hearings*, p. 54.

43. *New York Times*, October 28, 1974.

44. This is the view taken by Daniel Yergin, "Politics and Soviet-American Trade: The Three Questions," *Foreign Affairs* 55 (April 1977): 532.

45. John P. Hardt and George D. Holliday, "East-West Financing by Eximbank and National Interest Criteria," in Paul Marer, ed., *U.S. Financing of East-West Trade: The Political Economy of Government*

*Credits and the National Interest* (Bloomington, Ind.: International Development Research Center, Indiana University, 1975).

46. Foreign Broadcast Information Service, *Soviet Union-Daily Report* 74-245, December 19, 1974, p. B1 (hereafter cited as FBIS-SOV).

47. Ibid., p. B2.

48. FBIS-SOV-74-247, December 23, 1974, pp. B1-B7.

49. "Strelnikov Dispatch," FBIS-SOV-74-251, December 30, 1974, pp. B3-B4.

50. Press Conference given by Henry Kissinger, January 14, 1975, U.S. Department of State, Bureau of Public Affairs, transcript.

51. Dobrynin "had been head of the American division of the Soviet Foreign Ministry during that period, and he knew that Khrushchev seriously wanted an accommodation with the United States." Henry Kissinger, *White House Years* (Boston: Little, Brown, 1979), p. 113.

52. Quoted by William Zimmerman, *Soviet Perspectives on International Relations, 1956-1967* (Princeton: Princeton University Press, 1969), p. 224.

# CHAPTER 7

# SOVIET-AMERICAN CRISIS MANAGEMENT IN THE CUBAN MISSILE CRISIS AND THE OCTOBER WAR

On October 6, 1973, Syrian and Egyptian forces launched a simultaneous attack on Israel. The fourth Arab-Israeli war came as a shock to Nixon and Kissinger since the Soviets, at the very least, provided material support for the Arab forces. There were some indications that the Soviet Union even helped to plan the attack, an action that, if true, would be a violation of the détente agreements —the Basic Principles signed at the Moscow Summit and the Agreement on the Prevention of Nuclear War signed in June 1973. Clearly the war was the first significant test of détente, and some observers, in light of U.S. and Soviet actions during the war, agreed with André Fontaine of *Le Monde* that "détente is the cold war pursued by other means—and sometimes the same."[1]

The Cuban missile crisis and October War were similar in that both involved direct confrontations between the United States and the Soviet Union.[2] There were, however, a number of important differences in the two crises that complicate systematic comparison. First, the risk of nuclear war in the Cuban missile crisis was great; President Kennedy estimated it as between one out of three and even. Although the Soviet-American confrontation during the October War was serious and the possibility for escalation was substantial, the stakes and risks were not as great as those in the Cuban missile crisis. Second, the 1962 crisis was essentially a Soviet-American confrontation, and the Soviet Union's Caribbean client, Cuba, played a relatively unimportant role.[3] In the October War, the United States and the Soviet Union became involved as a result of the actions of their respective client states, which despite their dependence upon the superpowers for weapons and other military equipment were not under the strict control of the suppliers. Third, the international environments in which the two crises occurred were significantly different. In 1962, Soviet-American relations were still marked by cold war tensions; by 1973 many of these tensions had been lessened as a result of actions by decision makers in the two governments. Fourth, the domestic contexts of the two cases were different. In 1962, President Kennedy could depend upon public and congressional support of his actions during foreign policy crises; by 1973, due largely to the impact of Vietnam on the Congress and the public, this was no longer the case. Finally, there were important leadership changes in both the United States and the Soviet Union between 1962 and 1973, which affected American and Soviet perspectives on international relations.

## The Two Cases

### THE CUBAN MISSILE CRISIS

In August 1962, U.S. intelligence agencies obtained photographic evidence that the Soviet Union was installing surface-to-air missiles (SAM) in Cuba.[4] This evidence provided some justification for the public warnings made by conservative congressmen and journalists throughout September that the Soviet Union was equipping Cuba with sophisticated military equipment, which might include long-range surface-to-surface missiles capable of reaching the United States. On September 19, the U.S. Intelligence Board met to consider the implications of Soviet arms shipments to Cuba and ordered a formal national intelligence estimate (NIE) on the subject. According to Roger Hilsman, although the NIE acknowledged that the Soviet emplacement of intermediate- and medium-range ballistic missiles would significantly add to Soviet strategic capabilities and therefore might be attractive to Soviet decision makers, the report concluded that the Soviet Union would not opt for such action since it was likely that the United States would discover the missiles and react strongly.[5]

Soviet construction activity continued, and President Kennedy became concerned enough about the situation to order a U-2 overflight of Cuba, which took place on October 14. The next evening after the photographs were processed and analyzed, intelligence officials informed McGeorge Bundy, Dean Rusk, and Robert McNamara that the Soviet Union was attempting to introduce secretly and make operational some forty intermediate-range (IRBM) and medium-range ballistic missiles (MRBM).[6] Bundy informed the president of this finding the next morning, and Kennedy ordered a meeting with a group of his closest advisers (designated the Executive Committee, or ExCom, of the National Security Council) for later that day.

The ExCom was under considerable pressure to recommend an alternative course of action that would enable the United States to keep Soviet missiles from becoming operational. After seven days of intense discussions, it recommended a quarantine of Cuba as the appropriate response. On October 22 the president announced the quarantine, which went into effect two days later. The first and, as it turned out, the only ship to be inspected was boarded on October 26. That night as they discussed ways to increase the pressure on the Soviet Union, Kennedy and his advisers received a long, rambling letter from Khrushchev in which he proposed to remove the missiles in return for a promise from Kennedy not to invade Cuba.[7] At 10 A.M. on October 27, the ExCom received a second letter signed by Khrushchev (although some suspected that it was written by other members of the Soviet ruling hierarchy), which proposed the removal of the Soviet missiles in Cuba for an American pledge not to invade Cuba and the removal of American missiles in Turkey. Shortly after, the ExCom learned that an American U-2 had been shot down over Cuba, and some members of the group urged retaliation. Kennedy chose to ignore the second message and to accept the proposal contained in the October 26 letter. He also presented the Soviets with an ultimatum through Robert Kennedy's conversation with Dobrynin and gave the Soviets an informal assurance that the U.S. missiles in Turkey and Italy eventually would be removed.[8] Khrushchev accepted Kennedy's offer on October 28, and the crisis ended.

### THE OCTOBER WAR

On October 6, 1973, Egypt and Syria launched a simultaneous attack on Israel's northern and southern borders.[9] The leaders of both Israel and the United States were surprised by the attack and, in marked contrast to the 1967 June War, Arab forces performed very effectively and made striking gains during the first week of the war.

Prior to the outbreak of the war, the United States and Soviet Union had provided their respective allies in the Middle East with large amounts of military equipment; however, existing stocks of arms and ammunition were insufficient to fight the war, and the principal belligerents were in need of supplies after the first several days of fighting. The Soviets began airlifting arms to Egypt and Syria on October 10, and the United States began sending weapons to Israel three days later. During the first two weeks of the war, American and Soviet leaders exchanged a number of communications, but these interactions failed to produce a cease-fire.

On October 8, Israel launched a successful counterattack in the north against the Syrians. One week later the Israelis counterattacked in the south and crossed the Suez Canal. Within several days of the canal crossing, the advantage in the war had clearly shifted to Israel. In a move designed to support the Arab cause, the Organization of Arab Oil Producing Countries (OAPEC) announced, and the Soviet Union immediately endorsed, a cut in oil production until Israel withdrew from occupied territory.

Secretary Brezhnev sent President Nixon an urgent message on October 19 calling for immediate talks to end the hostilities. In response Kissinger flew to Moscow where the discussion resulted in a Soviet-American jointly sponsored resolution, which was accepted by the UN Security Council, Israel, and Egypt on October 22 (the Syrians did not agree to it until two days later). The cease-fire broke down soon after its acceptance, and the Israelis quickly completed the encirclement of the entire Egyptian Third Army, which was stranded on the East Bank. On October 24, Egyptian President Anwar Sadat requested joint Soviet-American intervention, but the White House refused. Brezhnev then sent a note to Nixon strongly suggesting joint intervention and, if the United States would not comply with this proposal, threatening unilateral Soviet intervention. The United States responded with a worldwide alert of its military forces just after midnight on October 25. The crisis ended later that day when the Soviet Union failed to intervene, and the Security Council approved a UN peace-keeping force to supervise the cease-fire.

## Analytical Comparison of the Cases

THE INTERNATIONAL ENVIRONMENTS

Although there was some concern about the role of China, American and Soviet decision makers in the early 1960s generally equated a state's power with the military forces possessed by that state. According to this criterion, there were two predominant actors in the international system, the United States and the Soviet Union. In the late 1950s, particularly following the launching of the first ICBM and Sputnik, Khrushchev gave the impression that the Soviet Union was equal, and perhaps even superior, to the United States. His boasting had the unintended consequence of stimulating a massive post-Sputnik effort within the United States to catch up with the Soviet Union. When the SAMOS reconnaissance satellite system became operational in early 1961, it became evident that Khrushchev's claims had been purely rhetorical.

At the end of 1962, the United States had approximately 1050 strategic nuclear delivery vehicles (294 ICBMs, 144 SLBMs, and 190 long-range bombers).[10] With well over three times the number of intercontinental strategic nuclear forces than the Soviet Union, the United States was clearly superior. However, in addition to their intercontinental nuclear forces, the Soviet Union had approximately 750 intermediate- (IRBMs) and medium-range ballistic missiles (MRBMs), designed and deployed for possible use in a European conflict. Because of their limited range, these missiles could not be used against the United States if they were deployed in the Soviet Union. However, if deployed in Cuba, they could easily reach most of the continental United States.[11] Thus with the clandestine deployment of IRBMs and MRBMs, the USSR could present the United States with a fait accompli and could move substantially closer to the achievement of nuclear parity.[12] Fidel Castro may also have been attracted to such a deployment because it would provide an effective deterrent to an attack on Cuba by the United States.

In the initial discussion of the ExCom, Robert McNamara

argued that "a missile is a missile. It makes no great difference whether you are killed by a missile from the Soviet Union or Cuba."[13] He pointed out that the Soviet Union already possessed ICBMs and that it would be a matter of a few years before it built even more. Dean Acheson, Paul Nitze, and Roswell Gilpatrick criticized McNamara's assertion and noted that the U.S. warning time would be cut from fifteen to three minutes and the missiles would have an effect on the perception of the strategic balance by foreign leaders, particularly in Latin America. The members of the ExCom accepted this line of reasoning, believing that were the United States to allow the Soviet missiles to remain in Cuba, U.S. vulnerability to attack would be increased and its political prestige decreased.

The deployment of strategic nuclear delivery vehicles to Cuba was very significant. This was the first deployment outside of the Soviet Union of land-based nuclear ballistic missiles and was a de facto admission by the Soviet Union that it was strategically inferior to the United States. Throughout the acute cold war, American and Soviet decision makers observed the sphere of influence of the other superpower. Thus the United States did not intervene, despite rhetorical assurances, in Hungary in 1956, and the Soviet Union did not directly intervene militarily during the Cuban revolution in 1959. The Soviet deployment in 1962 was, in effect, a violation of the implicit U.S.-Soviet rule against intervening into the sphere of influence of the other superpower.

In addition to the asymmetry in Soviet and American strategic forces in 1962, several other factors contributed to the U.S. advantage in the Cuban missile crisis. The most obvious was the geographic advantage held by the United States because of its proximity to Cuba. The Soviet Union's lines of communication were thousands of miles long, but American naval, air, and land forces were stationed within several hundred miles of Cuba, giving the United States a substantial advantage during the crisis and also contributing to the motivation of American decision makers to remove the missiles. Accentuating their logistical disadvantage, Soviet airlift and sealift capabilities were not well developed in the early 1960s.

In the October War, Soviet forces enjoyed a similar geographic advantage. For example, the Soviet Mediterranean Squadron was substantially strengthened during the war with naval units from the Black Sea. Even though many of the littoral states around the Mediterranean Sea were NATO members, these states did not cooperate with U.S. efforts to assist Israel due to fear of reprisals of oil cutbacks by OAPEC. Consequently American lines of communication during the October War were far longer than those of the USSR. By the early 1970s, the Soviet Union had developed sealift and airlift capabilities to the extent that they were able to resupply Arab forces effectively.

When the October War broke out, the major actors involved were Egypt, Syria, and Israel; however, because of their close ties with the belligerent states and their interests in the Middle East, the Soviet Union and the United States rapidly became involved. China remained uninvolved throughout the war, and most of the states of Western Europe and Japan also remained uninvolved, due primarily to the threats by OAPEC. Because of the vulnerability of Western states to an oil cutoff, OAPEC emerged during the October War as an influential actor in the international system. Thus a state's power in the early 1970s, in contrast to the acute cold war, depended upon the issue area and the situational conditions.

By the early 1970s the Soviet Union played a much more active role in world politics than it had during the previous decade. Soviet military and economic capabilities had increased substantially, better enabling the Soviet Union to confront potential enemies on its eastern and western borders. The Soviets' long-standing interest in the Middle East centered on Turkey and Iran from 1917 to 1945.[14] At the end of World War II, Stalin attempted to acquire a trusteeship over Libya, Eritrea, or Italian Somalia but was thwarted by the Western powers. In 1955, the Soviet Union indicated its intention to assist Arab countries militarily and economically and began sending arms to Egypt under the guise of an arms agreement between Egypt and Czechoslovakia. The USSR remained largely uninvolved (except rhetorically) in the 1956 Suez war. Throughout the late 1950s and 1960s, the Soviet Union continued to nurture its ties with the Arab states.

Unlike Cuba, which was clearly within the traditional American sphere of influence, the Middle East by the 1970s was not part of either great power's sphere of influence. Despite the Western colonial dominance of the Middle East in the past, Nixon recognized the right of the Soviet Union to maintain a presence in the area in his 1971 and 1973 foreign policy reports.[15] American acceptance of the Soviet Union in the Middle East, however, was conditioned on the warning that "attempts at exclusion or predominance are an invitation to conflict, whether local or global."[16]

There was a great deal more diplomatic flexibility by the early 1970s than during the acute cold war. Decision makers viewed international relations as a non-zero-sum game in which states could achieve mutual gains or losses. There was some flexibility in honoring commitments, and statesmen were not preoccupied solely with the need to maintain credibility. Thus, during the October War, the European NATO allies of the United States, with the exception of Portugal and the Netherlands, failed to support Israel and the United States for fear that OAPEC would cut off oil supplies.

In marked contrast to the international system of the early 1960s, by the early 1970s the system was no longer unambiguously bipolar. The USSR had achieved nuclear parity with the United States, and China, Great Britain, and France also possessed nuclear weapons. In nonstrategic-military issue areas, such as international economic relations, power was diffused and shared among a number of actors, including some nonstate actors such as multinational corporations. The two crises under examination occurred in two very different international milieus.

THE DOMESTIC CONTEXTS

Just as there were important differences in the international environments of the two cases, there were also significant differences in the domestic contexts, which affected the willingness of the Congress and the public to support the actions of U.S. decision-makers.

When the United States discovered that the Soviet Union was in fact installing intermediate- and medium-range ballistic missiles in Cuba, congressional elections were just three weeks away. Kennedy's attacks in the 1960 presidential campaign that the Republicans had done nothing about Cuba came back to haunt him in

1962. He had approved the disastrous Bay of Pigs invasion of April 1961, and the Republicans had announced that they were going to make Cuba the dominant issue of the 1962 campaign. Cuba was, in Theodore Sorensen's view, the Kennedy administration's "political Achilles heel."[17] In the course of the ExCom discussions, domestic political factors were mentioned on several occasions. Secretary of the Treasury Douglas Dillon, ironically a Republican himself, was concerned that the effect of inaction on the Democrats in the upcoming election could be disastrous.[18]

Once the president made his quarantine speech, his popularity ratings increased dramatically (although, curiously, not as high as his ratings following the Bay of Pigs crisis). Despite the public's support of Kennedy's decision to blockade Cuba, some congressional leaders, both Republicans and Democrats, felt that the blockade was not the best alternative. Kennedy was surprised, for instance, when the liberal chairman of the Senate Foreign Relations Committee, J. W. Fulbright, supported Senator Richard Russell's hawkish suggestion of an invasion. Despite some misgivings about the probable effectiveness of the blockade, Kennedy was nevertheless supported with some qualification by the Congress and to a greater extent by public opinion.[19]

Undoubtedly there is a relationship between a state's domestic and foreign policies, but the nature of this relationship and the degree to which domestic political considerations influence foreign policies, and vice-versa, is extremely complex.[20] The analysis of American actions during the October War presents a particularly troublesome problem since, at the time of the war, the Nixon administration faced serious domestic and international crises.

By the spring of 1973, the Watergate scandal dominated the news. On April 30, President Nixon dismissed advisers H. R. Haldemann and John Ehrlichman. By the end of May, Kissinger was being criticized for his role in the wiretapping of seventeen National Security Council employees and journalists. In June, Secretary Brezhnev visited the United States for a follow-up to the Moscow Summit of the previous year, but the products of this meeting were far more meager than the 1972 meeting. Some felt that Brezhnev was trying to help Nixon divert attention from Watergate, an objective that was transitory at best since John Dean began his testimony before the Senate Watergate Committee one week after the Brezhnev visit.

When the October War began on October 6, members of the U.S. government were deeply preoccupied with the disclosures of the Watergate and related scandals. As Nixon noted in his memoirs, "The immensely volatile situation created by the unexpected outbreak of this war could not have come at a more complicated domestic juncture."[21] On October 10, Spiro Agnew resigned as vice-president, pleading *nolo contendere* to a charge of tax evasion in Maryland. Tensions continued to mount on the domestic and international fronts; on October 20, as Kissinger conferred with Brezhnev in Moscow, Nixon fired Watergate Special Prosecutor Archibald Cox, an action that caused the attorney general, Elliot Richardson, and his deputy, William Ruckelshaus, to resign. When the Soviet Union threatened to intervene unilaterally four days later, Kissinger met with Secretary of Defense James Schlesinger, Director of the CIA William Colby, and Chairman of the Joint Chiefs of Staff Thomas Moorer. This group recommended that the president issue a worldwide alert of U.S. military forces. Nixon, who had not participated in the meetings on the war, accepted the group's recommendation and ordered the alert.

The alert created a great deal of controversy within the United States, as well as internationally. Many congressmen, government officials, journalists, and members of the public suspected that Nixon was trying to deflect attention from his Watergate problems. Indeed at his press conference to discuss the alert, Kissinger was asked if "the American alert might have been prompted as much perhaps by American domestic requirements as by the real requirements of diplomacy in the Middle East." Kissinger responded, "It is a symptom of what is happening to our country that it could even be suggested that the United States would alert its forces for domestic reasons."[22] In the aftermath of the crisis some critics of the administration charged that the alert was unnecessary and "over advertised."[23] Others argued that it was justified and needed but that the decision-making process leading up to the alert was overly centralized in Kissinger's hands.[24]

In contrast to Kennedy's rise in popularity following the Cuban missile crisis, the American alert superimposed on the background of Watergate raised more questions in the minds of many concerning Nixon's capabilities as president and commander-in-chief.

In the initial phases of the Cuban missile crisis, American and Soviet leaders depended almost exclusively on negative influence strategies. The Soviets deployed missiles to Cuba in order to achieve one or more of five objectives: to achieve a bargaining chip for future negotiations with the United States, to divert attention from Berlin, to deter a U.S. invasion of Cuba, to achieve a dramatic foreign policy success, and/or to gain strategic-military power.[25] The United States had an overriding objective: to remove the missiles from Cuba. Significantly both Soviet and American objectives during the initial phases were analogous to a two-actor zero-sum game in which a gain by one player results in a loss for the other player. As the crisis developed, Kennedy and Khrushchev searched for ways to resolve the conflict short of war. In his second letter of October 27, Khrushchev linked the Soviet removal of its missiles in Cuba with the removal of U.S. missiles in Italy and Turkey. While President Kennedy was unwilling to accept these terms, he was prepared to extend an informal assurance to the Soviets. According to Robert Kennedy, Dobrynin asked what offer the United States was prepared to make and Kennedy responded:

. . . There could be no *quid pro quo* or any arrangement made under this kind of threat or pressure, and that in the last analysis this was a decision that would have to be made by NATO. However, I said, President Kennedy had been anxious to remove those missiles from Turkey and Italy for a long period of time. He had ordered their removal some time ago, and it was our judgement that, within a short time after this crisis was over, those missiles would be gone.[26]

Thus in the concluding phase of the crisis, both Kennedy and Khrushchev compromised in order to avoid escalation and to maintain international stability. After the resolution of the crisis, according to Sorensen, Kennedy "laid down the line [to his staff] —no boasting, no gloating, not even a claim of victory. We had won by enabling Khrushchev to avoid complete humiliation—we should not humiliate him now."[27] Thus the concluding phase of the crisis, in contrast to the initial phase, was analogous to a nonzero-sum game in which each side achieved variable payoffs.

At the 1972 and 1973 summits, Nixon and Brezhnev explicated the crisis management and crisis prevention regime in the Basic Principles and the Agreement on the Prevention of Nuclear War. To what extent were the rules and procedures in this regime actually observed during the Cuban missile crisis and the October War?

## THE SUPERPOWERS' ROLES IN PRECRISIS PLANNING

Although the Soviets were directly and unambiguously involved in the planning and the attempt to install medium- and intermediate-range ballistic missiles in Cuba, their role in the preparation and execution of the Arab attack on Israel in October 1973 is far less clear. While the United States and the Soviet Union confronted each other directly in the Cuban missile crisis, during the October War they acted primarily as resuppliers for their respective client states until October 24, when the Soviet Union threatened to intervene. The nature of superpower involvement in the two crises therefore was very different.

Throughout the crisis, the Soviet Union maintained strict control over its missile installations in Cuba, and at the end of the crisis, Cuba was forced by the Soviets to return the long-range Ilyushin-28 bombers to the Soviet Union. In the Cuban case, Soviet policy-makers exercised firm policy control over their exported forces, and the Cubans had very little voice in the determination of how these forces were to be used. In the end, the forces were dismantled, packed up, and sent back to the Soviet Union, causing a minor rift in Cuban-Soviet relations.

The third point of the Basic Principles states that the United States and the Soviet Union will "do everything in their power so that conflicts or situations will not arise which would serve to increase international tensions." On October 7, one day after the start of the war, Kissinger gave Dobrynin a personal letter from Nixon to Brezhnev in which the president reminded the Soviet leader that they had agreed to two communiqués—the Basic Principles and the Agreement on the Prevention of Nuclear War—calling for Soviet-American cooperation to resolve threats to the peace. On several other occasions during the crisis, Nixon and Kissinger reminded the Soviet Union of its obligations under the 1972 and 1973 agreements.[28] For instance, after Nixon declared the

U.S. alert, he sent a message to Brezhnev stating that the intervention of Soviet troops in the Middle East would be considered a violation of article 2 of the Agreement on the Prevention of Nuclear War.[29] In the aftermath of the war, a number of critics argued that the fledgling rules of détente as set out in the two documents had been broken. For instance, Alvin Rubinstein contended that Soviet behavior during the October War "blatantly contradicted the principles agreed to by Brezhnev and Nixon at their summit meetings and indicated Soviet determination to back its clients to the utmost, short of nuclear war and in the expectation of continuing détente."[30]

Much of the debate concerning the alleged violation of the détente agreements centered on the question of how far in advance the Soviet Union knew about the impending Arab attack on Israel, since, according to the agreements, the leaders of both superpowers agreed to inform each other of any crisis that threatened peace. This principle, however, is negated in some instances by the last point in the Basic Principles, which states that "the basic principles set forth in this document do not affect any obligations with respect to other countries earlier assumed by the USA and the USSR."

It is unclear when the Soviet Union first learned when the Egyptian-Syrian attack on Israel would take place. In his memoirs, Sadat stated that on October 4 Syrian President Hafiz al-Asad informed the Soviets of the date of the attack.[31] This account is consistent with Soviet actions, for on October 4 the families of Soviet technicians and advisers were evacuated from Syria and Egypt; Soviet naval vessels left Alexandria and Port Said; and a Soviet reconnaissance satellite was launched. Considering these events and the *post hoc* testimony of Sadat, Hafiz Ishmail, and Mohamed Heikal, it is clear that the Soviet Union knew of the attack at least two days before it was launched.[32] Although some observers claim that the Soviet Union played an active role in assisting the Egyptians and Syrians plan their attack,[33] the evidence indicates that the initiative for the war rested with the Arabs, not the USSR.[34] Soviet military planners generally minimized risks during the cold war, and the fact that much of the Soviet equipment sent to the Arabs during the October War was taken from

Soviet and Warsaw Pact stocks provides evidence that the Soviets
did not have extensive foreknowledge.

Following the war, Soviet leaders argued that they had honored
their responsibilities under the Basic Principles and the Agreement
on the Prevention of Nuclear War. In fact, in his speech to the
World Peace Congress on October 26, 1973, Brezhnev stated,
"During recent years the Soviet Union has repeatedly, I stress
repeatedly, warned that the situation in the Near East was explo-
sively dangerous."[35] Furthermore, during his visit to Nixon's San
Clemente estate in June 1973, "for three hours, until past midnight," according to Nixon, "Brezhnev hammered me on the
Middle East."[36] Brezhnev wanted Nixon to agree to a set of principles concerning a Middle East settlement, and he proposed that
such principles should include the withdrawal of Israeli troops
from the occupied territories, free passage of ships through the
Suez Canal, the recognition of national boundaries, and international guarantees for any settlement.[37] According to Nixon,
Brezhnev "hinted that without such an agreement on principles he
could not guarantee that war would not resume."[38]

Former National Security Council and State Department official
Helmut Sonnenfeldt has commented, "We'll never know how early
the Soviets knew of the coming of the October War. The problem
is that they may have assumed that they had sufficiently fore-
warned us of Arab demands, and further assumed that we would
pass on the information to Israel."[39] Whatever the reason, it is
clear that in this case the rules and procedures for crisis prevention
were not sufficient to preclude a Soviet-American confrontation.

### FORCE DEPLOYMENTS AND ARMS DELIVERIES

An obvious, tangible means of assessing the importance of one
state's commitment to the defense of another is to analyze force
deployments. For example, a state that stations troops in a foreign
country indicates a relatively high level of commitment. American
forces in Western Europe and Soviet forces in Eastern Europe
indicate the high priority that the two superpowers place on avoiding disruption of the status quo in Europe. An analysis of the types
of force deployments that the superpowers have made during crises
may indicate the relative importance of the superpowers' objectives.

If a government's policymakers are unwilling to station troops in a foreign country, they may nevertheless be willing to give or sell weapons to that country. Since the end of World War II, the United States and the Soviet Union have sought to gain influence through arms transfers and sales; however, the quantity and the quality of the weapons that they have transferred vary significantly from country to country. Lacking a sophisticated theory explaining the superpowers' motivations in transferring arms to another country, one can assume that the number and quality of weapons sent to another state signify, at least in part, the importance that a particular country represents to the United States or the Soviet Union.

The Soviet decision to deploy IRBMs and MRBMs in Cuba was very significant since it was the first time that these weapons were deployed outside of the Soviet Union. In addition, the Soviets sent substantial numbers of their own personnel and a significant amount of first-line Soviet equipment, including forty-two Ilyushin-28 light bombers, forty-two MIG-21 interceptors, twenty-four SAM-2 missile sites, four coastal defense missile sites, and twelve KOMAR patrol boats equipped with antiship missiles.[40] It is estimated that by mid-October approximately 22,000 Soviet troops and technicians were in Cuba to assemble, operate, maintain, and defend these weapons.

In response to Soviet arms deliveries and the deployment of Soviet forces in Cuba, President Kennedy ordered that preparations be made for the invasion of Cuba. Twenty-four squadrons (14,000) men of air force reserve troop transport units were recalled to active duty, and some 200,000 troops gathered in Florida to prepare for the invasion. Tactical aircraft were moved to airports within striking distance of Cuba, and SAC B-52 bombers were dispersed. Kennedy also ordered a worldwide alert of U.S. military forces. Although these measures were undoubtedly designed, at least partially, as signaling measures to highlight American resolve to the Soviets, these actions were also actual preparations for war. Kennedy believed that, if the Soviet move was successful, it would "materially and politically change the balance of power" in the cold war, and he therefore deployed American forces to prepare for an invasion, if necessary, to remove the missiles.[41]

By the early 1970s, the Soviet Union had achieved nuclear parity with the United States. Since the Cuban missile crisis (some analysts say because of it), the Soviet Union had also improved its conventional forces, particularly its navy. In the Middle East, the two superpowers sought to gain influence by supplying their respective client states with military equipment. In their roles as arms suppliers, however, the United States and the Soviet Union faced a dilemma: each sought to maintain influence within its client states without stimulating a regional arms race that could lead to hostilities and a possible superpower confrontation. J. C. Hurewitz has described the superpowers' quandary in the Middle East in the following terms: "Involvement without commitment is irresponsible. On the other hand, if the superpowers are to avoid confrontation which might lead to the nuclear war, they must avoid such commitments. That is the responsible position to take. Responsibility in superpower politics becomes irresponsibility in regional politics."[42] The records of each superpower's deployment of forces and arms supplies prior to and during the war indicate the ways in which the United States and the Soviet Union sought to cope with this dilemma.

The Soviet Union began sending military equipment to the Middle East in 1955 under the guise of a Czech-Egyptian arms agreement. The weapons that they sent to their Middle Eastern clients from 1955 until 1962 were obsolete (even some left-overs from World War II) relative to other equipment in the Soviet inventory at that time. In 1962-1963, the Soviet Union began sending first-line equipment to the Middle East, including several of the best available Soviet systems (the MIG-21 and the T-54B tank). Throughout the 1955-1967 period, despite Arab requests, the USSR refused to supply its Arab clients with an effective offensive capability (tactical and medium-range FROG and SCUD missiles and large numbers of bombers).[43] Following the 1967 June War in which Israeli forces destroyed a great deal of Egypt's military equipment, the Soviet Union concentrated on the resupply of Egypt and Syria. During the war of attrition (1969-1970), the Soviet Union deployed fifteen thousand to twenty thousand troops and a sophisticated air defense network of SAM-3 missiles, which at that time had not even been supplied to North Vietnam. Soviet pilots began flying air defense missions over Egypt in mid-April, and in June, four Soviet-piloted

MIG-21s were shot down by Israeli planes.[44] During 1971-1972, the Soviet Union continued its deepening involvement in the Middle East. It supplied increasingly sophisticated weapons to the Arabs, including FROG surface-to-surface tactical missiles, the ZSU 23-24 radar-controlled anti-aircraft gun, and the SAM-6 mobile system. Additionally the Soviet Union deployed the MIG-25 Foxbat aircraft (with Soviet pilots) for the first time outside of the Soviet Union.

Despite the increased Soviet arms deliveries and involvement, Sadat was not satisfied; he repeatedly requested certain offensive weapons (SCUDS and MIG-23s), which he felt were necessary prerequisites for launching an attack on Israel. Having declared 1971 as the "year of decision" Sadat delayed the attack on Israel at Soviet urging through 1971 and half of 1972 for four basic reasons: he needed to obtain the backing of the Saudis, an objective he achieved in large part by expelling the Soviets from Egypt in July 1972; the Egyptian Army needed to devise a means of crossing the canal; the army needed to be strengthened; and the Soviet Union put some pressure on Sadat to delay the attack.[45] Soviet involvement in the Middle East from 1967 through July 1972 was characterized by support and restraint; the Russians supplied Egypt with sophisticated forces and even deployed Soviet personnel in combat roles, but they were unwilling to provide Sadat with a blank check for military equipment.

During the year following the expulsion of the Russians from Egypt, Sadat attempted, without success, to find alternative arms suppliers to provide the weapons that he believed Egypt needed prior to attacking Israel. At the same time, the Soviet Union sought to regain its pre-July 1972 position in Egypt and, in order to do so, agreed in mid-1973 to send Egypt twenty to thirty SCUD missiles, which had a range of 150 miles, enough to threaten Israeli cities from Egypt.[46] Sadat apparently felt that these weapons provided Egypt with an effective strategic deterrent; if Israel attacked Egyptian cities, he could retaliate with missiles. With his long-awaited offensive weapons in hand, Sadat made final preparations for the attack.

Soon after the war began, it became apparent that both sides would need large replenishments of ammunition, tanks, artillery, and other military equipment. On October 10 the Soviet resupply effort began with the arrival of twenty-one AN-12 transports to Damascus. Throughout 1973, the Soviet Union had been sending supplies to Egypt and Syria. It is estimated that the Soviet sealift to the Middle East during October alone resulted in deliveries of 63,000 tons of supplies to Arab forces,[47] while the Soviet airlift consisted of 934 round-trip flights and provided between 12,500 and 15,000 tons of equipment.[48]

The United States began replenishing Israel on October 10, with shipments sent from the United States on El Al planes. During the first week of the war, Nixon and Kissinger moved slowly on providing Israel with arms, particularly tanks and airplanes (A-4s and F-4s), hoping that a cease-fire could be arranged; however, on October 13 Sadat rejected the U.S. cease-fire proposal, and Nixon ordered the full-scale airlift to Israel. By the end of the war, El Al aircraft had carried between 5,500 and 11,000 tons of equipment,[49] and U.S. transports had carried approximately 22,400 tons, for a total of about 28,000 tons.[50] The United States also provided some supplies by ship and used three aircraft carriers as floating airfields for A-4 and F-4 aircraft being flown from the United States to Israel. The quality as well as the quantity of materiel that the United States supplied to Israel was significant; the American shipments included sophisticated electronic countermeasures equipment and precision-guided munitions.

On October 14 the decisive battle of the war was fought and won by Israel; a major Egyptian offensive toward the Mitla and Giddi passes was stopped. Assured of continuing U.S. supplies, the Israelis were no longer interested in a cease-fire. The next day Israeli forces crossed the canal, and by October 16 the war had clearly turned in Israel's favor. After several more days of fighting and frantic negotiations among the United States, Soviet Union, and their respective Middle Eastern clients, a cease-fire was arranged for October 22.

Just before the cease-fire went into effect, Egyptian forces launched several SCUD missiles against Israeli positions on the West Bank.[51] According to Sadat, "I wanted Israel to learn that such a weapon was indeed in our hands and that we could use it at a later stage of the war."[52] This event was very important since this was the first instance in which Soviet personnel had participated in an offensive activity (rather than defensive actions concerning air defense) and, according to one analyst, "may have marked an important escalation in the degree of direct Soviet military involvement in the Middle East."[53] Causing almost as much alarm, Western intelligence agencies detected neutron emissions, which indicated the possible presence of nuclear weapons, from a Soviet freighter crossing the Bosporus Strait on October 22. Some U.S. and Israeli officials feared that the Soviet Union would supply nuclear warheads for the SCUD missiles previously sent to Egypt; however, after the crisis, neutron emissions were recorded for the same ship returning from the Mediterranean to the Baltic Sea. In the aftermath of the war, Secretary Kissinger testified that there was no confirmed evidence that the Soviet Union had introduced nuclear weapons into Egypt.[54] Possibly the freighter carried warheads for the ship-based weapons of the Soviet Mediterranean Squadron or the Russians were "engaged in a dangerous form of psychological warfare aimed at making the Americans worry about the possibility of nuclear weapons in the area."[55]

The October 22 cease-fire did not hold, and Israel continued to isolate the Egyptian Third Army, which was stranded on the East Bank, and to seal off Suez City. Alarmed by potential Arab losses, the Russians placed all seven of their airborne divisions (approximately 50,000 troops and 100,000 support troops) on high alert. A break in the Soviet airlift led to speculations that the Soviet Union was planning to intervene. And some reports stated that the Soviet Union had made a request to Yugoslavia to overfly its territory and that the USSR had established an airborne command post in southern Russia. Additionally the Soviet Mediterranean Squadron was increased to over ninety ships, including eight troop and tank transports.

On the evening of October 24, Brezhnev sent a letter to Nixon in which he charged Israel with violating the cease-fire and threatened unilateral intervention by Soviet forces. In part the message read, "I will say it straight, that if you find it impossible to act together with us in this matter, we should be faced with the necessity urgently to consider the question of taking appropriate steps unilaterally. Israel cannot be allowed to get away with the violations."[56]

Presumably Brezhnev had threatened to intervene in order to prevent the capture of the 20,000 troops of the Egyptian Third Army and a possible Israeli attack on Cairo.

Within several hours of receiving Brezhnev's message, Kissinger and Schlesinger recommended and Nixon ordered a worldwide alert of U.S. military forces. Although critics contend that the U.S. worldwide alert was unnecessarily provocative, Helmut Sonnenfeldt believed that the alert was "a very mild" one designed to send "a clear signal to the Soviets that they should not send troops into Egypt. There was no expectation of actual fighting between Soviet and American forces."[57] General Brent Scowcroft, formerly the president's assistant for national security affairs, has characterized the alert as "an adjunct to the direct communication" and "a way of putting force" behind U.S. statements; in short, the alert was "an exclamation point, an underlining" to earlier U.S. messages.[58]

The United States and the Soviet Union were not only concerned with the actions of each other; each negotiated with and cajoled its respective allies in the Middle East. American leaders sought to convince Israeli decision makers that the Third Army must be spared. Reportedly Kissinger told Israeli Prime Minister Golda Meir:

The whole world is against you. Europe, Japan, the oil boycott. If you do not give the Egyptians a corridor to the Third Army, the Russians will come and do it with helicopters. What will you do? Will you shoot at them? And what do you think the United States will do? . . . The United States could not allow a one-sided Soviet action. . . . In order to prevent it the United States would have to send its own helicopters loaded with food to the Third Army.[59]

The United States, according to Nixon, gave the Israelis "an offer that they could not refuse."[60] They agreed to allow supplies to be sent to the Third Army, and the crisis ended.

U.S. and Soviet force deployments were quantitatively and qualitatively different in the Cuban missile crisis and the October War. In the Cuban crisis, the Soviet Union deployed strategic nuclear weapons to a foreign country; this was not done during the October War. Although U.S. force deployments in both cases were designed to send signals to the Soviet Union, U.S. maneuvers in the earlier crisis were taken in anticipation of a direct Soviet-American military engagement.

### U.S. AND SOVIET NAVAL INTERACTION

In both the Cuban missile crisis and the October War, the United States and the Soviet Union primarily employed naval forces in support of their respective foreign policy objectives. Virtually all of the military equipment delivered to Cuba during 1962 had been sent by sea, including forty-two IL-28 light bombers. In 1962 the Soviet navy was relatively weak; it was only five years earlier in 1957 that Soviet policymakers had decided to increase their naval forces significantly. The sea lines of communication between Cuba and the Soviet Union were long and vulnerable, and the Soviet Union was at a great geographic disadvantage relative to the United States in the Caribbean. As Theodore Sorensen noted, "A naval engagement in the Caribbean, just off our own shores, was the most advantageous military confrontation the United States could have, if one were necessary. Whatever the balance of strategic and ground forces may have been, the superiority of the American navy was unquestioned."[61] The local, overwhelming superiority of the U.S. Navy was one of the principal factors that made the quarantine of Cuba such an attractive alternative.

The Executive Committee discussed at least six alternatives of what to do about the Soviet deployment of IRBMs and MRBMs to Cuba, and President Kennedy decided to institute a quarantine. The quarantine was in effect a selective blockade of Cuba. President Kennedy chose to call the action a quarantine since a blockade was considered an act of war in international law. To implement the quarantine, the United States had over 150 ships in the Caribbean and southern Atlantic areas, including eight aircraft carriers. Sea-based naval forces were supplemented with sixty-eight aircraft squadrons.

Khrushchev reacted very strongly to the quarantine and informed Kennedy:

The Soviet Government considers that the violation of the freedom to use international waters and international air space is an act of aggression which pushes mankind toward the abyss of a world nuclear missile war. Therefore, the Soviet Government cannot instruct the captains of Soviet vessels bound for Cuba to observe the orders of American naval forces blockading that Island.[62]

On October 13, the day before the quarantine was to go into effect, Soviet submarines began to move into the Caribbean, and President Kennedy ordered the navy to give the highest priority to tracking them.

Although the evidence is fragmentary, it appears that the U.S. Navy effectively located six Soviet submarines and eventually forced at least several of them to surface.[63] The tactics used by U.S. naval units may have included the use of depth charges. One knowledgeable analyst of the crisis has concluded that "it appears likely that the decisive action that convinced Khrushchev to pull back was the navy's actions against Soviet submarines."[64] Not only were American anti-submarine warfare forces active; the navy's amphibious forces were preparing for an invasion of Cuba.[65]

In 1964 the Soviet Union began permanent deployment of Soviet warships to the Mediterranean.[66] By 1967 the Soviets maintained an average of twenty-five combat ships in the Mediterranean, an average that grew to thirty-five in 1968 and sixty-eight by 1972.[67] During the October War, the Soviet Mediterranean Squadron was increased to ninety ships. The U.S. Sixth Fleet at the time of the war consisted of forty to fifty ships, including two aircraft carriers with eighty-five to ninety-five aircraft on each, one helicopter carrier, and a number of escort ships (destroyers and frigates). By the end of the war the fleet had been augmented by a third aircraft carrier task group, a second helicopter carrier, and more escort vessels, for a total of sixty ships. Although it would appear that Soviet forces held significant advantages over U.S. forces (ninety ships for the USSR versus sixty for the U.S.), such a conclusion would be mistaken, for, as Vice-Admiral Daniel Murphy, the commander of the Sixth Fleet at the time of the October War, pointed out, approximately 40 percent of the Soviet fleet consisted of support ships, while only 20 percent of the U.S. fleet was composed of support ships.[68]

Soviet and American naval deployments during the war can be divided into three periods: October 6-12, October 13-24, and

October 25-November 17. Prior to the outbreak of the war, both Soviet and American naval units were in normal deployments; in fact, both of the Sixth Fleet's carriers as well as most of the Soviet Squadron's ships were in port.[69] Within twenty-four hours of the outbreak of war, an American naval task force consisting of the aircraft carrier *Independence* and three destroyers was sent to a holding position southeast of Crete, half-a-day's sailing time from the Suez Canal. Soviet ships followed the *Independence* task force to the area off Crete and at times even intermingled with U.S. warships, but they made no effort to interfere with Sixth Fleet operations.[70]

During the first week of the war, both sides adopted a "wait and see" posture. On October 12, however, Egypt and Syria declared substantial areas off their coasts as "dangerous to foreign shipping," and Soviet naval units moved into the area between Cyprus and the Syrian coast. This was probably the first time since World War II that the Soviet Navy moved combat forces into an active war zone.[71] This force was probably intended to ensure the maintenance of Soviet air and sea lines of communication to Syria. During this period, Soviet amphibious units began to move from the Black Sea into the Mediterranean.

On October 13, the *John F. Kennedy*, an aircraft carrier that had been in port in Scotland, was ordered south to augment the two carriers already in the Mediterranean. The *Franklin D. Roosevelt*, a carrier stationed in the western Mediterranean, moved east of Sicily. From October 15 through October 24, the three U.S. carriers played a major role in the effort to resupply aircraft for Israel by providing navigational assistance and refueling tankers for the aircraft.

During the two-and-a-half weeks following the outbreak of war, Soviet forces were substantially reinforced from the Black Sea, and Secretary of Defense Schlesinger listed the Soviet naval build-up as one of the major causes of concern leading to the U.S. alert on October 25.[72] Following the alert, the *JFK* entered the Mediterranean, and the *FDR* joined the *Independence* southeast of Crete. The helicopter carrier *Iwo Jima*, carrying eighteen hundred marines, entered the Mediterranean within hours of the alert. Soviet naval units responded to the alert by forming tactical task forces and moving into positions covering the three aircraft carriers and amphibious group.[73] After the alert, the Soviet Union substantially reinforced the squadron by sending sixteen more vessels (seven submarines, eight surface combatants, and one auxiliary) into the Mediterranean.[74] American and Soviet naval forces remained on alert until November 17 when the *JFK* left the Mediterranean and fleet operations returned to normal.

What roles did the Soviet and American fleets play in the war, and how can Soviet-American naval interaction best be characterized? Following the war, the commander-in-chief of U.S. naval forces in the Mediterranean, Admiral Worth Bagley, reported that the "Soviets weren't overly aggressive. It looked as though they were taking some care not to cause an incident. On the whole, their overt posture was restrained and considerate."[75] Compared to the actions of the Soviet Squadron in previous Middle Eastern crises, the modus operandi of the squadron during the October War differed in several respects.[76] Overall, however, the United States and the Soviet Union used their fleets for similar purposes: to protect their sea and air lines of communications, to support their respective resupply efforts, and to send diplomatic-political signals to the other side.

When compared to their actions during the Cuban missile crisis, the U.S. and Soviet navies behaved in a restrained manner during the October War. First, neither sought a confrontation; indeed it appears that both navies actively avoided confrontation. Second, neither navy acted in a tactically aggressive manner as U.S. anti-submarine forces had done during the Cuban missile crisis. Third, the Soviet navy made no attempt to interfere with U.S. ships involved with the resupplying of Israel. It is possible that the Incidents at Sea Agreement signed at the 1972 Moscow Summit meeting contributed in part to the restraint demonstrated by the American and Soviet navies during the October War.

## Conclusion

In comparing Soviet and American behavior in the two crises, clearly, both superpowers pursued more restrained policies in 1973 than in 1962. The role of the Soviet Union in precrisis planning was clear in the Cuban missile crisis and ambiguous in the October

War. Both the United States and the USSR deployed substantial military forces into the crisis area in 1962. With the exception of naval forces, neither deployed substantial forces into the Middle East in 1973. In both cases, the superpowers provided their respective allies with sophisticated military equipment; however, in 1962, this equipment included IRBMs and MRBMs, the first and only time that these weapons have been deployed outside the Soviet Union. In the Cuban missile crisis, a direct military confrontation between the naval forces of the two superpowers almost occurred. In the 1973 crisis, both navies were relatively restrained.

There were significant differences in Soviet and American foreign policy behavior in the two cases examined. In the analytical comparison of the two crises, three dimensions of superpower behavior were analyzed: the superpowers' roles in precrisis planning, force deployments, arms deliveries, and naval interaction. The research results of this study are summarized in table 15.

What are the most plausible reasons for these differences in behavior? First, the objectives of Soviet and American decision makers were more limited in the October War than in the Cuban missile crisis. Soviet objectives ranged from deterring an attack on Cuba to gaining a significant increment in strategic power. In order to accomplish their objective—to remove the missiles—American decision makers had to convince the Russians to undo their previous action. As Alexander George, David Hall, and William Simons have pointed out, this type of coercive diplomacy is difficult to achieve.[77]

Second, because of the proximity of Cuba to the United States and the potential political effect of the missiles upon the perceptions of foreign leaders, U.S. leaders were more motivated to achieve their objectives in 1962 than in 1973.

Third, the Cuban missile crisis was a direct American-Soviet confrontation, but the October War began as a conflict between the clients of the two superpowers. Thus, U.S. and Soviet leaders did not consider that their interests were as directly threatened in 1973 as in 1962.

Fourth, the United States was clearly superior to the Soviet Union in 1962 in both conventional and strategic military power. The favorable outcome of the crisis was partially, perhaps even

**Table 15**
**U.S. AND SOVIET BEHAVIOR IN THE CUBAN MISSILE CRISIS AND THE OCTOBER WAR**

|  | Cuban Missile Crisis | | October War | |
|---|---|---|---|---|
|  | *U.S.* | *USSR* | *U.S.* | *USSR* |
| Did the U.S. and/or USSR play an active role in precrisis planning? | Not applicable | Yes | No | Probably not |
| Did the U.S. and/or USSR deploy substantial military forces of their own into the crisis area? | Yes | Yes | No | No |
| Did the U.S. and/or USSR send first-line military equipment to their respective allies? | Not applicable | Yes | Yes | Yes |
| Did U.S. and/or Soviet naval forces aggressively seek out and harass the naval forces of the other superpower? | Yes | Yes | No | No |

most importantly, a result of the relative asymmetry of forces. By the early 1970s the Soviet Union possessed approximately equivalent strategic power to the United States and also possessed formidable conventional forces.

Fifth, while the United States enjoyed a geographic advantage in the Cuban missile crisis, the Soviet Union enjoyed a similar advantage in the 1973 crisis.

Sixth, the Congress and public strongly supported Kennedy's actions, while domestic support for Nixon's handling of the October War was, by comparision, relatively weak. Thus, even if Nixon and Kissinger had wanted to adopt a harder line, this would have been very difficult due to President Nixon's weakened domestic position.

Seventh, while military power was the most salient form of power in 1962, by 1973 economic power and, in particular, petropower, had become extremely important. The OAPEC states played a major role in deterring Western European states and Japan from supporting Israel.

Eighth, the United States and the Soviet Union had more difficulty in controlling their client states and enlisting the support of their non-Middle Eastern allies for their warring clients.

Ninth, the international contexts of the two crises help to explain the differences in Soviet and American behavior in the two cases. Soviet and American leaders had concluded a number of agreements in various areas in the early 1970s, and they no doubt believed that the future of détente would be affected by their behavior during the October War.

Attempting to avoid possible escalation to nuclear war, American and Soviet leaders developed a number of norms and procedures during the acute cold war for crisis management; however, this regime was not comprehensive enough to prevent serious U.S.-Soviet confrontations such as the Berlin crises and Cuban missile crisis.

During the early 1970s, American and Soviet leaders sought to explicate and expand the crisis management and crisis prevention norms and procedures in the Hot-Line Modernization Agreement, the Incidents at Sea Agreement, the Basic Principles, and the Agreement on the Prevention of Nuclear War. These agreements did not, however, prevent the U.S.-Soviet confrontation during the October War. The principles contained in the last two documents were nonoperational and were not adequately specified. Additionally each superpower believed that it must support its respective clients in the Middle East, even at the risk of injuring détente.

Despite the failure of these agreements to prevent the October War crisis, the crisis management norms nevertheless were important in restraining the actions of both sides in several ways. First, both superpowers sought to restrain their Middle Eastern clients by maintaining tight control over arms transfers. Second, Soviet-American naval interaction was restrained, and there were no major confrontations between the two navies during the war. Third, in contrast to previous crises, American and Soviet leaders communicated with one another quickly, effectively, and secretly throughout the October War. In fact, Secretary of State Kissinger

even flew to Moscow at the height of the war in order to consult
with Soviet leaders.

The first and most obvious lesson to be learned from Soviet-
American interaction in the Cuban missile crisis and the October
War is that the ability of Soviet and U.S. leaders to communicate
quickly, directly, and secretly with one another is a valuable asset.
During the Cuban missile crisis, a U.S. reconnaissance plane in-
advertently strayed into Soviet air space. Without a quick, reliable
means of communication, such an incident could have resulted in
disaster. As Khrushchev pointed out at the end of the crisis:

A . . . dangerous case occurred on 28 October, when one of your reconnaissance plans intruded over Soviet borders in the Chukotka Peninsula
area in the north and flew over our territory. The question is, Mr. President: How should we regard this. What is this: A provocation? . . . Is it not
a fact that an intruding American plan could be easily taken for a nuclear
bomber, which might push us to a fateful step?[78]

With the advent of the hot line, ambiguous situations such as this
could be clarified quickly, as the use of the hot line during the June
War demonstrated.

A second lesson concerns the difference between the crisis-
management and the crisis-prevention regimes. Crisis-prevention
norms and procedures appear to be more difficult to operationalize
for a number of reasons. The most basic reason is that the actions
of one's allies may simultaneously advance one's interests, as well
as catalyze a crisis. If the Soviet Union had warned the United
States of the Syrian-Egyptian attack on Israel, it would have
alienated its Arab allies and sacrificed its own potential gains to be
had from such a surprise attack. Even though crisis prevention
norms fail to prevent a confrontation, crisis management rules
nevertheless can help to restrain the behavior of the parties involved
and thereby contribute to a resolution of the crisis. This appeared
to be the case in the October War.

A third lesson concerns the need to operationalize crisis-management and crisis-prevention understandings. Both the Basic Principles and the Agreement on the Prevention of Nuclear War are
stated in general terms. What is needed is a set of norms applicable

to a number of diverse situations in which crises could develop. Such rules could, for example, be developed for southern Africa, the Middle East, Korea, or Yugoslavia.[79] Such norms would be context-specific rather than general and would account for the relative interests of the United States and the Soviet Union in various areas of the world.

As part of the process of operationalizing the crisis-prevention and crisis-management regimes, American and Soviet leaders should formally review the strong and weak points of existing agreements in order to remove existing ambiguities. Apparently this was not done following the October War, so the ambiguities of the Basic Principles and the Agreement on the Prevention of Nuclear War remain. A possible precedent of an organizational forum for such discussion is the Standing Consultative Commission, which was established by the ABM Treaty.

Finally one should not underestimate the difficulty of establishing norms and procedures for preventing and managing superpower crises since such confrontations involve the important interests of both powers. Soviet and American policymakers have been and will continue to be confronted with a dilemma: they may seek short-run benefits in third areas and risk a superpower crisis, or they may forestall a crisis and perhaps sacrifice some short-run, local interests.

## Notes

1. *Le Monde*, October 25, 1973.
2. For studies that have utilized the Cuban missile crisis in comparative case studies, see Alexander L. George, David Hall, and William Simons, *The Limits of Coercive Diplomacy: Laos, Cuba, Vietnam* (Boston: Little, Brown, 1971); Alexander L. George and Richard Smoke, *Deterrence in American Foreign Policy: Theory and Practice* (New York: Columbia University Press, 1974); Ole R. Holsti, *Crisis, Escalation, War* (Montreal: McGill-Queens University Press, 1972); Glenn D. Paige, "Comparative Case Analysis of Crisis Decisions: Korea and Cuba," in Charles F. Hermann, ed., *International Crises: Insights from Behavioral Research* (New York: Free Press, 1972); Glenn H. Snyder and Paul Diesing, *Conflict among Nations: Bargaining, Decision-Making, and System Structure in International Crises* (Princeton: Princeton University Press, 1977); Roberta Wohlstetter, "Cuba and Pearl Harbor," *Foreign Affairs* 43 (July 1965):

691-707; Oran Young, *The Politics of Force: Bargaining During International Crises* (Princeton: Princeton University Press, 1968).

3. For the most comprehensive discussion of Cuban-Soviet relations in 1962-1963, see Herbert S. Dinerstein, *The Making of a Missile Crisis: October 1962* (Baltimore: Johns Hopkins University Press, 1976).

4. For the most comprehensive case studies of the Cuban missile crisis, see Elie Abel, *The Missile Crisis* (Philadelphia: J. B. Lippincott, 1966), and Graham T. Allison, *Essence of Decision: Explaining the Cuban Missile Crisis* (Boston: Little, Brown, 1971).

5. Roger Hilsman, *To Move a Nation* (Garden City, N.Y.: Doubleday, 1967), p. 172.

6. The declassified intelligence reports to the ExCom from the Central Intelligence Agency are contained in Dan Caldwell, *Missiles in Cuba: A Decision Making Game* (New York: Learning Resources in International Studies, 1979), pp. 4-20.

7. The texts of the messages exchanged by President Kennedy and Chairman Khrushchev are reprinted in *Department of State Bulletin* (November 19, 1973): 635-55.

8. Robert F. Kennedy, *Thirteen Days* (New York: Signet Books, 1969), pp. 108-9.

9. For a useful overview of the war, see Insight Team of the London Sunday Times, *The Yom Kippur War* (Garden City, N.Y.: Doubleday, 1974).

10. Institute for Strategic Studies, *The Communist Bloc and the Western Alliance: The Military Balance, 1962-63* (London: Institute for Strategic Studies, 1963).

11. The medium-range ballistic missiles had a range of 1100 nautical miles, and the intermediate-range ballistic missiles had a range of 2200 nautical miles. Theodore Sorensen, *Kennedy* (New York: Harper and Row, 1965), pp. 761, 766.

12. Most analysts of the Cuban missile crisis have concluded that, in deploying missiles to Cuba, the Soviet Union sought to achieve a "quick fix" solution to its position of nuclear inferiority. See Abel, *Missile Crisis*, p. 28; Hilsman, *To Move a Nation*, p. 201; Jerome H. Kahan and Anne K. Long, "The Cuban Missile Crisis: A Study of Its Strategic Context," *Political Science Quarterly* 87 (December 1972): 568; and Arnold Horelick, "The Cuban Missile Crisis: An Analysis of Soviet Calculations and Behavior," *World Politics* 16 (April 1964).

13. Quoted by Abel, *Missile Crisis*, p. 51.

14. This paragraph is based on information from Alvin Z. Rubinstein,

*Red Star on the Nile: The Soviet-Egyptian Influence Relationship since the June War* (Princeton: Princeton University Press, 1977), pp. 3-8.

15. Richard M. Nixon, *U.S. Foreign Policy for the 1970's: Building for Peace* (Washington, D.C.: Government Printing Office, 1971), p. 129; *U.S. Foreign Policy for the 1970's: Shaping a Durable Peace* (Washington, D.C.: Government Printing Office, 1973), p. 140.

16. Nixon, *U.S. Foreign Policy (1973)*, p. 139.

17. Sorensen, *Kennedy*, p. 670.

18. Ibid., p. 688.

19. Sorensen notes that the Republican congressmen (including Keating) called for complete support of the president the day after his quarantine speech. Telegrams received at the White House supported the president's move by a ratio of ten to one. Ibid., p. 797.

20. For general treatments of this subject, see Henry A. Kissinger, "Domestic Structure and Foreign Policy," in *American Foreign Policy* (New York: W. W. Norton, 1969), and James N. Rosenau, ed., *Domestic Sources of Foreign Policy* (New York: Free Press, 1967). For studies of the relationship between foreign and domestic policies in the Soviet Union, see Wolfgang Leonhard, "The Domestic Politics of the New Soviet Foreign Policy," *Foreign Affairs* (October 1973), and Morton Schwartz, *The Foreign Policy of the U.S.S.R.: Domestic Factors* (Encino, Calif.: Dickenson Publishing Company, 1974).

21. Richard Nixon, *RN: The Memoirs of Richard Nixon* (New York: Grosset and Dunlap, 1978), p. 922.

22. Quoted by Marvin Kalb and Bernard Kalb, *Kissinger* (Boston: Little, Brown, 1974), pp. 494-95.

23. Testimony by Herbert Dinerstein in U.S. Congress, House of Representatives, Committee on Foreign Affairs, *Hearings on United States-Europe Relations and the 1973 Middle East War*, Hearings, 93d Cong., 1st and 2d sess., 1974; and George Liska, *Beyond Kissinger: Ways of Conservative Statecraft* (Baltimore: Johns Hopkins University Press, 1974), p. 70.

24. Ray S. Cline, "Policy Without Intelligence," *Foreign Policy* 17 (Winter 1974-1975), and Admiral Elmo R. Zumwalt, Jr., *On Watch: A Memoir* (New York: Quadrangle/New York Times Book Co., 1976), p. 448.

25. These five possible objectives are presented and discussed by Allison, *Essence of Decision*, pp. 43-56.

26. Kennedy, *Thirteen Days*, pp. 108-9.

27. Sorensen, *Kennedy*, p. 809.

28. Author's interviews with senior members of the National Security Council.

29. William B. Quandt, *Decade of Decisions: American Policy toward the Arab-Israeli Conflict, 1967-1976* (Berkeley: University of California Press, 1977), p. 197.

30. Rubinstein, *Red Star on the Nile*, p. 271.

31. Anwar el-Sadat, *In Search of Identity: An Autobiography* (New York: Harper and Row, 1977), p. 246.

32. Ibid.; Mohamed Heikal, *The Road to Ramadan* (New York: Quadrangle/The New York Times Book Co., 1975).

33. See, for instance, Foy D. Kohler, Leon Gouré, and Mose L. Harvey, *The Soviet Union and the October 1973 Middle East War: The Implications for Detente* (Washington, D.C.: Center for Advanced International Studies, University of Miami, 1974); and Harvey Sicherman, *The Yom Kippur War: End of Illusion?* Foreign Policy Papers, vol. 1, no. 4 (Beverly Hills, Calif.: Sage, 1976).

34. William E. Griffith, "The Fourth Middle East War, the Energy Crisis and U.S. Policy," *Orbis* 17 (Winter 1974): 1166, and William B. Quandt, *Soviet Policy in the October 1973 War*, Rand Report R-1864-ISA (Santa Monica, Calif.: Rand Corporation, May 1976).

35. Quoted in Lawrence L. Whetton, *The Arab-Israeli Dispute: Great Power Behavior*, Adelphi Paper 128 (London: International Institute for Strategic Studies, Winter 1976-1977), p. 27.

36. "Excerpts of Frost Interview with Nixon," *New York Times*, May 1, 1977.

37. Nixon, *Memoirs*, p. 885.

38. Ibid.

39. Comments by Helmut Sonnenfeldt at a seminar sponsored by the Woodrow Wilson International Center for Scholars, Washington, D.C., August 30, 1977, transcript, p. 4.

40. U.S. Congress, House, Committee on Appropriations, Subcommittee on Department of Defense Appropriations, *Hearings*, 88th Cong., 1st sess., 1963, pp. 1-21.

41. Sorensen, *Kennedy*, p. 770.

42. Comment by J. C. Hurewitz in *Hearings on United States-Europe Relations and the 1973 Middle East War*, pp. 24-25.

43. Jon D. Glassman, *Arms for the Arabs: The Soviet Union and War in the Middle East* (Baltimore: Johns Hopkins University Press, 1975), pp. 24-33.

44. Abraham S. Becker, *The Superpowers in the Arab-Israeli Conflict,*

*1970-1973*, Paper P-5167 (Santa Monica, Calif.: Rand Corporation, December 1973), pp. 1-4.

45. Interview with Dr. William Quandt, Washington, D.C., August 29, 1977.

46. Kalb and Kalb, *Kissinger*, p. 454, and *Aviation Week and Space Technology* (November 4, 1973): 12 claim that SCUDs were sent to Egypt in September. Israeli sources, however, date the shipments from June; see Quandt, *Soviet Policy*.

47. Quandt, *Soviet Policy*, p. 23.

48. Ibid., p. 25, reported 12,500 tons, while the International Institute for Strategic Studies reported 15,000 tons; *Strategic Survey 1973* (London International Institute for Strategic Studies, 1974), p. 27.

49. The International Institute for Strategic Studies (*Strategic Survey 1973)* reported that El Al aircraft carried 5500 tons of equipment, while *Aviation Week and Space Technology*, December 10, 1973, reported a figure of 11,000 tons.

50. International Institute for Strategic Studies, *Strategic Survey, 1973*, p. 27.

51. *New York Times*, December 29, 1973.

52. Sadat, *In Search of Identity*, p. 265.

53. Glassman, *Arms for the Arabs*, p. 138.

54. John W. Finney, "Officials Suspect Russians Sent Atom Arms to Egypt," *New York Times*, November 22, 1973, p. 1; Michael Getler, "A-Arms Believed in Egypt: SCUD Missiles Seen under Soviet Control," *Washington Post*, November 21, 1973.

55. William Quandt discusses both of these hypotheses; *Soviet Policy*, p. 31, and *Decade of Decisions*, p. 198.

56. Quoted by Kalb and Kalb, *Kissinger*, p. 490.

57. Comments by Helmut Sonnenfeldt at a seminar sponsored by the Woodrow Wilson International Center for Scholars, Washington, D.C., August 30, 1977, transcript, p. 4.

58. Comments by General Brent Scowcroft, at a seminar sponsored by the Woodrow Wilson International Center for Scholars, Washington, D.C., August 30, 1977, transcript, p. 5.

59. Quoted by Matti Golan, *The Secret Conversations of Henry Kissinger: Step-by-Step Diplomacy in the Middle East* (New York: Bantam, 1976), p. 108.

60. "Excerpts of Frost Interview with Nixon," *New York Times*, May 13, 1977.

61. Sorensen, *Kennedy*, p. 776.

62. Chairman Khrushchev to President Kennedy, October 24, 1962 (official translation), *Department of State Bulletin* (November 19, 1973): 822.

63. Kennedy, *Thirteen Days*, p. 61. References to the anti-submarine warfare activities of the U.S. Navy are found in Abel, *Missile Crisis*, p. 155; Hilsman, *To Move a Nation*, p. 214; and Arthur Schlesinger, *A Thousand Days* (Boston: Houghton Mifflin, 1965), p. 822.

64. Alexander L. George, "The Cuban Missile Crisis," in George, Hall, and Simons, *Limits of Coercive Diplomacy*, p. 112.

65. For a *post hoc* official review of U.S. military actions during the Cuban missile crisis, see Dan Caldwell, ed., "Department of Defense Operations During the Cuban Crisis: A Report by Adam Yarmolinsky, 13 February 1963," *Naval War College Review* 32 (July-August 1979): 83-99.

66. For a brief but informative review of the growth of the Soviet navy, see Barry M. Blechman, *The Changing Soviet Navy* (Washington, D.C.: Brookings Institution, 1973).

67. Admiral Isaac C. Kidd, Jr., "View from the Bridge of the Sixth Fleet Flagship," *U.S. Naval Institute Proceedings* 98 (February 1972).

68. *New York Times*, November 9, 1973.

69. For the most comprehensive account of U.S. and Soviet naval operations during the war, see Robert G. Weinland, *Superpower Naval Diplomacy in the October 1973 Arab-Israeli War*, Professional Paper 221 (Arlington, Va.: Center for Naval Analyses, 1978).

70. *New York Times*, October 8, 1973.

71. Weinland, *Superpower Naval Diplomacy*, p. 51.

72. Press conference, Secretary of Defense James Schlesinger, in *Washington Post*, October 27, 1973.

73. Report by Vice-Admiral Daniel Murphy, quoted in Zumwalt, *On Watch*, p. 447.

74. Weinland, *Superpower Naval Diplomacy*, p. 45.

75. "Interview with Admiral Worth Bagley," *U.S. News and World Report*, December 24, 1973, pp. 27-28.

76. Weinland, *Superpower Naval Diplomacy*, pp. 59-61.

77. George, Hall, and Simons, *Limits of Coercive Diplomacy*, pp. 24-25.

78. Chairman Khruschev to President Kennedy October 28, 1962, reprinted in *Department of State Bulletin* 69 (November 19, 1973): 651.

79. Alexander L. George, "Towards a Soviet-American Crisis Prevention Regime: History and Prospects" (unpublished paper, February 1980).

# PART III

# CONCLUSION

# CHAPTER 8

# AMERICAN-SOVIET RELATIONS AND THE NIXON-KISSINGER GRAND DESIGN AND GRAND STRATEGY

This study began as an examination of U.S.-Soviet détente, defined in the classical diplomatic lexicon as the lessening of tensions between two or more states. It is clear, however, that the Nixon-Ford-Kissinger conception of détente went well beyond the classical definition and referred instead to a complex process of regime and system development. In part I, the norms to manage interactions in the economic, crisis management, and strategic-military issue areas were described. The comparative studies contained in part II illustrate how the norms of the regimes under investigation were established and observed or violated in particular cases of U.S.-Soviet interaction. This concluding chapter examines the differences in American and Soviet foreign policy behavior across the cases according to issue areas, presents reasons for these differences, assesses the degree to which Nixon, Ford, and Kissinger were able to cope with and encourage the development of interdependence between the United States and the Soviet Union, and analyzes the reasons for the collapse of the Nixon-Ford-Kissinger détente policies.

## Issue Area Variation within Foreign Policy

World politics can be compared to the structure and operation of a casino.[1] On the ground floor are hundreds of players involved in a great variety of different games (slot machines, black jack, roulette, bingo), which are analogous to different issue areas in world politics. Many players possess one type of currency (such as quarters and half-dollars) and can play only a few games. Those who have greater resources can play any game that they wish and can afford. As one leaves the buzzing confusion of the ground floor of the casino and enters the second floor, the stakes increase and the number of players decreases. On the top floor of the casino, all players are required to possess substantial financial holdings, and all bets are a minimum of a thousand dollars. Given these stakes, the number of players is very limited. One can easily imagine a poker game in which the stakes become too high for all of the players but two—the house and a very wealthy player, perhaps the owner of another casino.

The casino is analogous to the international system, the games are analogous to issue areas, and the rules of the different games are similar to international regimes. All of the players have the resources to play at least a few games, the slot machines. Some players have enough money to purchase chips and can play a greater number of games. Some games, however, have very high stakes, and there are few players. Soviet-American strategic nuclear relations are analogous to the two-player, high-stake game; only the United States and the Soviet Union have the capability to kill hundreds of millions of people. The strategic military game is not the only game that the United States and the USSR play; in fact, because of their substantial resources and interests, they play in almost all of the games or issue areas in the international system.

A number of political scientists have employed the issue area approach in their analyses of disparate political phenomena. Robert Dahl found in his examination of three types of issues (urban redevelopment, education, and nominations) in New Haven, Connecticut, that the "overlap among leaders and subleaders" on these issues involved only 3 percent of his sample.[2] In effect, these findings indicated that, rather than one political system in New Haven, there were at least three, corresponding to the three issue areas he examined. Theodore Lowi has identified three "arenas of power" (analogous to issue areas) evident in domestic politics: distribution, regulation, and redistribution.[3] Although Lowi excluded foreign policy from his analytical framework, he noted that it constituted a fourth issue area.

James Rosenau and William Zimmerman have focused on the differences in policy making in the domestic and foreign policy issue areas.[4] Although this work is suggestive, the two categories—domestic and foreign—are too broad to be of much analytical value. In addition, the distinction between these two categories is increasingly breaking down. In their analysis of international inter-dependence, Robert Keohane and Joseph Nye have examined the oceans and monetary issue areas in U.S.-Canadian and U.S.-Australian relations.[5] What is needed, and is all too rare in the present international relations literature, is an analysis of how different political systems vary from one foreign policy issue to another, for as Rosenau has suggested, "the functioning of the U.S.-U.S.S.R. international system in the Berlin issue-area bears little resemblance to the processes through which it allocates values and mobilizes support for the attainment of its goals in the dis-armament or wheat production areas."[6]

The issue area concept has been valuable in this study. Rather than analyzing domestic and foreign policy issue areas, I have focused on three issue areas within foreign policy and found that American and Soviet foreign policy differed across issue areas, as well as across time. Therefore it is somewhat misleading to write of Soviet cold war policy since Soviet policies during the cold war differed by issue area. The analysis contained in this study provides a more differentiated and discriminating view of U.S.-Soviet relations.

Issue areas do not exist autonomously; rather they are related in two ways. The first type of linkage, which I call natural linkage, occurs between or among issue areas that are related because they concern similar phenomena (such as the political-military and strategic-military issue areas). The second type of linkage, policy linkage, is a product of policymakers' attempts to relate two or more issue areas that may or may not be inherently related. Nixon, Ford, and Kissinger often linked SALT with other issues such as Berlin and U.S.-Soviet trade negotiations. The opponents of détente also employed policy linkage as illustrated by the Jackson-Vanik Amendment. Although there is some form of common currency within a particular issue area, there are neither common currencies nor recognized exchange rates between or among issue areas. This is the major reason that policy linkage of unrelated issue areas is more difficult to achieve successfully than policy linkage within the same or closely related issue areas.

Natural linkage is a physical fact of international interdependence, and policy linkage is the result of decision makers' actions. Leaders may use policy linkage in several different ways. First, it may be used to deter an action of another state's leaders. Second, it may be employed to coerce an opponent to stop short of a goal or to persuade an opponent to undo a particular action.[7] When Nixon ordered the U.S. SALT delegation to stall the SALT negotiations in December 1971, he was attempting to coerce Soviet leaders to restrain their Indian allies in the Indo-Pakistani war.[8] Finally, it may be used to facilitate negotiations in different issue areas; according to this usage, decision makers offer positive inducements in one issue area for concessions in another. Nixon and Kissinger apparently believed that agreements in the scientific, technological, and cultural issue areas would facilitate agreement in what they viewed as the more important areas of arms control and economics.

What were the differences in American and Soviet foreign policy behavior in the crisis management, arms control, and economic issue areas? The most obvious difference in behavior in the three matched pairs of cases examined concerns the outcome of negotiations and/or interactions in the three issue areas analyzed. Broadly viewed, American and Soviet decision makers developed the crisis management regime during the acute cold war, the arms control regime during the limited détente period, and the economic regime during the détente era. Of course, each of these regimes had historical antecedents in previous periods, but nevertheless, the evidence of the sequential development of these regimes is striking. Why did these three regimes develop during different periods?

Soon after the end of World War II, American and Soviet decision makers recognized the dangers inherent in a direct U.S.-Soviet military confrontation and began to develop implicit rules and procedures for the management of superpower crises. The crisis management regime evolved throughout the acute cold war, and it was given its most serious test in the Cuban missile crisis, which revealed that, despite the existence of the regime, a U.S.-Soviet confrontation could escalate to general war. In essence, the Cuban missile crisis accentuated Soviet and U.S. decision makers' dissatisfaction with the acute cold war and raised their motivation to develop new system-wide and regime rules to preserve the stability of the international system.

Nuclear war, as Kennedy and Khrushchev discovered, could result from misperception or miscalculation. In order to provide a means of communicating with one another rapidly and secretly, U.S. and Soviet leaders negotiated the Hot Line Agreement in early 1963. The hot line could be used not only to communicate during crises but also to clarify ambiguous or threatening situations prior to the development of a crisis. In this sense the agreement represented an extension of the crisis management regime that included the physical capability for crisis prevention.

The crisis management and strategic-military issue areas were naturally linked; if a Soviet-American crisis was not properly controlled, it could escalate into a Soviet-U.S. nuclear exchange. Because of this natural linkage, some of the procedures and rules in the crisis management regime were similar to or even synonymous with the norms developed to manage and control nuclear weapons in the nuclear deterrence and arms control regimes. American involvement in Vietnam and leadership changes in the Soviet Union and the United States in 1963-1964 forestalled the full development of the arms control regime until the late 1960s. Worsening relations with China, the Soviet achievement of parity, and the rising costs of defense in both the United States and the Soviet Union led American and Soviet leaders to agree to open negotiations regarding the limitation of strategic weapons in 1968, but the Soviet intervention in Czechoslovakia caused U.S. leaders to postpone the talks.

The political-military (including crisis management) and strategic-military issues were naturally linked during the acute cold war and limited détente periods. Whereas outstanding political-military issues, particularly concerning Germany, precluded agreement on any strategic-military issues at the UN Disarmament Subcommittee negotiations from 1955 through 1957, this was not the case in the early 1970s. There was still a natural linkage between the two issue areas, but disagreements in the political-military arena no longer blocked any agreement in the strategic-military issue area. For instance, in May 1972, as U.S. planes bombed Hanoi and completed the mining of Haiphong, the Russians greeted Nixon in Moscow for the final negotiations and signing of the SALT I agreements. Thus it seems that American and Soviet decision makers viewed the strategic-military issue as so important that they decoupled it from other issues.

Khrushchev sought to develop an economic regime with the United States in the 1958-1961 period, but Eisenhower was unwilling to loosen cold war trade restrictions and to expand economic relations with the Soviet Union. The principal reason for Eisenhower's action was his belief (shared by most other policymakers during the acute cold war) that the United States should seek to isolate the Soviet Union in all issue areas and thereby weaken it. The U.S. cold war policy was, in essence, a form of policy linkage designed to hurt the Soviet Union rather than to achieve some specific policy objective. Due in large part to the undifferentiated nature of the U.S. cold war economic policy goal and to the availability of alternative suppliers in Western Europe and Japan, U.S. policy in this issue area was ineffective. It did, however, prevent the development of a Soviet-American regime, perhaps to the economic detriment in comparative advantage terms of both the United States and the Soviet Union.

The 1963-1964 grain trade agreement between the Soviet Union and U.S. grain-exporting companies established a precedent for significant economic intercourse between the two superpowers; however, a number of significant obstacles blocked the further expansion of trade. In the early 1970s Soviet leaders were very interested in increasing their imports of advanced Western technology, and after the disastrous harvest of 1972 they were also interested in importing U.S. grain. Nixon and Kissinger were motivated to increase American-Soviet trade as part of their grand design and grand strategy; by expanding their trade, the two countries would become economically tied to one another over time. Thus, for their own reasons, Soviet and American leaders sought to create and develop an economic regime.

The Trade Agreement resolved the major obstacles that had

blocked the growth of U.S.-Soviet trade during the acute cold war and limited détente periods. Although the Trade Agreement was signed, it was not implemented, primarily because of the coercive policy linkage of the Jackson-Vanik Amendment. While the Soviets expanded U.S.-Soviet trade, they were not willing to grant the concessions called for in order to gain MFN status. Thus, while there were no common currencies or exchange rates for different issue areas, decision makers nevertheless subjectively determined the relative value of achieving certain objectives in one issue area at the cost of concessions in another. For domestic political reasons peculiar to each country, the United States and the Soviet Union were not willing to pay the cost to implement the Trade Agreement.

## The Reasons for Different Regime Outcomes

There are several major reasons why U.S. and Soviet leaders were able to establish regimes in the crisis management and arms control issue areas and why they failed to implement an economic regime. Developments in the international system contributed to the creation of the two successfully implemented regimes.

The international system is influenced by three major variables: the number of actors in the system, the distribution of power among the major actors, and the milieu and regime objectives of the principal actors. At the end of World War II, the two most powerful states were the United States and the Soviet Union, both of which implicitly agreed on a number of rules and procedures in order to avoid and to lessen the probability of escalation in direct superpower confrontations. When this regime proved insufficient to prevent the development of the 1962 Cuban crisis, American and Soviet leaders expanded the crisis management regime and strengthened the arms control regime. Two developments in the international system—the Soviet achievement of parity and the worsening of the Sino-Soviet split—contributed to the explication and expansion of the arms control regime during the détente period.

International systemic variables are not the only constraints on the choices of statesmen; domestic political variables also limit the choice of decision makers. There is, of course, a great deal of variation longitudinally and cross-nationally concerning the degree to which domestic factors influence decision making, but there is little doubt that domestic factors exert some influence upon foreign policymaking in all states.

Domestic factors undoubtedly play much less of a role in the Soviet Union than in the United States; however, particularly since the death of Stalin, domestic factors have increasingly influenced the conduct of Soviet foreign policy. Khrushchev's desire to increase trade with the West during the late 1950s was motivated largely by Soviet domestic factors, specifically, Khrushchev's desire to increase the Soviet standard of living. Similarly it appears that the Brezhnev-Kosygin foreign policy of increased contact with the West was motivated at least partially by the desire to increase the Soviet standard of living and to modernize Soviet industry.

Whereas domestic political variables did not appreciably influence the development of the crisis management or arms control regimes (with the possible exception of the Limited Test Ban Treaty), they played a major role in blocking the development and implementation of an economic regime.[9] One of the reasons for greater public and congressional involvement in the development of the economic regime is the perception of U.S. domestic political actors that economic affairs have a more direct and immediate effect on their interests than does crisis management or arms control. As Rosenau has pointed out, "The more an issue encompasses a society's resources and relationships, the more will it be drawn into the society's domestic political system and the less it will be processed through the society's foreign political system."[10] Not only did domestic political actors within the United States perceive that the creation of a Soviet-American economic regime would affect their interests; they also had the capabilities to influence policy in the Congress, which by law must approve all commerce bills. It appears that issue areas that directly affect the interests of the attentive public and organized interest groups are most susceptible to politicization; however, even those that are not perceived as directly affecting particular public or private interests may be politicized, as demonstrated by Senator Jackson's politicization of SALT after the ABM Treaty and Interim Agreement were signed.

Decision-making variables can influence the course and outcome of U.S.-Soviet negotiations and/or interactions in different issue areas. For instance, as Graham Allison has persuasively shown, the outcomes of various decisions made during the Cuban missile crisis can be explained through the examination of intragovernmental bargaining among important decision makers and organizational participants.[11] In the case studies examined here, perhaps the most striking instance of decision-making factors' influencing the outcome of negotiations was Harold Stassen's unauthorized circulation of an informal paper at the UN Disarmament Subcommittee talks. The U.S. withdrawal of this paper angered the Soviet Union and contributed to the demise of the negotiations.

Are particular types of variables (international system, domestic, or decision making) of greater ability in explaining the outcomes of interaction in different issue areas? Although it is obvious that the three types of variables discussed in this book somehow influence interactions in all three of the issue areas analyzed, it is nevertheless possible on the basis of the case materials to hypothesize the relative importance of different variables in analyzing outcomes— in the crisis management, arms control, and economic issue areas. Table 16 summarizes these relationships.

The number of actors and the distribution of power among them appears to play an important role in decision makers' willingness to participate in arms control negotiations. Domestic political actors perceive of their interests as most affected by negotiations and changes in the economic issue area. During crises, decision makers have the greatest amount of flexibility in bargaining, and, therefore, decision-making variables (both individual and organizational) seem to be most relevant for the analysis of the crisis management issue area.

## The Impact of the Nixon-Kissinger Grand Design and Grand Strategy

While Nixon and Kissinger were in office, they sought to construct "a new structure of peace." Their grand design consisted of three essential components: the acceptance of a tripolar configuration of power in the military-security issue area and a multipolar international economic system, the development of a moderate international system supported by the United States, the Soviet

**Table 16**

**HYPOTHESIZED RELATIONSHIPS BETWEEN TYPES OF EXPLANATORY VARIABLES AND ISSUE AREAS**

| | Variables | | |
|---|---|---|---|
| | *International System* | *Domestic* | *Decision Making* |
| Arms Control | ✕ | | |
| Economic | | ✕ | |
| Crisis Management | | | ✕ |

Union, and China, and the halting of the spread of communism within the Western sphere of influence while simultaneously avoiding a direct military confrontation with the Soviet Union. Nixon and Kissinger believed that these objectives could be achieved through the implementation of a grand strategy, which included such measures as the acceptance of strategic nuclear parity, the maintenance of firm alliance commitments, the development of regimes in important issue areas, and the maintenance of U.S. foreign policy commitments with reduced public and congressional support (for a summary of the elements of the Nixon-Kissinger grand design and grand strategy, see table 17).

The Nixon-Ford-Kissinger grand design and grand strategy contrasted markedly with that of the acute cold war period. Alexander George has characterized the elements of the U.S. cold war grand design and grand strategy and shows that cold war policy was simpler and less complex than that of Nixon, Ford, and Kissinger

## Table 17
### U.S. DÉTENTE POLICY

**Grand Design**

Accept the emergence of a tripolar configuration of power in the security issue area and a multipolar international economic system

Encourage the development of a moderate international system supported by the U.S., USSR, and the PRC

Stop the spread of communism to areas of the world in the traditional Western sphere of influence but avoid direct military confrontation with the USSR

**Grand Strategy**

Accept Soviet achievement of nuclear parity; strive for the limitation of strategic arms (SALT)

Contain the spread of communism through deterrence of military aggression, the use of positive incentives, mixed strategies employing positive and negative sanctions, and covert operations

Maintain firm collective security arrangements with the NATO alliance and Japan; other alliance commitments should be more flexible; all allies should pay a greater proportion of the cost of defense as well as providing manpower (Nixon Doctrine)

Deal with tension between grand design objectives of containing communism to traditionally Western areas and avoiding direct military confrontation with the USSR through communication and consultation with the USSR; threaten or use U.S. force only if necessary

Employ careful, presidentially controlled crisis management of confrontations and limited wars to prevent escalation; communicate and consult with other relevant states in crisis situations (Basic Principles and Agreement on the Prevention of Nuclear War)

Recognize the boundaries of post-World War II European states and the Soviet sphere of influence in Eastern Europe while attempting to encourage freer interchange between Eastern and Western Europe (Helsinki Agreement)

Encourage ties between the United States and the Soviet Union through the conclusion of a number of cooperative projects in the economic, cultural, scientific, and technological areas

Develop regimes (agreed rules, procedures, and institutions) in important issue areas

Attempt to mesh the various regimes into an overall grand strategy; use asymmetrical advantage in one regime to influence other issue areas

Maintain U.S. foreign policy commitments with reduced public and congressional support

(see table 18). Stanley Hoffmann, Richard Falk, and Robert Osgood have argued that the Nixon-Kissinger foreign policy did not
differ significantly from that followed by the United States during
the cold war;[12] however, tables 17 and 18 point out important
differences. For instance, the cold war system was bipolar, while
the détente system was composed of an actual bipolar security
system, an incipient tripolar security system, and a multipolar
economic system. While the United States maintained strategic
nuclear superiority over the Soviet Union for most of the cold war,
the Soviet Union achieved parity by the late 1960s. In general,
U.S. policy during the cold war was defensive and rigid, whereas
the Nixon-Kissinger grand design and grand strategy were more
positive and called for greater flexibility and maneuverability.

## The Demise of Détente

By early 1976, a number of politicians and observers were critical
of the Nixon-Ford-Kissinger détente policies. In reaction, in March
1976 President Ford ordered members of his administration to
drop the use of the word "détente" and to replace it with the more
awkward phrase "peace through strength." This action contrasted
markedly with the 1972 presidential campaign in which Nixon
pointed to détente as one of the most significant accomplishments
of his first term in office.

There were systemic, domestic, and international reasons for the
transmogrification of détente. A number of events in the international system occurred that called into question the premises
upon which Nixon and Kissinger had based their grand design and
grand strategy for U.S. foreign policy. First, the 1972 sale of wheat
to the Soviet Union, which initially appeared to be a convenient
way for the U.S. government to dispose of surplus grain, turned
into a fiasco in which the U.S. government lost money, the Soviets
made money, and grain prices within the United States increased
dramatically. Second, the October War raised questions concerning
Soviet complicity in Arab planning for the war and Soviet compliance of the rules and procedures of the crisis management and
crisis prevention regime. Third, despite their support of the war for
over six years, Nixon's, Ford's, and Kissinger's policies in South-

**Table 18**

### U.S. COLD WAR POLICY

---

**Grand Design**

Accept (and expedite to some extent) the emergence of a bipolar structuring of the international system into two opposing hostile camps; maintain the stability and unity of the "free world" bloc

Stop the spread of communism but also avoid World War III

**Grand Strategy**

Strive to maintain U.S. military superiority (later, accept "balance of terror" between U.S. and Soviet strategic capabilities; still later, strive for and accept stable mutual strategic deterrence and improve U.S. limited war capabilities)

Contain spread of communism through deterrence of military aggression and through political-economic-military measures to reduce vulnerability of small, weak countries to internal or external subversion

Form a "free world" network of collective security alliances led by the United States

Deal with tension between grand design objectives of "stop spread of communism" and "avoid World War III," when it occurs in a specific situation, by judging implications of what is at stake for the balance of power

Employ careful, presidentially controlled crisis management of confrontations and limited wars to prevent escalation to a world war

Avoid de facto as well as de jure recognition of Soviet postwar territorial acquisitions and Soviet sphere of influence in Eastern Europe; defer serious negotiations of outstanding issues in U.S.-USSR relations (with emerging exception of arms control) until the West achieves "positions of strength"

---

*Source:* Alexander L. George, "The Role of Cognitive Beliefs in the Legitimation of a Long-Range Foreign Policy: The Case of F. D. Roosevelt's Plan for Post-War Cooperation with the Soviet Union" (Paper presented to the Conference on Approaches to Decision-Making, August 9-12, 1977, Oslo, Norway).

east Asia were not able to prevent the fall of South Vietnam in April 1975. Fourth, the Portuguese military took over the Portuguese government in April 1974, and this led to a series of coups. There were reports that the Soviet Union provided support for the communist party in Portugal, and these reports caused further anxiety over Soviet foreign policy objectives. Fifth, following the governmental changes in Portugal, leaders of various nationalist factions in Angola began fighting among themselves, believing that independence would soon be granted by Portugal. Both the United States and the Soviet Union clandestinely provided military aid to different factions throughout 1975; however, in August 1975 some Soviet military advisers and a larger number of Cuban combat troops arrived in Angola to help the procommunist forces, an action that raised even more questions about the viability of détente.[13]

Within the United States, several political developments weakened public and congressional support for the Nixon-Ford-Kissinger détente policy. From late 1972 until President Nixon's resignation in August 1974, the Watergate and related scandals of the Nixon administration dominated the news. Although Watergate primarily concerned domestic issues, it nevertheless had a spillover effect on the public and congressional evaluation of Nixon's conduct of foreign policy. Curiously Kissinger was able to disassociate himself from the various inquiries and investigations, with the exception of the investigation concerning his role in the wiretapping of seventeen former NSC staff members and journalists.

During the 1976 presidential campaign, Ronald Reagan, Henry Jackson, George Wallace, and to a lesser extent, Jimmy Carter criticized the Nixon-Ford-Kissinger détente policy on a number of grounds. Reagan attacked Ford and Kissinger for "giving away everything and getting nothing in return from the Soviet Union."[14] Jackson was more specific in his criticism; he believed that the SALT I agreements favored the Soviet Union by allowing it a larger number of strategic nuclear launch vehicles and that Nixon, Ford, and Kissinger placed too little emphasis on human rights in their détente policy. On the global level, Carter argued that "we must replace balance of power politics with world order politics,"[15] and regarding U.S.-Soviet relations, he argued that the United States must "try to make detente broader and more reciprocal."[16]

In response to these criticisms, Ford moved to the right and eventually accepted the Republican party's platform, which contained a number of direct criticisms of his détente policy.

In addition to influencing U.S. domestic opinion concerning détente, campaign rhetoric also had an effect in the Soviet Union. Writing in *Pravda*, Georgi Arbatov noted, "The elections pass, but the consequences of pre-election demagogy and the concessions made in the course of the election campaign continue to influence American policy sometimes creating serious difficulties."[17] It was unclear whether Arbatov was referring to problems faced by prodétente factions within the Soviet Union, the United States, or both countries. Possibly he meant to warn American presidential candidates that their campaign rhetoric might have unintended consequences: the strengthening of hard-line factions and the weakening of prodétente forces within the Soviet Union. By mid-1976, Soviet publications contained many articles critical of the United States and détente, a marked contrast to the 1972-1973 period. Prodétente Soviet writers, such as Arbatov, justified their stance on the grounds that it reduced the probability of nuclear war. This was a minimal defense of détente and significantly contrasted with the more grandiose claims of the early 1970s. Interestingly this limited justification closely resembled the more limited view held by Ford and Kissinger throughout 1975 and 1976.

When asked what the Nixon and Ford administrations could have done differently in the 1973-1976 period with the benefit of hindsight, a former high-ranking member of Kissinger's staff remarked that "this question cannot be isolated from three factors: the collapse of the Nixon Administration, the way the Vietnam War ended, and the outbreak of the October War."[18] He went on to note four changes that he would have made. First, the Nixon and Ford administrations should have moved more rapidly on SALT in order to maintain forward momentum. Second, the administrations should not have negotiated with Senator Jackson over the Trade Agreement. Third, grain subsidies were retained too long. Fourth, Nixon should not have created unrealistic expectations concerning the benefits of détente, which critics focused on when evaluating that policy. Perhaps these changes would have made a difference and prolonged the life of détente. But even if they had

256                                                           CONCLUSION

been implemented, a serious weakness still would not have been resolved: the failure to legitimate the new grand design and grand strategy.

## The Problem of Legitimation

Nixon and Kissinger sought to formulate and implement a long-range strategy for regime and system development, but they encountered a number of obstacles in this effort. Although the Nixon-Kissinger approach to the Soviet Union was a long-range strategy, for domestic political reasons Nixon and Kissinger needed short-term payoffs to demonstrate the advantages of their policy. In describing the payoffs of their grand design and grand strategy, Nixon and Kissinger tended to distort and oversimplify. The China trip, according to Nixon, was "the week that changed the world";[19] the SALT agreements marked the codification of parity; and the Agreement on the Prevention of Nuclear War marked the end of the cold war. Nixon and Kissinger undoubtedly realized that U.S.-Soviet relations were characterized by both cooperative and conflictual interactions, but by emphasizing the former, they contributed to the unrealistic expectations for détente held by many Americans. The problem that Nixon and Kissinger faced of how to legitimate their grand design and grand strategy without distorting or oversimplifying was not unique, for as Theodore Lowi has pointed out, "overselling of package doctrines had been repeated over and over again in the years since the postwar period."[20] The cause that has made oversell necessary in the United States, according to Lowi, is the lack of coherence that characterizes the organization of the American government. Public expectations were shattered by the various reversals in U.S.-Soviet relations, such as the grain deal, the October War, and Angola.

During their first several years of office, Nixon and Kissinger were able to gain public and congressional support for their foreign policy by making short-term promises (for example, U.S. withdrawal from Vietnam) and by holding out the prospect of "a new international system." Nixon's dramatic visits to Peking in February 1972 and to Moscow in May also helped gain support for his policies.

By late 1973 public and congressional opinion turned against the Nixon-Kissinger foreign policies. The most important reason for the waning of détente was Nixon and Kissinger's failure to meet the normative and cognitive requirements necessary to achieve policy legitimacy. In seeking to gain public and Congressional support in the short run, Nixon and Kissinger neglected the need to attend to long-range considerations. This is an ironic finding since in his academic career Kissinger had been acutely aware of the danger inherent in policy making; that urgent day-to-day problems could eclipse longer-range, more important problems.[21] Even though he was aware of the further danger of neglecting domestic actors in foreign policymaking (this, according to Kissinger, had been Metternich's and Castlereagh's greatest shortcoming), Kissinger failed to appreciate adequately the need for the legitimation of foreign policy. Thus, one must conclude that the Nixon-Kissinger grand design and grand strategy was not adequately tested as a foreign policy; it failed primarily for domestic political reasons and was not in effect for a long enough period to be developed, tested, and refined.

The Nixon-Kissinger failure to legitimate their grand design and grand strategy raises an important and disturbing question: How can a president and his administration gain public and congressional support of his policies without oversimplification and distortion? Marshall Shulman has provided a tentative answer: "Even the wisest of policies cannot be effective if public support has to be won for them by the manipulation of outworn and oversimplified themes. The public should share in the difficult revision of thought which experience has been forcing on the decision makers."[22] This solution is theoretically possible but practically infeasible, for as many public opinion studies have shown, most Americans, including congressmen, are not interested in foreign policy issues unless they directly affect their interests. It is possible that, as domestic issues become internationalized and as international issues become domesticated, public and congressional interest in and knowledge of foreign policy issues will increase.

Lowi has suggested that "under crisis conditions our government has operated pretty much as it was supposed to operate" and that

since our record of response to crisis is good, then the men in official positions have been acting and are able to act rationally. If, when there is no crisis, officials and their policies appear to be less rational, then we must conclude that something is wrong with the structures and institutions within which they operate.[23]

Thus, according to Lowi, the problem is that "interest-group liberals display too little trust in the formal institutions of democracy."[24] The solution, Lowi contends, "will be found in restoring respect for formal institutions and the roles assigned to them before the outbreak of war."[25] As Lowi recognizes, his proposed solution to the problem of achieving coherence in foreign policy is both elitist and formalistic. Interestingly, the Nixon-Kissinger foreign policy system under Nixon and Ford was both highly centralized and formalistic, and yet the Nixon-Ford-Kissinger system did not meet the requirements of legitimacy.

The task facing American presidents of legitimating a particular foreign policy is not an easy one for, as Alexander George has pointed out, they must "invoke national values and elements of ideology that make it more attractive in the eyes of the public."[26] Even if this requirement is met, the policy may not be acceptable to foreign leaders. For example, by appealing to important underlying American values in his emphasis on human rights, President Carter was able to gain domestic support for his foreign policy from conservatives and liberals alike; however, Carter's stress on human rights was totally unacceptable to Soviet leaders. There are no panaceas or easy solutions to the problem of achieving foreign policy legitimation, and the intractability of the problem should not divert attention and analysis away from this vital subject.

## Notes

1. This analogy was stimulated by a passage from Patrick Morgan, *Theories and Approaches to International Politics: What Are We to Think?* (San Ramon, Calif.: Consensus, 1973), pp. 227-28: "Think of the international system as a game table. . . . Now think of the international system as a series of game tables with different games for varying stakes."
2. Robert A. Dahl, *Who Governs? Democracy and Power in an American City* (New Haven: Yale University Press, 1961), pp. 174-75.
3. Theodore J. Lowi, "American Business, Public Policy, Case Studies and Political Theory," *World Politics* 16 (July 1964).
4. James N. Rosenau, "Pre-Theories and Theories of Foreign Policy,"

in *Approaches to Comparative and International Politics*, ed. R. Barry Farrell (Evanston, Ill.: Northwestern University Press, 1966); James N. Rosenau, "Foreign Policy as an Issue Area," in *Domestic Sources of Foreign Policy* (New York: Free Press, 1967); William Zimmerman, "Issue Area and Foreign-Policy Process: A Research Note in Search of a General Theory," *American Political Science Review* 67-4 (December 1973).

5. Robert O. Keohane and Joseph S. Nye, *Power and Interdependence: World Politics in Transition* (Boston: Little, Brown, 1977).

6. Rosenau, "Pre-Theories," p. 73.

7. Alexander L. George, David K. Hall, and William R. Simons, *The Limits of Coercive Diplomacy: Laos, Cuba, Vietnam* (Boston: Little, Brown, 1971), p. 24.

8. Interview with a former National Security Council staff member who worked on SALT.

9. By the mid-1950s scientists reported that increasing amounts of strontium 90, an isotope with a half-life of thirty years, were being detected in the bones of children. This finding stimulated some public interest in and support for a test ban, which became a political issue in the 1956 presidential election.

10. Rosenau, "Foreign Policy as an Issue Area," p. 49.

11. Graham T. Allison, *Essence of Decision: Explaining the Cuban Missile Crisis* (Boston: Little, Brown, 1971).

12. Richard Falk contends, "Despite the general impression that conflict among principal states in the world has entered a moderate phase, it is difficult to discuss any modification of foreign policy objectives and world order design implicit in the Nixon-Ford/Kissinger-Brezhnev diplomacy." "Arms Control, Foreign Policy, and Global Reform," in Franklin Long and George Rathjens, eds., *Arms, Defense Policy, and Arms Control. Daedalus* 104 (Summer 1974): 38; see also Robert Osgood, "Introduction: Reappraisal of American Foreign Policy," in Osgood, ed., *America and the World: From the Truman Doctrine to Vietnam* (Baltimore: Johns Hopkins University Press, 1970); and Stanley Hoffmann, "Flaws and Omissions in the New Foreign Policy," in Fred Warner Neal and Mary Kersey Harvey, eds., *The Nixon-Kissinger Foreign Policy: Opportunities and Contradictions* (Santa Barbara, Calif.: Center for the Study of Democratic Institutions, 1974).

13. To protest Soviet military involvement in Angola, the United States decided to delay its participation in three of the nine commissions established for joint cooperation in various issue areas. See Bernard Gwertzman, "U.S. Angered over Angola, to Delay Three Soviet Meetings," *New York Times*, March 17, 1976, p. 1.

14. *Washington Post*, February 24, 1976, p. A15.

15. Quoted in Leslie Gelb, "Carter, Ford May Differ Widely on Foreign Policy," *New York Times*, August 1, 1976, sec. 4, p. 1.

16. Quoted in Robert Shogan, "Carter Seeks to Prove He's Not 'Fuzzy on Issues,' " *Los Angeles Times*, May 9, 1976, p. 22.

17. Quoted in David K. Shipler, "Moscow Is Said to Modify Expectations of Detente," *New York Times*, April 15, 1976, p. 6.

18. Author's interview with a former staff member of the National Security Council and the Department of State.

19. Richard Nixon, *RN: The Memoirs of Richard Nixon* (New York: Grosset and Dunlap, 1978), p. 580.

20. Theodore Lowi, *The End of Liberalism: Ideology, Policy and the Crisis of Public Authority* (New York: W. W. Norton, 1969), p. 178.

21. Kissinger has pointed out, "The staffs on which modern executives come to depend develop a momentum of their own. What starts out as an aid to decision-makers turns into a practically autonomous organization whose internal problems structure and sometimes compound the issues which it was originally designed to solve." Henry A. Kissinger, "Domestic Structure and Foreign Policy," *American Foreign Policy* (New York: W. W. Norton, 1969), p. 20.

22. Marshall D. Shulman, *Beyond the Cold War* (New Haven: Yale University Press, 1966), p. 110.

23. Lowi, *End of Liberalism*, p. 160.

24. Ibid., p. 157.

25. Ibid., p. 187.

26. Alexander L. George, "American Foreign Policy: The Problem of Legitimacy" (Paper presented to the Symposium on U.S. Foreign Policy in the Next Decade, University of Missouri-St. Louis, April 15, 1977), p. 22.

# AFTERWORD

It has been tempting to include in this study some analysis of the Carter and Reagan Administrations' approaches to the Soviet Union since they contrast so markedly with that of the Nixon and Ford administrations. Whereas the Nixon-Ford-Kissinger approach was guided by a desire to implement a new grand design and grand strategy, the Carter administration's approach was *ad hoc* and at times even inconsistent. The emphasis on human rights by President Carter also contrasted with the *realpolitik* orientation of Nixon, Ford, and Kissinger. A detailed comparison of the Nixon-Ford foreign policy toward the Soviet Union with those of the Carter and Reagan administrations is beyond the scope of this book and must await systematic analysis.

The final version of this book was written during the last half of 1980 following the Soviet invasion of Afghanistan, the withdrawal of the SALT II agreement from Senate consideration, and the election of Ronald Reagan. These events resulted in an overall cooling of American-Soviet relations, causing some observers to note the emergence of "a new cold war." Some commentators even announced "the death of détente."[1]

If détente died in 1980, it had suffered from a malingering illness for some time. The passage of the Jackson-Vanik Amendment, the vociferous denunciations of the USSR by the presidential candidates in 1976 and 1980, the Soviet Union's interventions in Third

World countries, particularly its invasion of Afghanistan, and the demise of SALT II all contributed to the crisis atmosphere surrounding U.S.-Soviet relations as the 1980s began. George Kennan, one of the most respected observers of American-Soviet interaction, ominously noted early in 1980:

We are now in the danger zone. I can think of no instance in modern history where such a breakdown of political communication and such a triumph of unrestrained military suspicions as now marks Soviet-American relations has not led, in the end, to armed conflict. . . . If there was ever a time for realism, prudence and restraint in American statesmanship, it is this one.[2]

During the 1980 presidential election, the major candidates strongly criticized the USSR for its invasion of Afghanistan. President Carter substantially increased the 1981 defense budget, and following his election Ronald Reagan called for an even greater increase. Although differing in degree, both Carter and Reagan sought to deal with the Soviet Union by relying more heavily than during the previous ten years on deterrence, which is best summarized in the old Roman maxim, "If you want peace, prepare for war."

The central reality of the nuclear age is stark: should deterrence fail, war between the United States and the Soviet Union would break out, and the resulting devastation would be unprecedented.

Throughout the post-World War II era, competition and cooperation have characterized U.S.-Soviet relations. During the acute cold war, the USSR and the United States competed with one another in a number of geographic regions and functional areas. The two superpowers also implicitly cooperated to develop rules designed to manage crises and to deter the use of nuclear weapons.

Nixon, Ford, and Kissinger successfully and substantially expanded U.S.-Soviet cooperative relations in a number of different issue areas. They did not resolve the "rules of the game" concerning Third World areas, where the limitations of détente first became evident: the October War, Angola, Ethiopia, and Afghanistan. In the future, American and Soviet leaders must devote time and energy to efforts designed to develop an effective crisis prevention regime in these areas in order to avoid escalation.

The Soviet-American relationship is an inherently competitive one, but this competition must be kept within limits. In addition, it should not preclude important cooperative efforts, particularly attempts to stabilize the strategic military balance. In an elemental sense, the future of the world is tied to the relationship between the United States and the Soviet Union.

## Notes

1. Dimitri Simes, "The Death of Détente?" *International Security* 5-1 (Summer 1980).

2. *Los Angeles Herald Examiner*, February 4, 1980, p. A17.

# BIBLIOGRAPHY

## U.S. Government Publications

(The following sources were published by the U.S. Government Printing Office, Washington, D.C.)

Nixon, Richard M. *U.S. Foreign Policy for the 1970s* (series title, individual report titles follow).
_____. *A New Strategy for Peace*. February 18, 1970.
_____. *Building for Peace*. February 25, 1971.
_____. *The Emerging Structure of Peace*. February 9, 1972.
_____. *Shaping a Durable Peace*. May 3, 1973.
U.S. Arms Control and Disarmament Agency. *Annual Report*, 1969-1976. Annual.
_____. *Arms Control and Disarmament Agreements: Texts and History of Negotiations*. 1977.
U.S. Congress. Congressional Research Service. Library of Congress. *U.S. Foreign Policy for the 1970's: An Analysis of the President's 1973 Foreign Policy Report and Congressional Action*. Report prepared for the House Committee on Foreign Affairs, 93d Congress, 1st session, 1973.
_____. House. Committee on Foreign Affairs. *Détente*. Hearings, 93d Congress, 2d session, 1974.
_____. Senate. Committee on Armed Services. *Military Implications of the Treaty on Limitation of Anti-Ballistic Missile Systems and the Interim Agreement on Limitation of Offensive Arms*. Hearings. 92d Congress, 2d session, 1972.

_____. Senate. Committee on Foreign Relations. *East-West Trade.* Hearings. 88th Congress, 2d session, 1964.

_____. Senate. Committee on Foreign Relations. *Strategic Arms Limitation Agreements.* Hearings. 92d Congress, 2d session, 1972.

_____. Senate. Committee on Foreign Relations. *Nomination of Henry A Kissinger.* Hearings. 93d Congress, 1st session, 1973.

_____. Senate. Committee on Foreign Relations. *Détente.* Hearings. 93d Congress, 2d session, 1974.

_____. Senate. Committee on Finance. *Nominations of Helmut Sonnenfeldt, Donald C. Alexander, and Edward C. Schmults.* Hearings. 93d Congress, 1st session, 1973.

_____. Senate. Committee on Finance. *The Trade Reform Act of 1973.* Hearings. 93d Congress, 2d session, 1974.

_____. Senate. Committee on Government Operations. *Hearing on Sale of Grain to the Soviet Union,* 93d Congress, 2d session, 1974.

U.S. Congress, Joint Economic Committee. *New Directions in the Soviet Economy.* Special Studies. 89th Congress, 2d session, 1967.

_____. *Soviet Economic Prospects for the Seventies.* Compendium of Papers. 93d Congress, 1st session, 1973.

_____. *Soviet Economic Outlook.* Hearings. 93d Congress, 1st session, 1973.

U.S. Department of Commerce. *U.S.-Soviet Commercial Relationships in a New Era.* Report by Secretary of Commerce Peter G. Peterson. August 1972.

_____. *The United States' Role in East-West Trade: Problems and Prospects.* Report by Secretary of Commerce Rogers Morton. August 1975.

_____. Foreign Broadcast Information Service. *Daily Report, Soviet Union.* 1969-1976.

_____. Domestic and International Business Administration. Bureau of East-West Trade. *Selected Trade and Economic Data of the Centrally Planned Economies.* September 1976.

U.S. Department of Defense. *Annual Defense Department Report* ("Posture Statement"). 1970-1976. Annual.

U.S. Department of State. *Disarmament: The Intensified Effort, 1955-1958.* Publication 6676. 1958.

_____. *Documents on Disarmament 1945-1959.* 1961.

_____. *Department of State Bulletin.* 1969-1976. Weekly.

_____. Bureau of Public Affairs. Office of Media Services. News Releases, October 1973-December 1976.

U.S. Office of the Federal Register. *Public Papers of the Presidents of the United States.* 1970-1976. Annual.

_____. *Weekly Compilation of Presidential Documents.* 1969-1976. Weekly.

U.S. White House Disarmament Staff. *Pathway to Peace.* 1957.

## Books and Articles

Abel, Elie. *The Missile Crisis.* Philadelphia: J. B. Lippincott, 1966.

Acheson, Dean. *Present at the Creation: My Years in the State Department.* New York: W. W. Norton, 1969.

Adomeit, Hannes. *Soviet Risk-Taking and Crisis Behaviour.* Adelphi Paper 101. London: International Institute for Strategic Studies, 1973.

_____. "Soviet Risk-Taking and Crisis Behaviour: A Theoretical and Empirical Analysis." Ph.D. dissertation, Columbia University, 1977.

Allison, Graham T. *Essence of Decision: Explaining the Cuban Missile Crisis.* Boston: Little, Brown, 1971.

_____. "Cold Dawn and the Mind of Kissinger." *Washington Monthly* (March 1974): 39-47.

Alroy, Gil Carl. *The Kissinger Experience: American Experience in the Middle East.* New York: Horizon Books, 1975.

Barton, John H., and Weiler, Lawrence D., eds. *International Arms Control: Issues and Agreements.* Stanford: Stanford University Press, 1976.

Bechhoefer, Bernhard G. *Postwar Negotiations for Arms Control.* Washington, D.C.: Brookings Institution, 1961.

Bell, Coral. *The Conventions of Crisis: A Study in Diplomatic Management.* London: Oxford University Press, 1971.

_____. *The Diplomacy of Detente: The Kissinger Era.* New York: St. Martin's Press, 1977.

Bloomfield, Lincoln P.; Clemens, Walter C., Jr.; and Griffiths, Franklyn, *Khrushchev and the Arms Race: Soviet Interest in Arms Control and Disarmament, 1954-1964.* Cambridge: MIT Press, 1966.

Brandon, Henry. *The Retreat of American Power.* Garden City, N.Y.: Doubleday, 1972.

Brennan, Donald G., ed. *Arms Control, Disarmament, and National Security.* New York: George Braziller, 1961.

Brown, Seyom. *The Faces of Power: Constancy and Change in United States Foreign Policy from Truman to Johnson.* New York: Columbia University Press, 1968.

_____. *The Crises of Power: An Interpretation of United States Foreign Policy During the Kissinger Years.* New York: Columbia University Press, 1979.

Brzezinski, Zbigniew. *Alternative to Partition: For a Broader Conception of America's Role in Europe.* New York: McGraw-Hill, 1965.

_____. "The Balance of Power Delusion." *Foreign Policy* 7 (Summer 1972): 54-59.

Buchan, Alastair. "A World Restored?" *Foreign Affairs* 50-4 (July 1972).

_____. *Power and Equilibrium in the 1970's.* New York: Praeger, 1973.

Bull, Hedley. *The Control of the Arms Race.* New York: Praeger, 1961.

Cox, Arthur Macy. *The Dynamics of Detente.* New York: Norton, 1976.

Dallin, Alexander. *The Soviet Union, Arms Control and Disarmament.* New York: School of International Affairs, Columbia University, 1964.

_____, ed. *The Twenty-Fifth Congress of the CPSU: Assessment and Context.* Stanford, Calif.: Hoover Institution Press, 1977.

Dinerstein, Herbert S. *The Making of a Missile Crisis: October 1962.* Baltimore: Johns Hopkins University Press, 1976.

Draper, Theodore. "From 1967 to 1973: The Arab-Israeli Wars." *Commentary* (December 1973).

_____. "Détente." *Commentary* 57 (June 1974): 25-47.

_____. "Appeasement and Détente." *Commentary* 59 (February 1976): 27-38.

Edmonds, Robin. *Soviet Foreign Policy 1962-1973: The Paradox of Super Power.* London: Oxford University Press, 1975.

Eisenhower, Dwight D. *The White House Years: Mandate for Change: 1953-1956.* Garden City. N.Y.: Doubleday, 1963.

_____. *Waging Peace, 1956-1961.* Garden City, N.Y.: Doubleday, 1965.

Ford, Gerald. *A Time to Heal.* New York: Berkley Books, 1980.

Friesen, Connie M. *The Political Economy of East-West Trade.* New York: Praeger, 1976.

Frye, Alton. *A Responsible Congress: The Politics of National Security.* New York: McGraw-Hill, 1975.

Garrett, Stephen A. "Nixonian Foreign Policy: A New Balance of Power —or a Revived Concert?" *Polity* 8-3 (Spring 1973): 389-421.

Garthoff, Raymond. "SALT and the Soviet Military." *Problems of Communism* (January-February 1974).

_____. "Negotiating with the Russians: Some Lessons from SALT." *International Security* 1 (Spring 1977).

George, Alexander L.; Hall, David K.; and Simons, William R. *The Limits of Coercive Diplomacy: Laos, Cuba, Vietnam.* Boston: Little, Brown, 1971.

George, Alexander L., and Smoke, Richard. *Deterrence in American Foreign Policy: Theory and Practice.* New York: Columbia University Press, 1974.

Girling, J. L. S. " 'Kissingerism': The Enduring Problems." *International Affairs* 51-3 (July 1975).

Glassman, Jon D. *Arms for the Arabs: The Soviet Union and the War in the Middle East.* Baltimore: Johns Hopkins University Press, 1975.

Goldman, Marshall I. *Détente and Dollars: Doing Business with the Soviets.* New York: Basic Books, 1975.

Golan, Galia. *Yom Kippur and After: The Soviet Union and the Middle East Crisis.* Cambridge: Cambridge University Press, 1977.

Golan, Matti. *The Secret Conversations of Henry Kissinger: Step-by-Step Diplomacy in the Middle East.* New York: Bantam, 1976.

Graubard, Stephen R. *Kissinger: The Portrait of a Mind.* New York: W. W. Norton, 1973.

Gulick, Frances Anderson. "United States Policy on Disarmament: 1955-1958." Ph.D. dissertation, Fletcher School of Law and Diplomacy, Tufts University, 1960.

Halle, Louis J. *The Cold War as History.* New York: Harper and Row, 1967.

Hammond, Paul Y. *The Cold War Years: American Foreign Policy Since 1945.* New York: Harcourt, Brace and World, 1969.

Hartley, Anthony. *American Foreign Policy in the Nixon Era.* Adelphi Paper 110. London: International Institute for Strategic Studies, 1975.

Heikal, Mohamed. *The Road to Ramadan.* New York: Quadrangle Books, 1975.

Hermann, Charles F., ed. *International Crises: Insights from Behavioral Research.* New York: Free Press, 1972.

Herzog, Chaim. *The War of Atonement.* Boston: Little, Brown, 1975.

Hilsman, Roger. *To Move a Nation.* Garden City, N.Y.: Doubleday, 1967.

Hoffmann, Stanley. *Gulliver's Troubles, or the Setting of American Foreign Policy.* New York: McGraw-Hill, 1968.

———. *Primacy or World Order: American Foreign Policy since the Cold War.* New York: McGraw-Hill, 1978.

Holsti, Ole R. *Crisis, Escalation, War.* Montreal: McGill-Queens University Press, 1972.

Holzman, Franklyn D. *International Trade under Communism: Politics and Economics.* New York: Basic Books, 1976.

———, and Legvold, Robert. "The Economics and Politics of East-West Relations." *International Organization* 29 (Winter 1975).

Horelick, A. "The Cuban Missile Crisis: An Analysis of Soviet Calculations and Behavior." *World Politics* 16 (April 1964).

——— and Rush, M. *Strategic Power and Soviet Foreign Policy.* Chicago: University of Chicago Press, 1965.

Insight Team of the London Sunday Times. *The Yom Kippur War.*
Garden City, N.Y.: Doubleday, 1974.
Johnson, Lyndon B. *The Vantage Point: Perspectives on the Presidency.*
New York: Holt, Rinehart, and Winston, 1971.
Kahan, Jerome H. *Security in the Nuclear Age: Developing U.S. Strategic
Arms Policy.* Washington, D.C.: Brookings Institution, 1975.
_____, and Long, Anne K. "The Cuban Missile Crisis: A Study of Its
Strategic Context." *Political Science Quarterly* 87-4 (December
1972).
Kalb, Marvin, and Kalb, Bernard. *Kissinger.* Boston: Little, Brown, 1974.
Kaplan, Morton A., ed. *SALT: Problems and Prospects.* Morristown,
N.J.: General Learning Press, 1973.
Kennan, George F. "Peaceful Coexistence: A Western View." *Foreign
Affairs* 38-2 (January 1960).
Kennedy, Robert F. *Thirteen Days.* New York: W. W. Norton, 1966.
Keohane, Robert O., and Nye, Joseph S. *Power and Interdependence:
World Politics in Transition.* Boston: Little, Brown, 1977.
Khrushchev, Nikita S. "On Peaceful Coexistence." *Foreign Affairs* 38-1
(October 1959).
_____. *Khrushchev Remembers.* 2 vols. Edited and translated by Strobe
Talbott. Boston: Little, Brown, 1970, 1974.
Kintner, William R., and Pfaltzgraff, Robert L., Jr. eds. *SALT: Implica-
tions for Arms Control in the 1970's.* Pittsburgh, Pa.: University
of Pittsburgh Press, 1973.
Kissinger, Henry A. *A World Restored: Metternich, Castlereagh, and the
Problems of Peace, 1812-1822.* New York: Houghton Mifflin, 1957.
_____. *Nuclear Weapons and Foreign Policy.* New York: Harper, 1957.
_____. *The Necessity for Choice: Prospects of American Foreign Policy.*
New York: Harper, 1961.
_____. *The Troubled Partnership: A Reappraisal of the Atlantic Alliance.*
New York: McGraw-Hill, 1965.
_____. *American Foreign Policy: Three Essays.* New York: Norton, 1969.
_____. "The Viet Nam Negotiations." *Foreign Affairs* 47-2 (January
1969): 211-34.
_____. "The White Revolutionary: Reflections on Bismarck." In Dank-
wart A. Rustow, ed., *Philosophers and Kings: Studies in Leader-
ship*, pp. 317-53. New York: George Braziller, 1970.
_____. *White House Years.* Boston: Little, Brown, 1979.
Kohl, Wilfrid. "The Nixon-Kissinger Foreign Policy System and U.S.-
European Relations: Patterns of Policy Making." *World Politics*
27 (October 1975): 1-43.

Kohler, Foy D.; Gouré, Leon; and Harvey, Mose L. *The Soviet Union and the October 1973 Middle East War: The Implications for Detente.* Washington, D.C.: Center for Advanced International Studies, University of Miami, 1974.

Kolko, Joyce, and Kolko, Gabriel. *The Limits of Power.* New York: Harper and Row, 1972.

Kolkowicz, Roman; Gallagher, Matthew P.; and Lambeth, Benjamin S. *The Soviet Union and Arms Control: A Superpower Dilemma.* Baltimore: Johns Hopkins University Press, 1970.

Kolodziej, Edward A. "Foreign Policy and the Politics of Interdependence: The Nixon Presidency." *Polity* 9-2 (Winter 1976): 121-57.

Kruzel, Joseph J. "The Preconditions and Consequences of Arms Control Agreements." Ph.D. dissertation, Harvard University, 1975.

LaFeber, Walter. *America, Russia, and the Cold War, 1945-1971.* 2d ed. New York: John Wiley, 1972.

Landau, David. *Kissinger: The Uses of Power.* Boston: Houghton Mifflin, 1972.

Leacacos, John P. "Kissinger's Apparat." *Foreign Policy* 5 (Winter 1971-1972).

Liska, George. *Beyond Kissinger: Ways of Conservative Statecraft.* Baltimore: Johns Hopkins University Press, 1975.

Long, Franklin, and Rathjens, George, eds. *Arms, Defense Policy, and Arms Control.* New York: Norton, 1975.

Marantz, Paul. "Prelude to Detente: Doctrinal Change under Khrushchev." *International Studies Quarterly* 19 (December 1975).

Monroe, Elizabeth, and Farrar-Hockley, A. H. *The Arab-Israeli War, October 1973: Background and Events.* Adelphi Paper 111. London: International Institute for Strategic Studies, 1975.

Morgenthau, Hans J. "Henry Kissinger, Secretary of State: An Evaluation." *Encounter* (November 1974): 57-61.

———. "The Question of Detente." *Worldview* 19-3 (March 1976): 7-13.

Morris, Roger. *Uncertain Greatness: Henry Kissinger and American Foreign Policy.* New York: Harper and Row, 1977.

Nagorski, Zygmunt, Jr. *The Psychology of East-West Trade: Illusions and Opportunities.* New York: Mason and Lipscomb, 1974.

Neal, Fred Warner and Harvey, Mary Kersey, eds. *The Nixon-Kissinger Foreign Policy: Opportunities and Contradictions.* Santa Barbara, Calif.: Center for the Study of Democratic Institutions, 1974.

Newhouse, John. *Cold Dawn: The Story of SALT.* New York: Holt, Rinehart and Winston, 1973.

Nixon, Richard M. "Asia After Viet Nam." *Foreign Affairs* 46-1 (October 1967): 111-25.

_____. *RN: The Memoirs of Richard Nixon*. New York: Grosset and Dunlap, 1978.

_____. *The Real War*. New York: Warner Books, 1980.

Nutter, G. Warren. *Kissinger's Grand Design*. Washington, D.C.: American Enterprise Institute, 1975.

Osgood, Robert, ed. *America and the World: From the Truman Doctrine to Vietnam*. Baltimore: Johns Hopkins University Press, 1970.

_____. *America and the World*. Volume 2: *Retreat from Empire? The First Nixon Administration*. Baltimore: Johns Hopkins University Press, 1973.

Petrov, Vladimir. *U.S.-Soviet Detente: Past and Future*. Washington, D.C.: American Enterprise Institute, 1975.

Pisar, Samuel. *A New Look at Trade Policy toward the Communist Bloc*. Report prepared for the Joint Economic Committee. Washington, D.C.: Government Printing Office, 1961.

_____. *Coexistence and Commerce*. New York: McGraw-Hill, 1970.

Platt, Alan. *The U.S. Senate and Strategic Arms Policy, 1969-1977*. Boulder, Colo.: Westview Press, 1978.

_____, and Weiler, Lawrence D., eds. *The Congress and Arms Control*. Boulder, Colo.: Westview Press, 1978.

Quandt, William B. *Decade of Decisions: American Policy Toward the Arab-Israeli Conflict, 1967-1976*. Berkeley: University of California Press, 1977.

Quester, George H. *Nuclear Diplomacy: The First Twenty-Five Years*. New York: Dunellen, 1970.

Rosenau, James N., ed. *Domestic Sources of Foreign Policy*. New York: Free Press, 1967.

Rubinstein, Alvin Z. *Red Star on the Nile: The Soviet-Egyptian Influence Relationship since the June War*. Princeton: Princeton University Press, 1977.

Sadat, Anwar. *In Search of Identity: An Autobiography*. New York: Harper and Row, 1977.

Safran, Nadav. "The War and the Future of the Arab-Israeli Conflict." *Foreign Affairs* 52-2 (January 1974).

_____. "Trial by Ordeal: The Yom Kippur War, October 1973." *International Security* 2-2 (Fall 1977).

Schelling, Thomas C. *Arms and Influence*. New Haven: Yale University Press, 1966.

_____, and Halperin, Morton. *Strategy and Arms Control*. New York: Twentieth-Century Fund, 1961.

Schlesinger, Arthur. *A Thousand Days*. Boston: Houghton Mifflin, 1965.

Sheehan, Edward R. F. *The Arabs, Israelis, and Kissinger: A Secret History of American Diplomacy in the Middle East*. New York: Reader's Digest Press, 1976.

Shulman, Marshall D. *Stalin's Foreign Policy Reappraised*. Cambridge: Harvard University Press, 1963.

_____. *Beyond the Cold War*. New Haven: Yale University Press, 1966.

_____. "Toward a Western Philosophy of Coexistence." *Foreign Affairs* 51-1 (October 1973).

Smith, Gerard. *Doubletalk: The Story of the First Strategic Arms Limitation Talks*. Garden City, N.Y.: Doubleday, 1980.

Sobel, Lester, ed. *Kissinger and Detente*. New York: Facts on File, 1975.

Solzhenitsyn, Aleksandr. "Detente and Democracy." *Society* 13-1 (November-December 1975): 14-47.

Sonnenfeldt, Helmut. "The Meaning of 'Détente.' " *Naval War College Review* 28-1 (Summer 1975): 3-8.

_____. "American-Soviet Relations: Informal Remarks." *Parameters* 6-1 (1976): 12-17.

Sorensen, Theodore C. *Kennedy*. New York: Harper and Row, 1965.

Starr, Harvey. "The Kissinger Years: Studying Individuals and Foreign Policy." *International Studies Quarterly* 24-2 (December 1980).

Steibel, Gerald. *Detente: Promises and Pitfalls*. New York: Crane, Russak, 1975.

Stern, Paula. *Water's Edge: Domestic Politics and the Making of American Foreign Policy*. Westport, Conn.: Greenwood Press, 1979.

Stoessinger, John G. *Henry Kissinger: The Anguish of Power*. New York: W. W. Norton, 1976.

Strong, John W., ed. *The Soviet Union under Brezhnev and Kosygin*. New York: Van Nostrand Reinhold Company, 1971.

Sutton, Anthony C. *Western Technology and Soviet Economic Development*. Volume 1, *1917-1930*; volume 2, *1930-1945*; volume 3, *1945-1965*. Stanford, Calif.: Hoover Institution Press, 1968, 1971.

Tatu, Michel. *Power in the Kremlin*. New York: Viking, 1969.

Triska, Jan F., and Finley, David D. *Soviet Foreign Policy*. New York: Macmillan, 1968.

Trout, B. Thomas. "Rhetoric Revisited: Political Legitimation and the Cold War." *International Studies Quarterly* 19-3 (September 1975): 251-84.

Truman, Harry S. *Memoirs*. Volume 2, *Years of Trial and Hope, 1946-1952*. Garden City, N.Y.: Doubleday, 1956.

Ulam, Adam B. *Expansion and Coexistence: Soviet Foreign Policy, 1917-73*. 2d ed. New York: Praeger, 1974.

Urban, G. R., ed. *Détente*. New York: Universe Books, 1976.

Vincent, R. J. "Kissinger's System of Foreign Policy." *The Yearbook of World Affairs 1977*. Boulder, Colo: Westview Press, 1977, pp. 8-26.

Walker, Stephen G. "The Interface between Beliefs and Behavior: Henry Kissinger's Operational Code and the Vietnam War." *Journal of Conflict Resolution* (March 1977).

Ward, Dana. "Kissinger: A Psychohistory." *History of Childhood Quarterly* 2-3 (Winter 1975): 287-348.

Wilczynski, Jozef. *The Economics and Politics of East-West Trade*. New York: Praeger, 1969.

Williams, Phil. *Crisis Management: Confrontation and Diplomacy in the Nuclear Age*. New York: John Wiley, 1976.

Willrich, Mason, and Rhinelander, John B., eds. *SALT: The Moscow Agreements and Beyond*. New York: Free Press, 1974.

Wohlstetter, Albert. "Threats and Promises of Peace: Europe and America in the New Era." *Orbis* 17-4 (Winter 1974).

_____ and Wohlstetter, Roberta. *Controlling the Risks in Cuba*. Adelphi Paper 17. London: Institute for Strategic Studies.

Wolfe, Thomas. *The SALT Experience*. Cambridge, Mass.: Ballinger Publishing Company, 1979.

Yergin, Daniel, "Great Expectations: Trade with Russia." *Yale Review* 65 (December 1975).

_____. "Politics and Soviet-American Trade: The Three Questions." *Foreign Affairs* 55 (April 1977).

York, Herbert F., ed. *Arms Control: Readings from Scientific American*. San Francisco: W. H. Freeman, 1973.

Young, Elizabeth. *A Farewell to Arms Control?* London: Penguin, 1972.

Young, Oran. *The Politics of Force: Bargaining During International Crises*. Princeton: Princeton University Press, 1968.

Zagoria, Donald S. *Vietnam Triangle: Moscow, Peking, Hanoi*. New York: Pegasus, 1967.

Zimmerman, William. *Soviet Perspectives on International Relations, 1956-1967*. Princeton: Princeton University Press, 1969.

_____. "Issue Area and Foreign Policy Process: A Research Note in Search of a General Theory." *American Political Science Review* 67-4 (December 1973).

Zumwalt, Elmo R., Jr. *On Watch: A Memoir*. New York: Quadrangle/ New York Times Book Company, 1976.

# INDEX

DAN CALDWELL is Associate Professor of Political Science at Pepperdine University in Malibu, California. He is the author of the monograph *Food Crises and World Politics* and has written on arms control and disarmament, decision-making theory, and East-West trade for scholarly books and periodicals.